I0795759

IMAGES
of Rail

RAILROAD DEPOTS OF CENTRAL FLORIDA

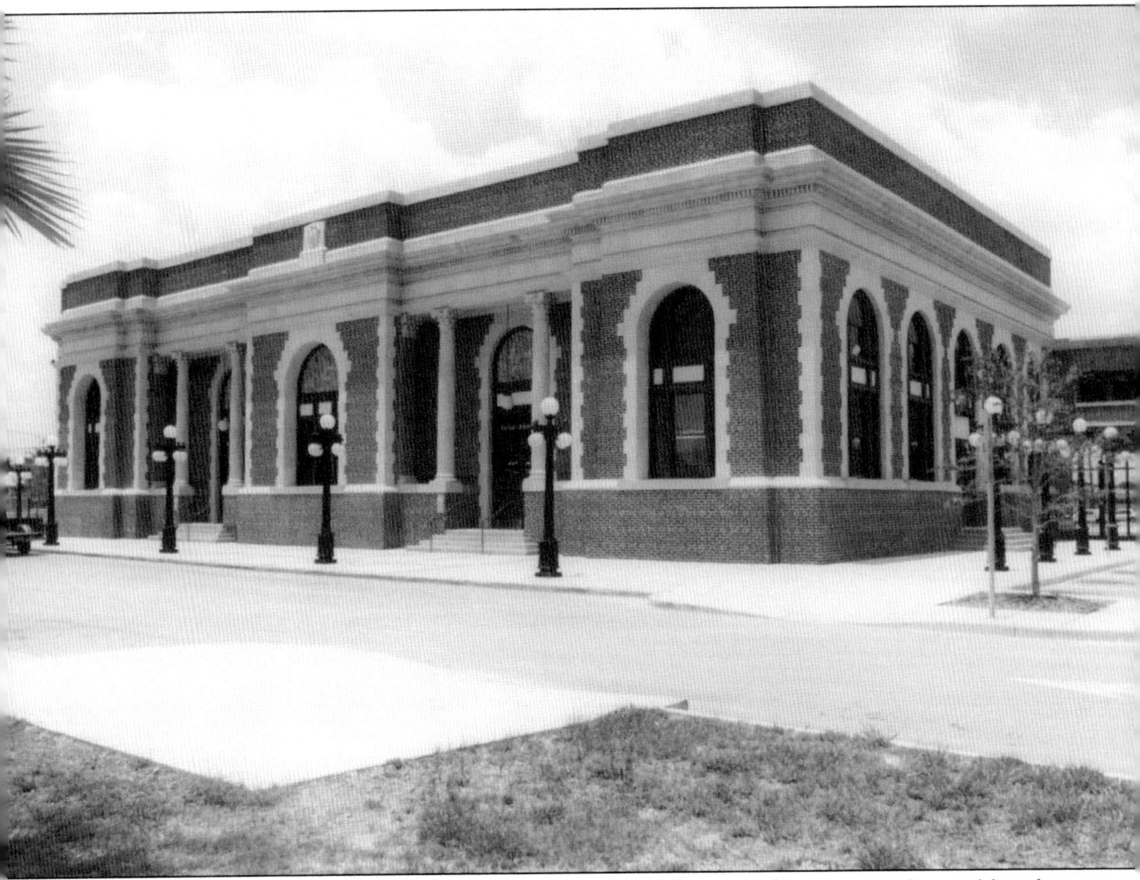

Tampa Union Station. In 1998, Tampa's Union Station reopened to the traveling public after a $2.1 million restoration and renovation project returned the building to its original splendor. The building closed in 1984 after years of neglect made it no longer capable of serving the traveling public. Customers were served by a temporary adjacent facility located by the track platforms. This scene shows the station has it appeared in June 2000. (Courtesy of Mike Mulligan.)

On the Cover: Amtrak's northbound *Silver Meteor* is easing into Ocala's Union Depot on a hot summer afternoon in 1975. In pre-Amtrak days, the depot served the Atlantic Coast Line Railroad (ACL) and the Seaboard Air Line Railroad (SAL). The *Meteor* is running on former Seaboard tracks. The other rail forming the crossing is the former Atlantic Coast Line. These lines merged to form Seaboard Coast Line Railroad on July 1, 1967. (Courtesy of Fred Clark Jr.)

IMAGES
of Rail

RAILROAD DEPOTS OF CENTRAL FLORIDA

Michael Mulligan

ARCADIA
PUBLISHING

ISBN 978-0-7385-5390-0

Published by Arcadia Publishing
Charleston, South Carolina

Printed in the United States of America

Library of Congress Catalog Card Number: 2007942745

For all general information contact Arcadia Publishing at:
Telephone 843-853-2070
Fax 843-853-0044
E-mail sales@arcadiapublishing.com
For customer service and orders:
Toll-Free 1-888-313-2665

Visit us on the Internet at www.arcadiapublishing.com

I dedicate this book to my wife, Laurie, who encouraged and supported me with this project. I also dedicate this book to the photographers of yesteryear and today for going out and documenting with images our nation's railroading history. Without their effort, this book would not have been possible.

Contents

ACKNOWLEDGMENTS

A book of this nature can only be produced with the assistance of many people. I am grateful for the assistance provided to me. I thank Fred Clark Jr. of Clearwater, Florida, for sharing his time, stories, and railroad photography with me on my visits to his home. My thanks to Paul Coe of Pinellas Park, Florida, for spending a morning with me and searching his 35-mm slide material for images I could use. A big thank-you to Randy Stevens of Lutz, Florida, for allowing me to purchase and use his Florida depot 35-mm slide collection, which provided the bulk of photographic material used in the book. I offer my gratitude to Tom King of Kingsport, Tennessee, for his efforts to arrange my acquisition of Randy's collection. I thank Clayton Bishop, Lake County historian, for allowing me the use of his collection, the interesting stories he shared, and information he provided.

I also acknowledge the assistance of the following individuals: Tom Muir, curator with the Polk County Historical Museum; Adam Watson, Florida State Archives; Ken Murdock, Central Florida Chapter, National Railway Historical Society (NRHS); Elaine Levey, Avon Park Depot Museum; Wenxian Zhang, Rollins College; Diane Cripps, Ormond Beach Historical Society; Janice Mahaffey, Putnam County Library; Laurie Diestler, Old Courthouse Heritage Museum; Ashley Miller, Brevard County Historical Commission; Stephanie Gaub, Orange County Regional History Center; Joe Spann, Polk County Historical and Genealogical Library; David Salter; Gregg Turner; Howard Melton, historian of Arcadia, Florida; Jeanne Hickam, Southwest Florida Chapter, NRHS; Carole Goad, Sebring Historical Society; Louise Carter, Eustis Historical Museum; Jonathan Nelson; and many others who were willing to assist me with the production of this book. I thank you all!

Introduction

It seems I have always had a liking for railroad depots or stations. I spent my first 13 years growing up in Richmond, Virginia, which exposed me to that city's grand Broad Street Station, which served the Richmond, Fredericksburg, and Potomac; Atlantic Coast Line; Seaboard Air Line; and Norfolk and Western Railroads. I boarded my first train at Broad Street Station in 1968 for a fifth-grade class day-trip to Washington, D.C. Upon arriving in Washington, I experienced that city's monumental Union Station. I would often pass by Richmond's ornate Main Street Station, which served the Chesapeake and Ohio Railroad (C&O) as well as the Seaboard before it relocated operations to Broad Street in 1959. Its unique architecture and clock tower always caught my attention. Even the Southern Railroad's Hull Street Station was regularly observed on my trips out and about in the city. By that time, the Southern had long since ceased using the building, but the structure intrigued me nonetheless. Perhaps it was the architecture of the buildings or the sense of history that seemed to emanate from them that piqued my interest.

In September 1969, my family relocated to Florida. We didn't live anywhere near a railroad line, much less a depot, so my days taking in the railroad scene and depots seemed at an end. However, I was lucky enough to visit the Fort Myers Mission Revival–style Seaboard Coast Line depot a month or so later when my brother was to make his way to Florida by train. We waited for some time for the train to arrive, and I took the time to explore the facility. My brother never arrived, as he changed his mind about traveling by train and took the bus instead. Oh, well! I enjoyed the outing and was thrilled to see a depot. I regret I didn't have a camera to record that day, as the depot would lose all passenger service on April 30, 1971.

Railroads and depots faded from my world through my teen years. I was not able to reconnect with my interest in railroads and depots until a young adult. In the early 1980s, my wife and I started using Amtrak to travel along the East Coast. Our first trip was a short one between Richmond's new Amtrak station and Colonial Williamsburg. One big reason for taking this short trip was to pass by the old C&O Main Street Station on-board a train and experience it in a different way. Shortly after this excursion, I took a day trip from Tampa to Lakeland for my first train-riding experience in Florida. I was impressed by Tampa's Union Station even though it was in rough shape from years of neglect. I pondered what its future would hold and whether there was any effort to restore it. Tampa's station contrasted sharply from the modern Lakeland facility I visited later that day, which had been built in the 1960s.

A few years later, we began traveling by train from Florida to Virginia and New Jersey to visit relatives in our respective home states. These trips exposed me to a variety of Florida railroad depots as well as stations in other states. I appreciated the vast difference in styles of the structures as well as their current condition. It was interesting to see those no longer in rail service and what other uses they had been converted to.

Our first Amtrak trip north called for boarding the train at Sebring's former Seaboard depot. This station had been built in 1926. The Seaboard had pushed an aggressive line expansion down the Florida peninsula to reach Miami starting in 1924. The simple Mediterranean Revival–style stucco structure was showing its years by 1983, but I took in all of its features while we waited. I took notice of other depots as we headed north on the train. The first station observed was Sebring's near twin at Avon Park. We then passed by the forlorn West Lake Wales depot, which appeared to be in the middle of nowhere. Winter Haven was the next station stop, and the train seemed squeezed between the depot and the adjacent citrus-processing facility that unbeknownst to me hid an earlier Winter Haven depot. The next station stop was Wildwood, where my eyes were drawn more to the massive adjacent freight yard rather than to the 1940s-era depot. After Wildwood was Ocala's impressive former Union Station, built in 1917. Then farther on was the simple wood frame structure at Waldo. A short time later, we arrived at Jacksonville's Amtrak station before leaving the Sunshine State.

That first Amtrak trip was followed by four more round-trips from 1984 to 1987. We covered both routes Amtrak used at that time through the central section of the state leaving from and returning to Sebring, but we once used Tampa Union Station as our departure and return point. This exposure to passenger trains and the depots associated with it left me wanting to discover more about Florida's railroading past and the depots that served it. When children arrived in the home, the train travel came to an end for a while, but I was determined to get out on the road as soon as time and money would allow photographing the remaining depots in the state.

My work presented me with opportunities to travel around the state and seek out railroad depots. Whatever areas my work did not take me to I would cover on my own in my mission to photograph the remaining depots in the state. This was before the Internet provided easy information. I knew of depots that existed along rail lines I had ridden, but I had few clues to go by for all the other depots that existed elsewhere. I used copies of Delamore maps for the locales I would explore and to help navigate and determine where the depots might be. Delamore maps showed where existing and abandoned rail lines were located.

I photographed many depots over the years, some shortly before they were demolished. I researched the history of the stations as well as the communities they served. I discovered articles like "The Railroad Depot: A Photo Essay" by R. Randolph Stevens, produced for the University of South Florida's *Tampa Bay History*; the Florida State Photograph Archive; various local historical societies; and private photograph collections. These resources and Arcadia Publishing's Images of Rail series make it possible for a novice to produce a book like this.

This pictorial book covers the central region of the state, which includes the following counties: Levy, Alachua, Putnam, Citrus, Marion, Volusia, Hernando, Sumter, Lake, Seminole, Orange, Pasco, Polk, Osceola, Brevard, Pinellas, Hillsborough, Manatee, Hardee, Highlands, Sarasota, and Desoto.

One

Atlantic Coast Line and Predecessors

The Atlantic Coast Line Railroad entered Florida in a big way when it purchased the Plant System of railroads in 1902. The Plant System operated a network of rail lines that served south, central, and coastal Georgia with lines extending down into Florida all the way to Port Tampa and Punta Gorda.

The Savannah, Florida, and Western (SF&W) Railway's 1,721-mile network was the main component of the Plant System of railroads in Florida. The SF&W was used to consolidate various lines acquired by the Plant System. These earlier lines consisted of the South Florida Railroad, which operated a main line between Sanford and Tampa over a distance of 114 miles; St. Cloud and Sugar Belt Railway, operating 14 miles between Kissimmee and Narcossee; Jacksonville, Tampa, and Key West Railway, running over a main line of 125 miles between Jacksonville and Sanford; the Sanford, Silver Springs, Ocala, and Gulf Railroad with lines running from Ocala west to Dunnellon then south to Inverness (approximately 50 miles total); and the Tampa and Thonotosassa Railroad, running over 13 miles between its namesake communities.

In addition to the SF&W Railway, over 500 additional miles of track in Florida was brought under Atlantic Coast Line control when the Plant System was acquired. These lines consisted of the 27-mile Barrs Tram, running in the High Springs area; Florida Midland Railroad, operating 44 miles between Kissimmee and Longwood; Florida Southern Railroad's 250 miles of track in two sections between Palatka and Punta Gorda; St. Johns and Lake Eustis Railroad, extending from Astor to Leesburg for 49 miles; Sanford and Lake Eustis, running over 29 miles of track between Sanford and Tavares; Sanford and St. Petersburg Railway (formerly known as the Orange Belt Railway), operating over 150 miles of track between its namesake cities; and the Winston and Bone Valley Railroad, which ran over 25 miles of track in the phosphate-mining area between Winston and Phosphoria.

The Plant System railroads were all physically connected, providing service that covered the Central Florida region. All of these acquired lines were built from the 1880s through the 1890s up to the time obtained by the Atlantic Coast Line. Numerous line extension projects would expand the system to its greatest extent by 1929. Atlantic Coast Line merged with Seaboard Air Line Railroad on July 1, 1967.

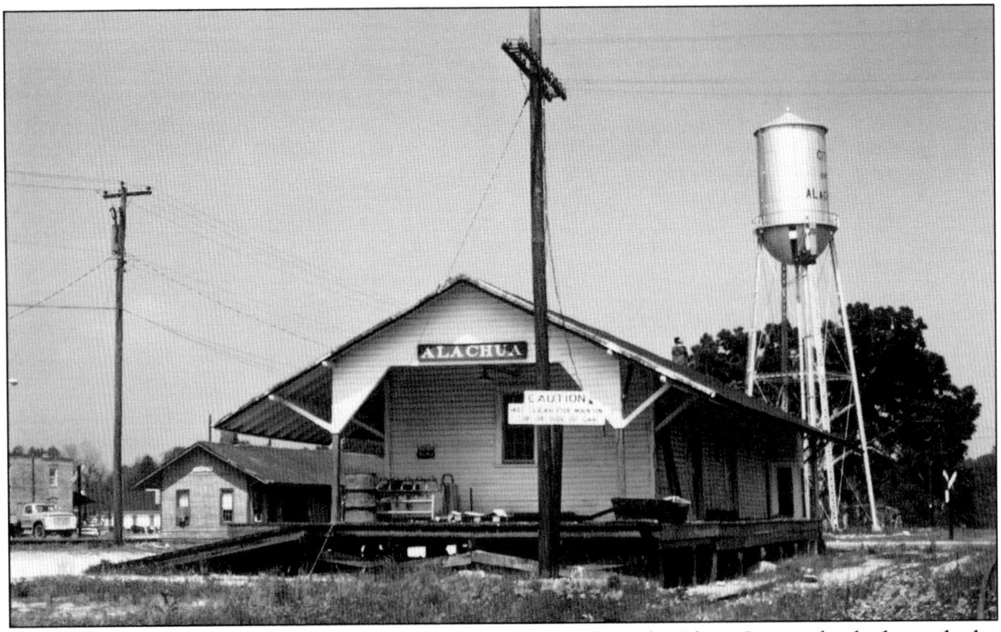

ALACHUA. The town of Alachua was founded in 1884, when the Plant System built through the area. In past years, large amounts of tobacco, Sea Island cotton, winter vegetables, and watermelons were shipped north to markets. This view from early 1971 shows the freight end of the station with competitor Seaboard Air Line's depot located in the background. The caution sign reads, "Not clear for man on top or side of car." (Courtesy of R. Randolph Stevens.)

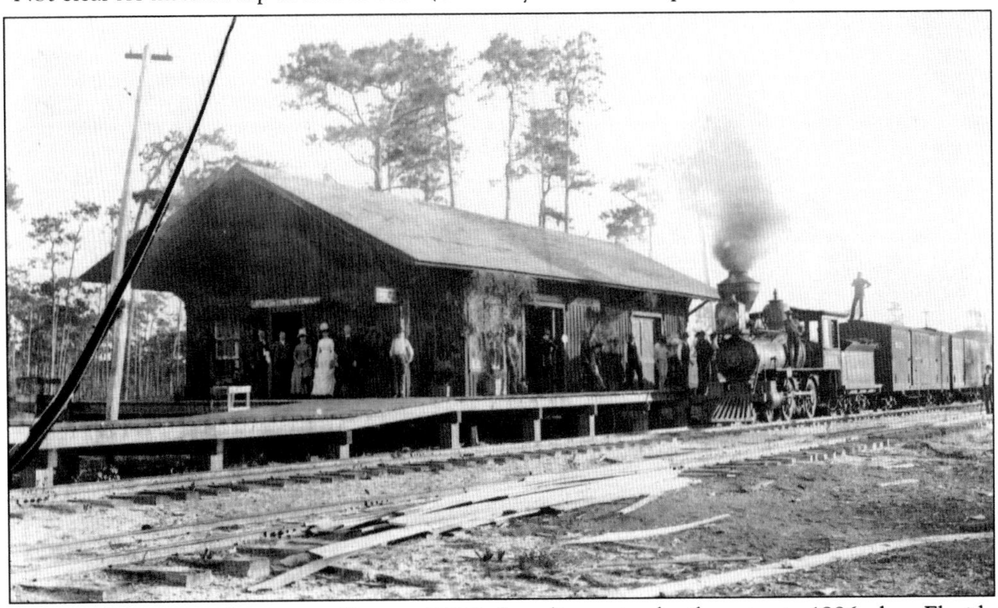

ARCADIA'S FLORIDA SOUTHERN DEPOT, 1890. Arcadia received rail service in 1886 when Florida Southern Railway's 3-foot-gauge line was extended south from Bartow. The following year, Arcadia incorporated with a population of 400. The narrow gauge converted to standard gauge in 1892. The town's original depot is seen in this rare view when the railway was narrow gauge. Express package services were provided by Southern Express Company. Locomotive No. 8, built in 1884, powered the train. (Courtesy of Polk County Historical Museum.)

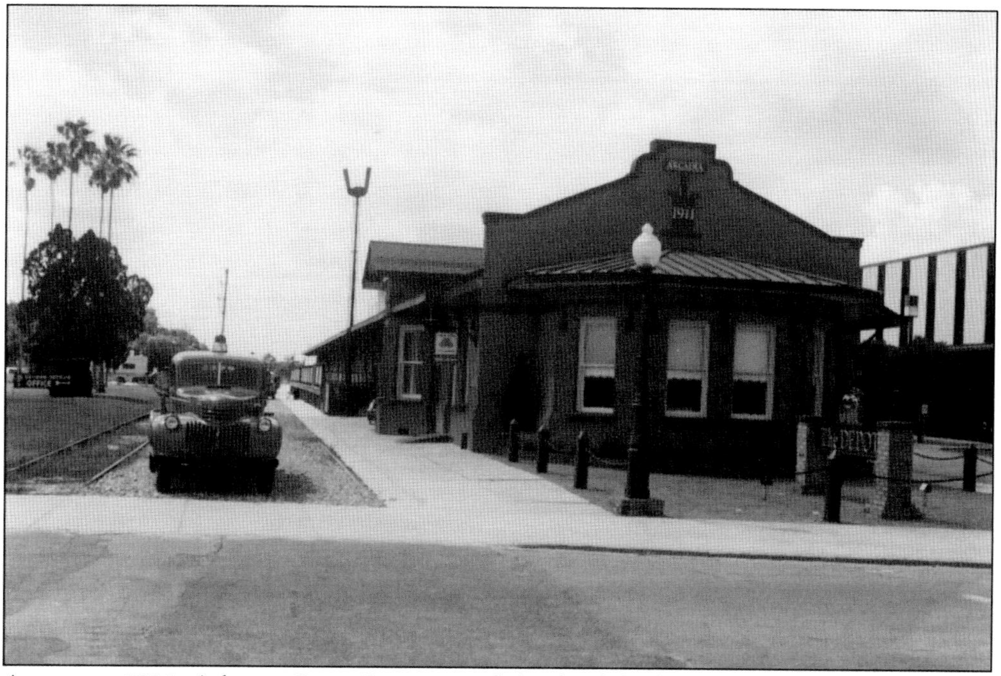

ARCADIA, 1911. Atlantic Coast Line opened this brick building to serve Arcadia in 1911. Passenger service ended on April 30, 1971. The rail line would be removed around 1980. Developers renovated the building a few years later at a cost of $250,000 to provide commercial office space, retail outlets, and a small local history museum. The photograph shows the building as it appeared early 1990. The structure is still in use. (Courtesy of Mike Mulligan.)

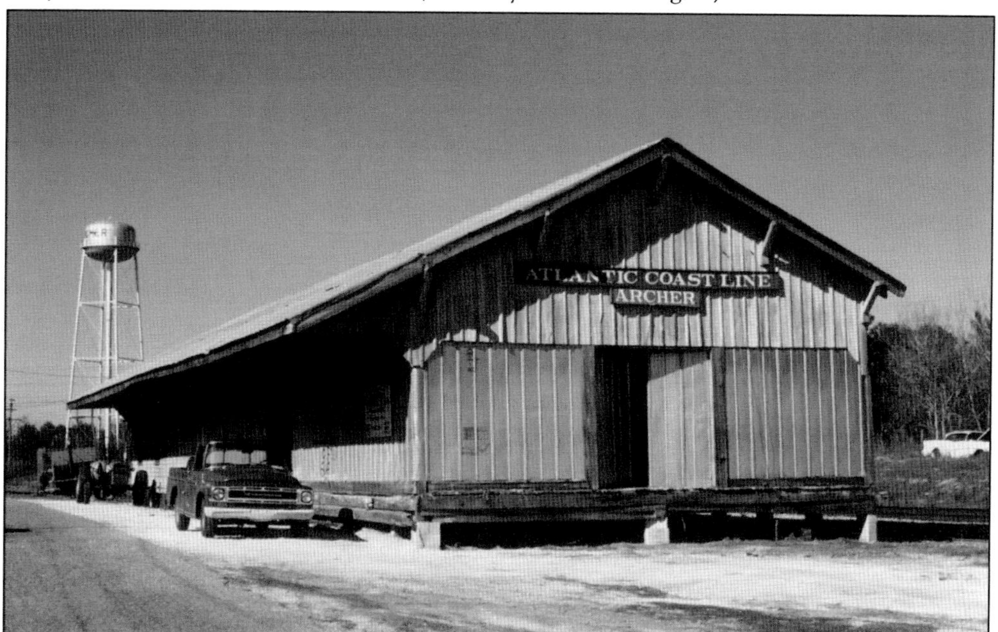

ARCHER. This structure served as the freight depot from 1914 to the 1960s. This photograph is from 1971, at which time the building was used for storage for non-railroad purposes. It was later moved to another site and consumed by fire in the mid-1980s. (Courtesy of R. Randolph Stevens.)

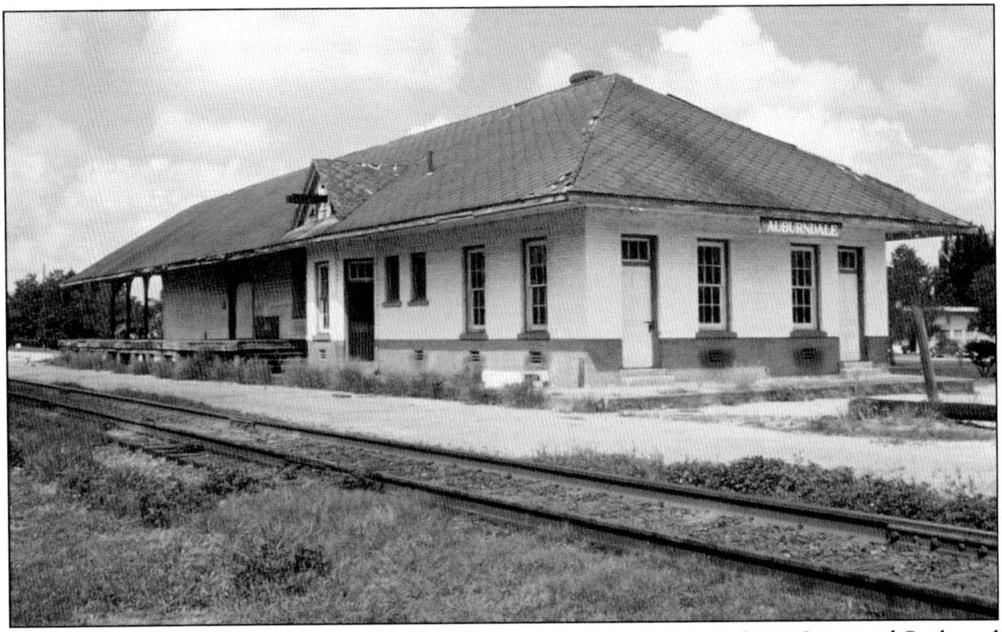

AUBURNDALE. One year after the July 1, 1967, merger of the Atlantic Coast Line and Seaboard Air Line, the former ACL depot sits neglected. The merger made a lot of track, buildings, and other infrastructure superfluous. The lower part of the exterior walls and trim are painted in ACL purple. Sometime in the next few years, the building was demolished. (Courtesy of R. Randolph Stevens.)

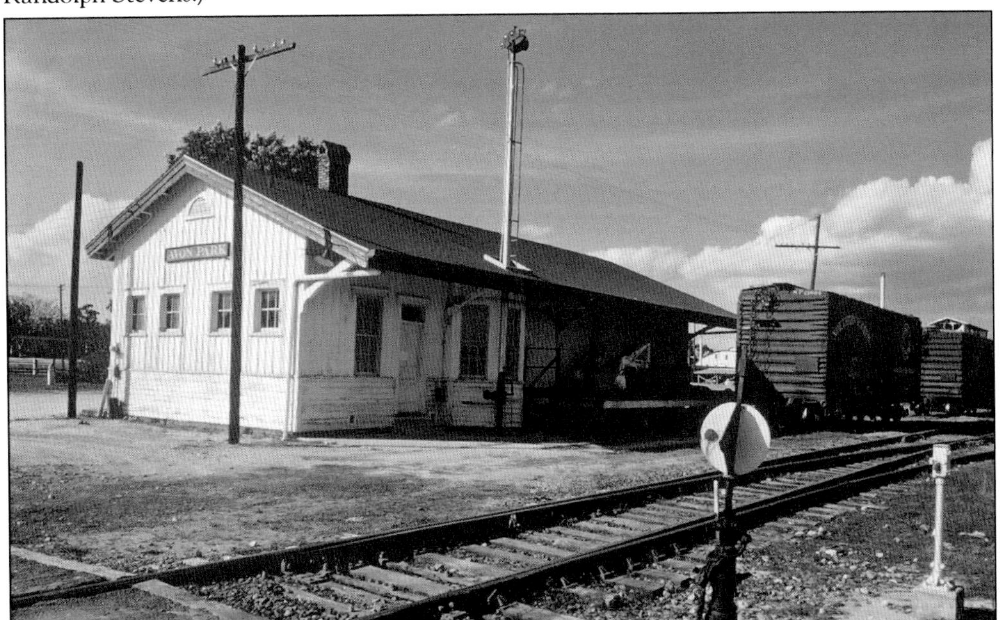

AVON PARK. Rail service came to the struggling community of Avon Park in 1912. Reliable transportation spurred development, with town incorporation taking place the following year. By 1929, the town population stood at 1,534. The Northern Pacific boxcar in this view from the beginning of 1969 suggests the depot is still used by the railroad. However, any further company use would be brief, as the building was torn down in 1970. (Courtesy of R. Randolph Stevens.)

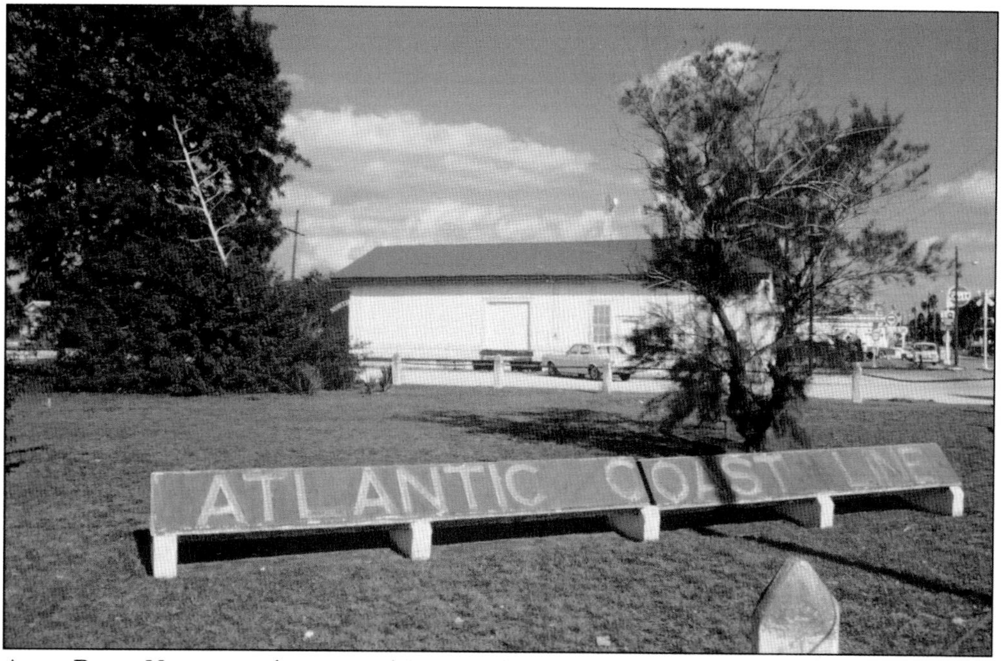

AVON PARK. Here is another view of Avon Park taken in 1969 showing the pride the railroad displayed in the service they provided communities. Seaboard Air Line's depot was located a short distance away as shown in a double-page spread featured later in the book. (Courtesy of R. Randolph Stevens.)

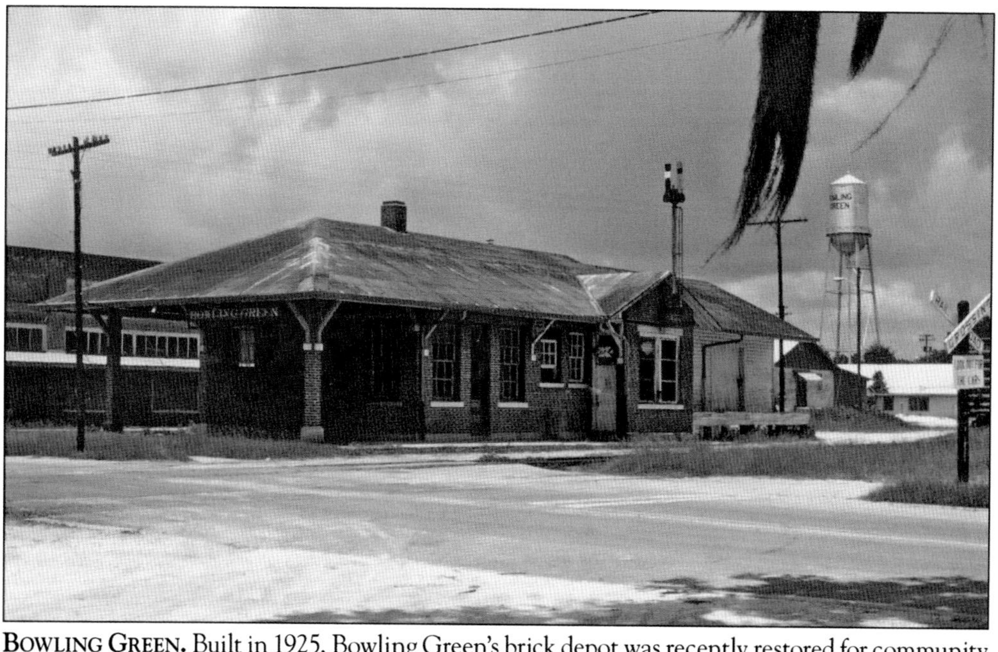

BOWLING GREEN. Built in 1925, Bowling Green's brick depot was recently restored for community use. Tracks were pulled up around 1980, and currently the end of the line is a short distance north of the building. This scene is from mid-1969, shortly after the railroad no longer manned the station. A restored Atlantic Coast Line caboose is on display between the depot and the end of tracks. (Courtesy of R. Randolph Stevens.)

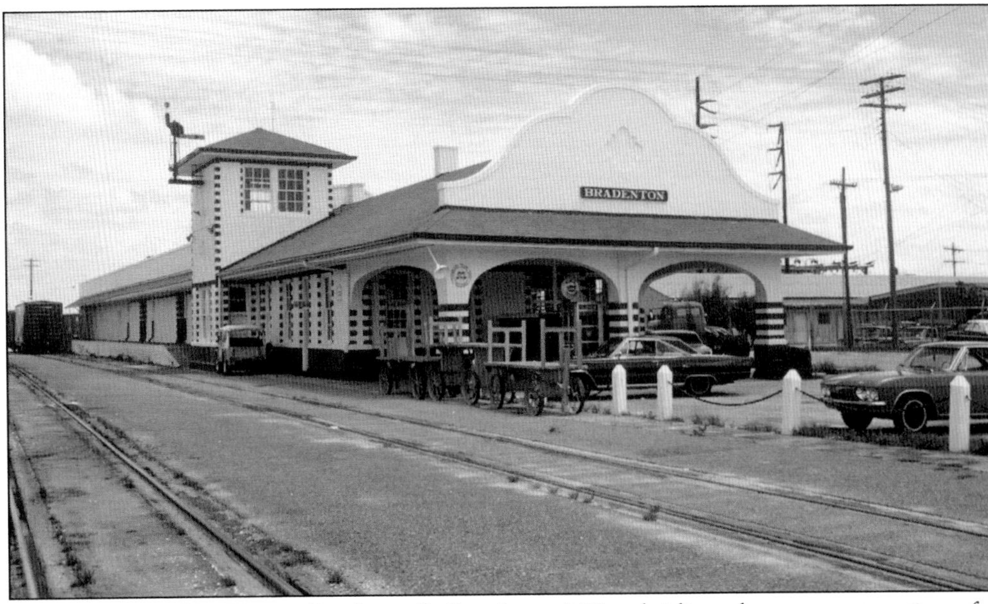

BRADENTON ACL. Tampa Southern Railroad, an ACL subsidiary, began construction of a line south to Bradenton from a point east of Tampa in 1919. This Mission Spanish/Colonial Revival–style station cost approximately $80,000, serving passengers until 1971. It was used for railroad purposes into the 1990s. When the railroad vacated the building, it fell into disrepair. It is restored as a medical office. This view is from 1968. (Courtesy of R. Randolph Stevens.)

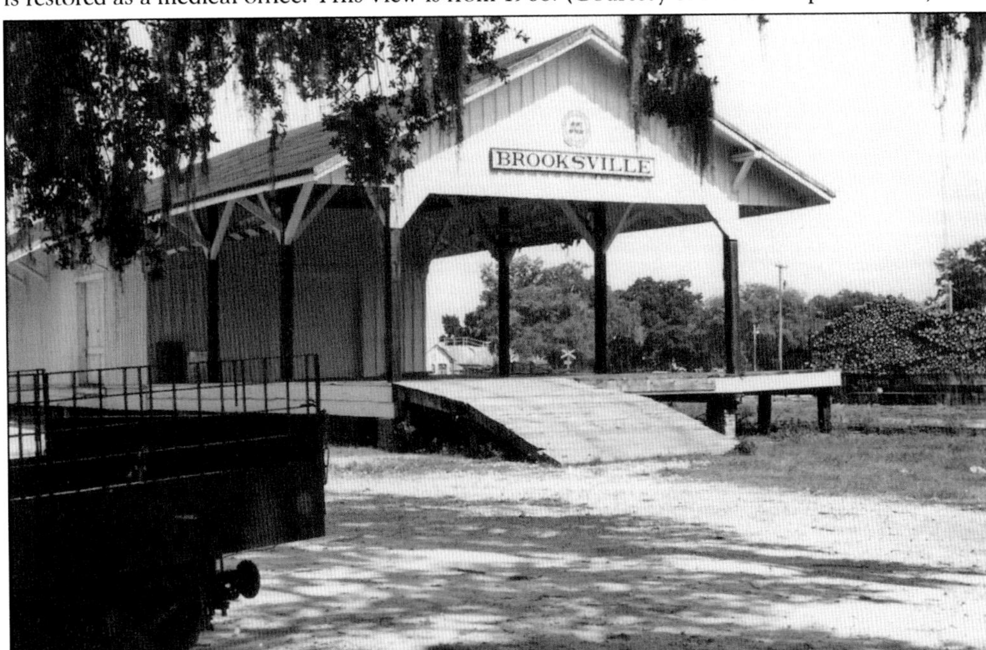

BROOKSVILLE. Everything looks neat and orderly at the Brooksville depot loading platform on this day in 1975. Florida Southern Railroad brought rail service to the town in 1885 and built this wooden-frame, board-and-batten building. Tracks were taken up in the 1970s, but the depot is still with us as the home of Hernando Historical Museum's Genealogical Center. It is the trailhead for Brooksville's Good Neighbor Trail. (Courtesy of Fred Clark Jr.)

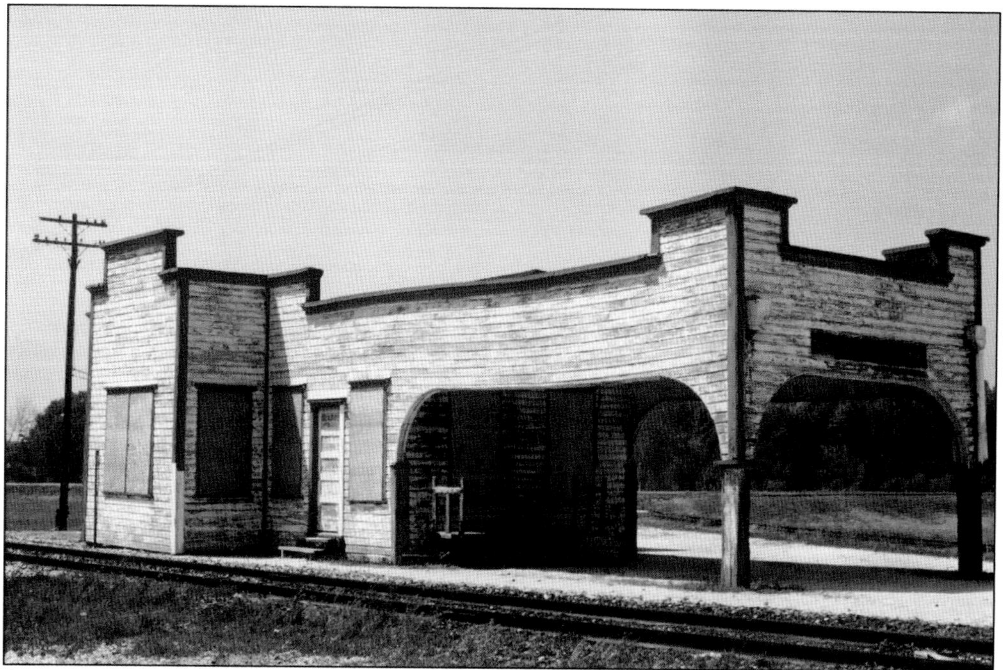

BURNETTS LAKE. Any further use is doubtful, for the Burnetts Lake boarded-up depot in this early-1971 scene. Freight trains of CSX transportation still rumble through the area, but the wooden depot has been gone for many years. (Courtesy of R. Randolph Stevens.)

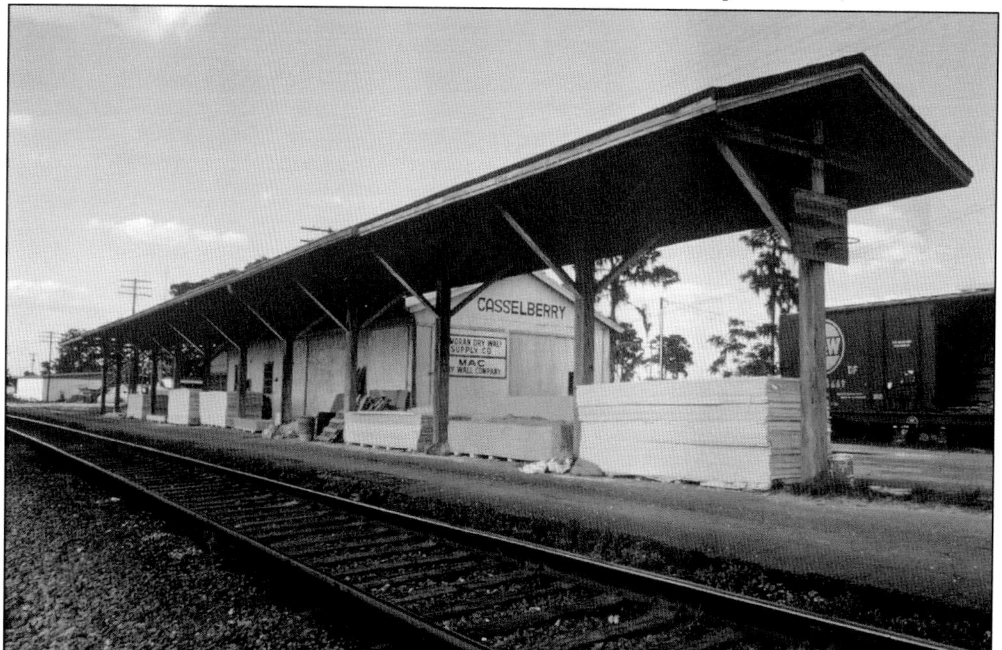

CASSELBERRY. Casselberry's depot has ceased service to the railroad, but it found another use as a drywall supply company. Stacks of wallboard take up space underneath the former passenger shed, as seen here in April 1969. In 1950, the town of Casselberry had a population of 407. The town had grown to a city of about 25,000 by 2005. (Courtesy of R. Randolph Stevens.)

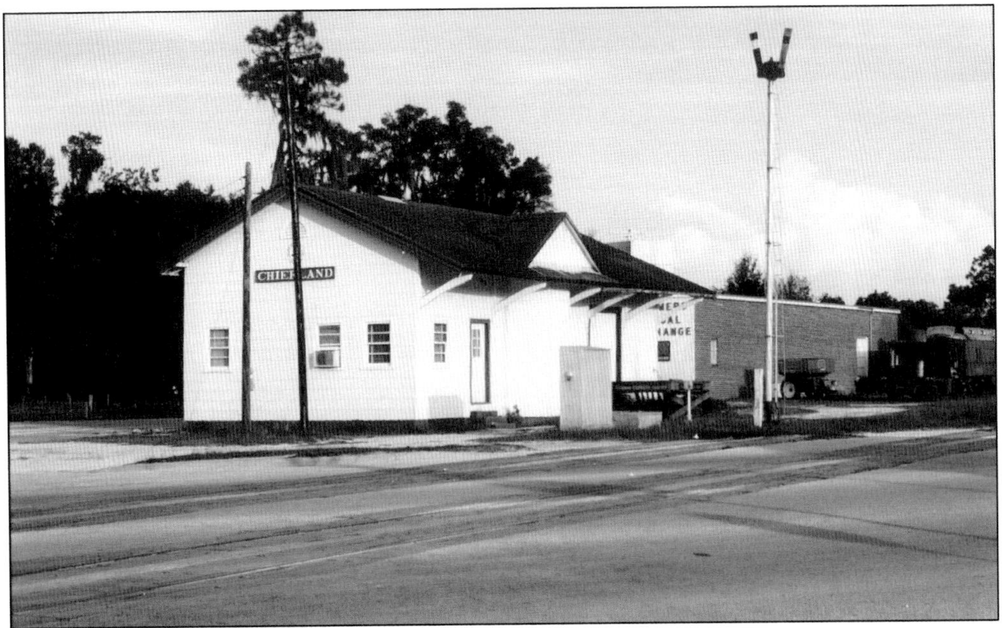

CHIEFLAND. The railroad came to Chiefland in 1913 when the ACL built the 108-mile Perry Cutoff between Perry and Dunnellon. This depot was built to serve the town, which was incorporated in 1929. U.S. Highway 19 lies in the foreground of this September 1972 image. The depot was sold and moved. Later it was brought back to its original location to serve as the local history museum. (Courtesy of Jonathan Nelson, Jonathan Nelson Collection.)

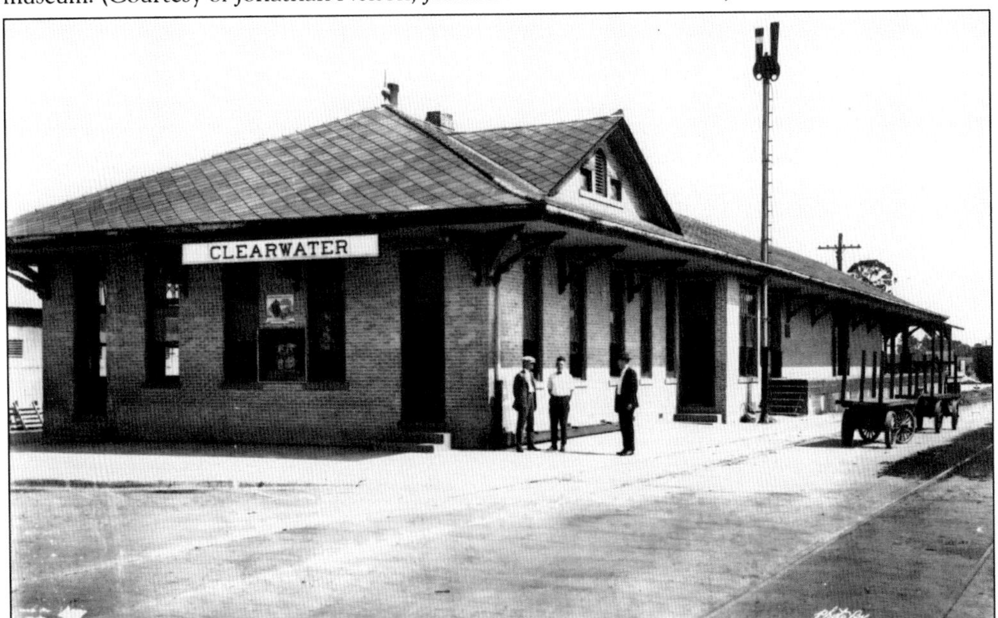

CLEARWATER. Clearwater's new brick station opened in 1910 and would serve until shortly after the 1967 merger between the ACL and Seaboard. The redundant track was removed soon afterward, and the building was razed in the early 1970s. This c. 1920 image was taken by Tampa's Burgert Brothers studio. The sign just above the train bulletin board urges motorists to "Cross Crossings Cautiously." (Courtesy of Tampa-Hillsborough Public Library.)

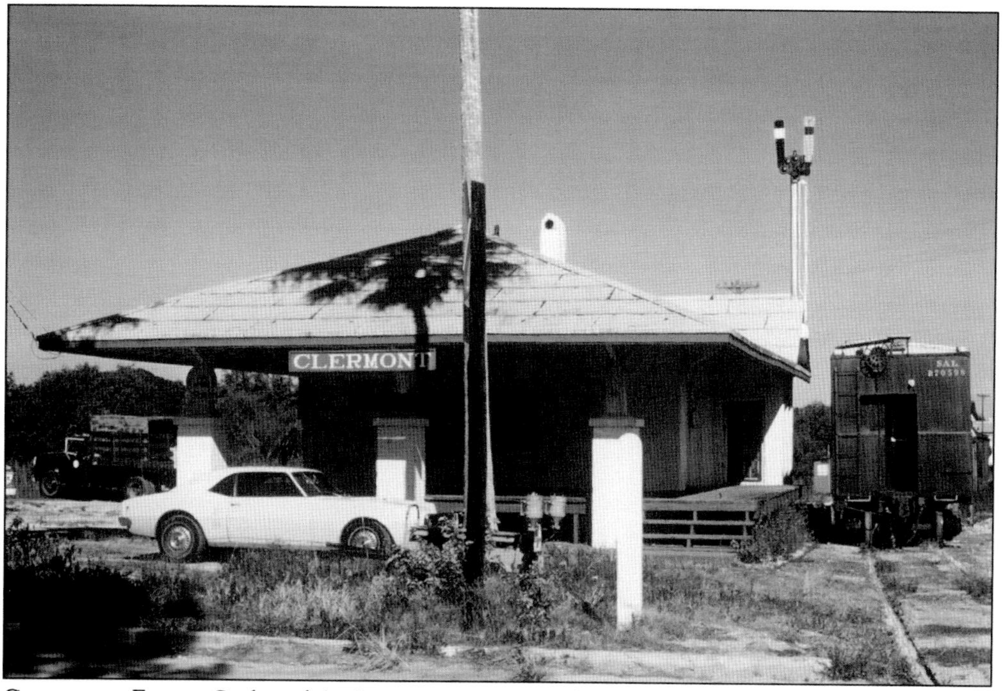

CLERMONT. Former Seaboard Air Line maintenance-of-way foreman's car R70598 sits beside the depot in this scene from mid-1969. Two years after the merger, the car is still lettered for the SAL. The depot was built around 1925. Rails through Clermont were taken up by 1984. The building was used as a barbecue restaurant before becoming a feature in Clermont's Historical Village Park after a 2008 restoration. (Courtesy of R. Randolph Stevens.)

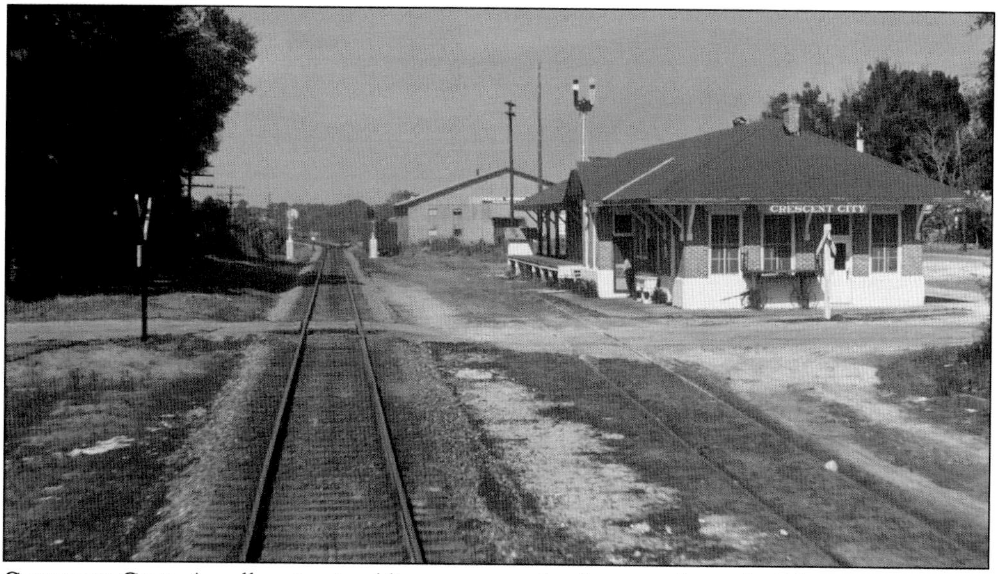

CRESCENT CITY. A well-maintained line runs past the depot in this early-1970 view. Passengers have not used the building in many years, and it appears by this time it was used for sporadic freight service only. Crescent City is 76 rail miles south and an over-two-hour train ride from Jacksonville's Union Terminal, according to the May 1927 passenger timetable. Reportedly the structure was dismantled for salvage in 1982. (Courtesy of R. Randolph Stevens.)

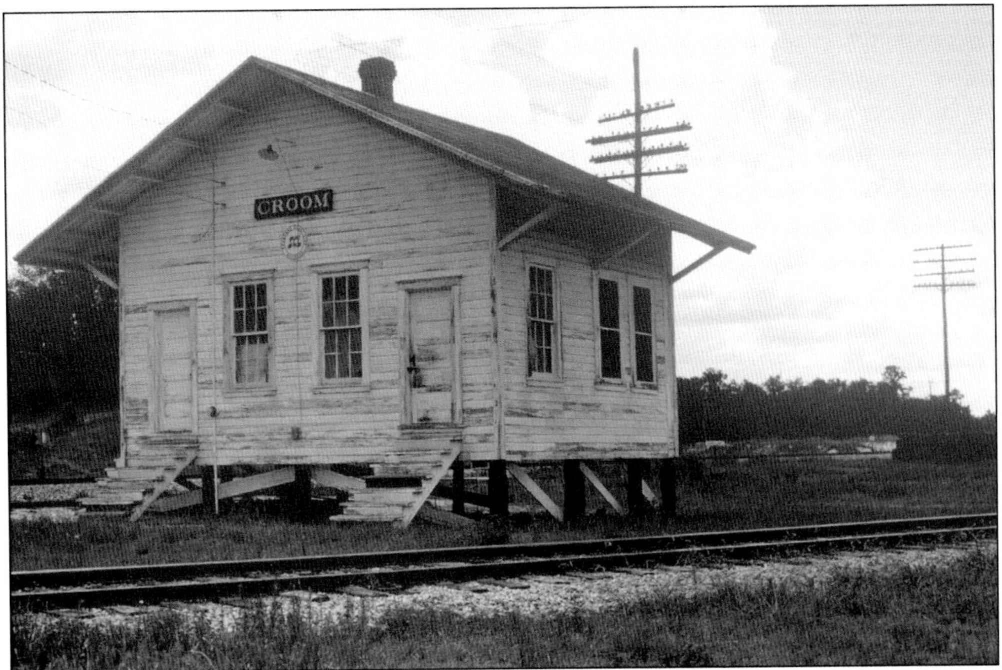

Croom. This simple wooden depot provided express, telegraph, and postal services for the railroad town of Croom in bygone days. By the time of this mid-1969 image, it had become inconsequential to the railroad. This community was known as Pemberton's Ferry when predecessor Florida Southern served the area. Croom was a rail junction and had a small yard. Today there is scant evidence any railroad activity ever took place here. (Courtesy of R. Randolph Stevens.)

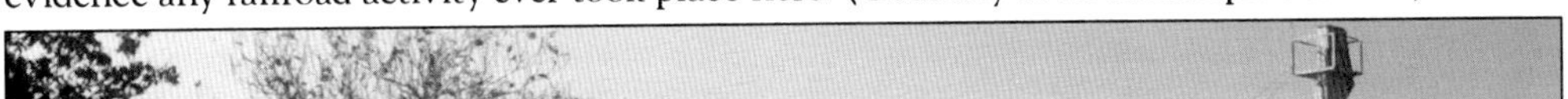

Crystal River. The Silver Springs, Ocala, and Gulf Railroad built a 50-mile line southwesterly from Ocala to Homosassa around 1888. Crystal River was located at milepost 40. The timetable of May 1927 indicates a daily train in each direction. A suitable depot was constructed around 1910. Currently this structure is leased from the city by the Lions Club and is seen as it looked in May 1971. (Courtesy of R. Randolph Stevens.)

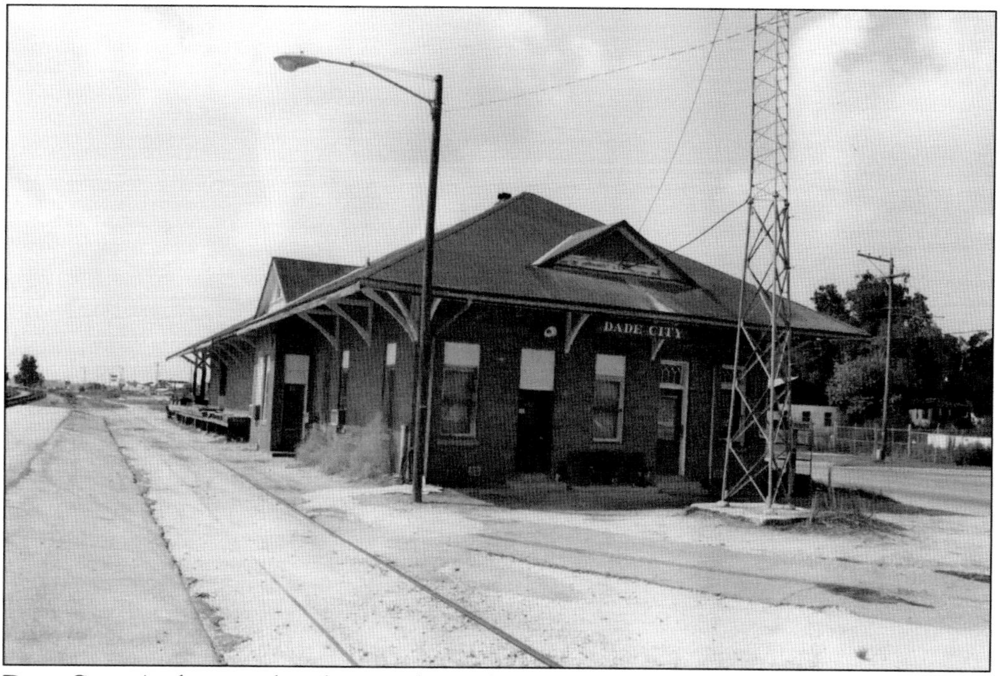

Dade City. At the time this photograph was shot on July 25, 1992, the depot was used by CSX Transportation for maintenance-of-way purposes. The next year, it became a station stop for Amtrak and was acquired by the city. It was renovated and restored in 1996–1997. Amtrak service was terminated in 2004. Built in 1912, it became Pasco County's first site to be placed on the National Register of Historic Places. (Courtesy of Mike Mulligan.)

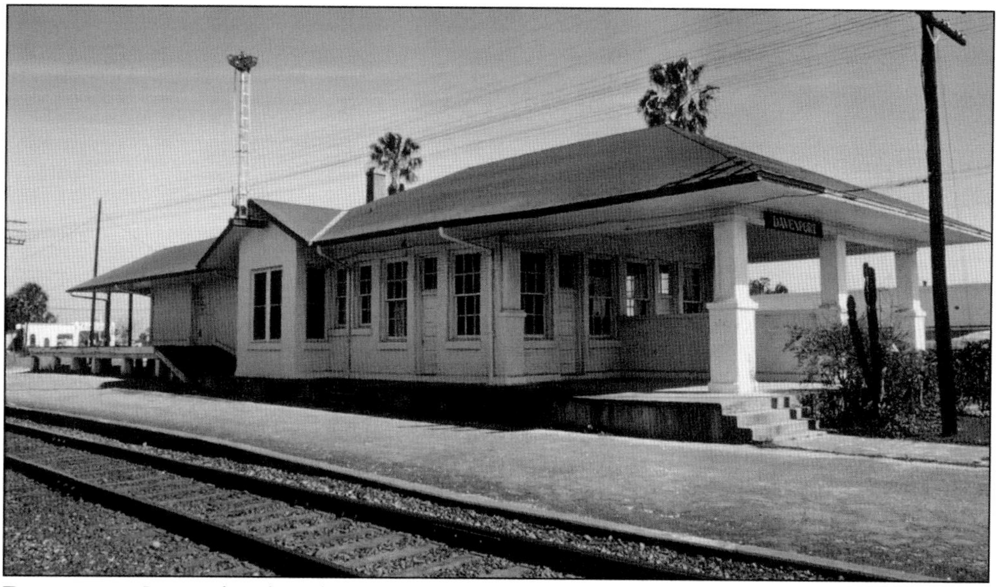

Davenport. Located midway between Orlando and Lakeland on the mainline, Davenport was once a prosperous citrus area with canning plants and fruit-packing facilities. In 1939, the town population stood at 650. The town's second depot was built around 1915 after the first station succumbed to fire. It is seen here early in 1969. It was razed in the late 1980s. (Courtesy of R. Randolph Stevens.)

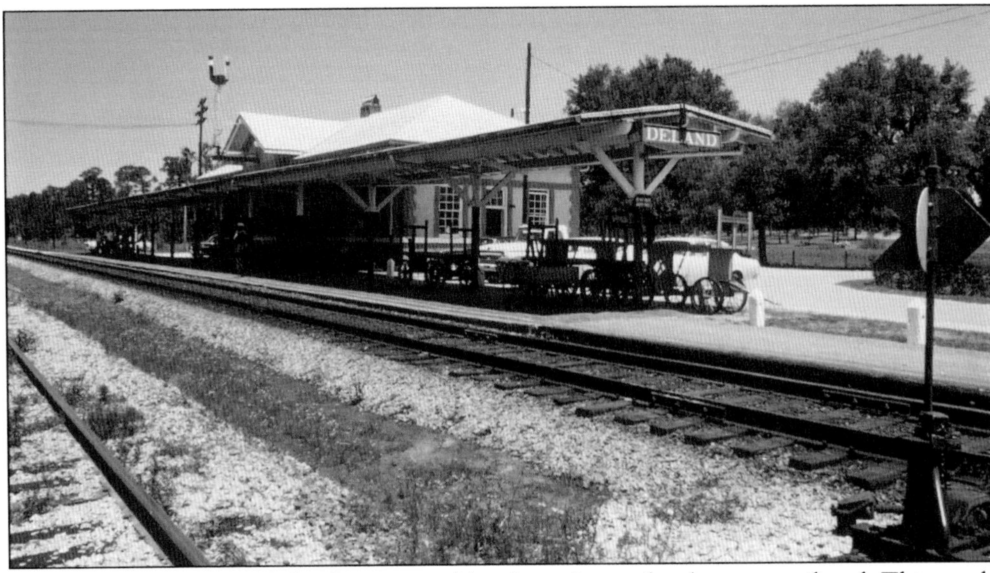

DELAND. At one time, Deland was served by three depots for the same railroad. This rarely happened in communities with fewer than 6,000 people. Stations were provided at Deland Junction, Stetson University, and Amelia Avenue. Amelia Avenue was lost to fire in 1911 and replaced by Michigan Avenue. The last Deland Junction building is shown in early 1969. Built in 1918, this current Amtrak station was renovated with $425,000 and rededicated December 21, 2006. (Courtesy of R. Randolph Stevens.)

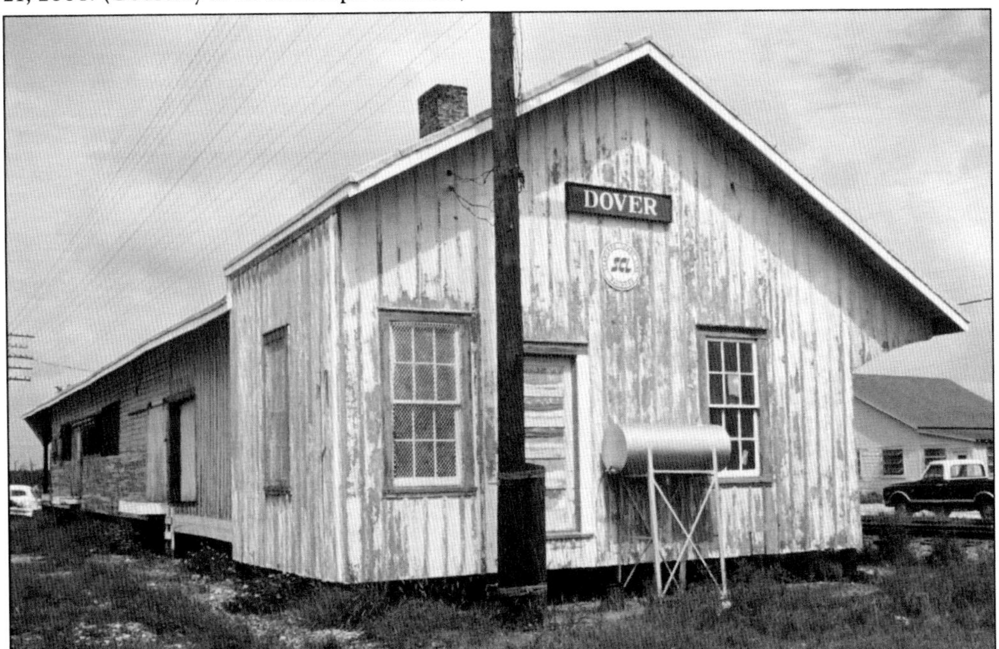

DOVER. This post-merger view of Dover from July 1968 displays the new Seaboard Coast Line logo on the building, which is in need of painting. Obviously railroad management knew its days of service were soon coming to an end. Dover is located in Hillsborough County, just 14 railroad miles from Tampa's Union Station. The building was taken down sometime in the 1970s. (Courtesy of R. Randolph Stevens.)

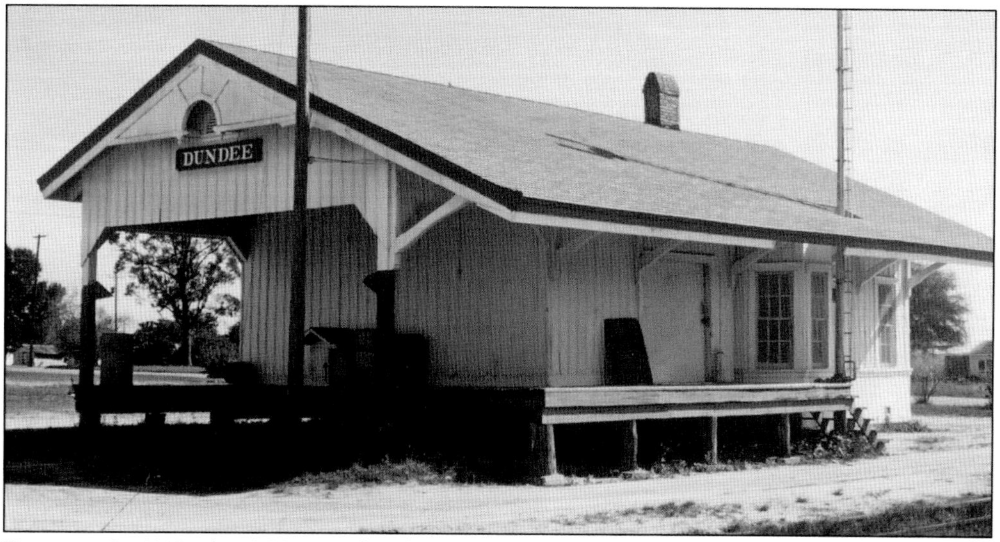

DUNDEE. In 1912, the ACL completed a branch line coming off the main at Haines City and extending down 46 miles near Sebring. This branch brought the railroad to Dundee, and this depot was built to serve the town. Passenger rail service concluded around 1954, and freight services ended around 1975. The depot was later moved a short distance to serve as the local history museum. This photograph dates to early 1969. (Courtesy of R. Randolph Stevens.)

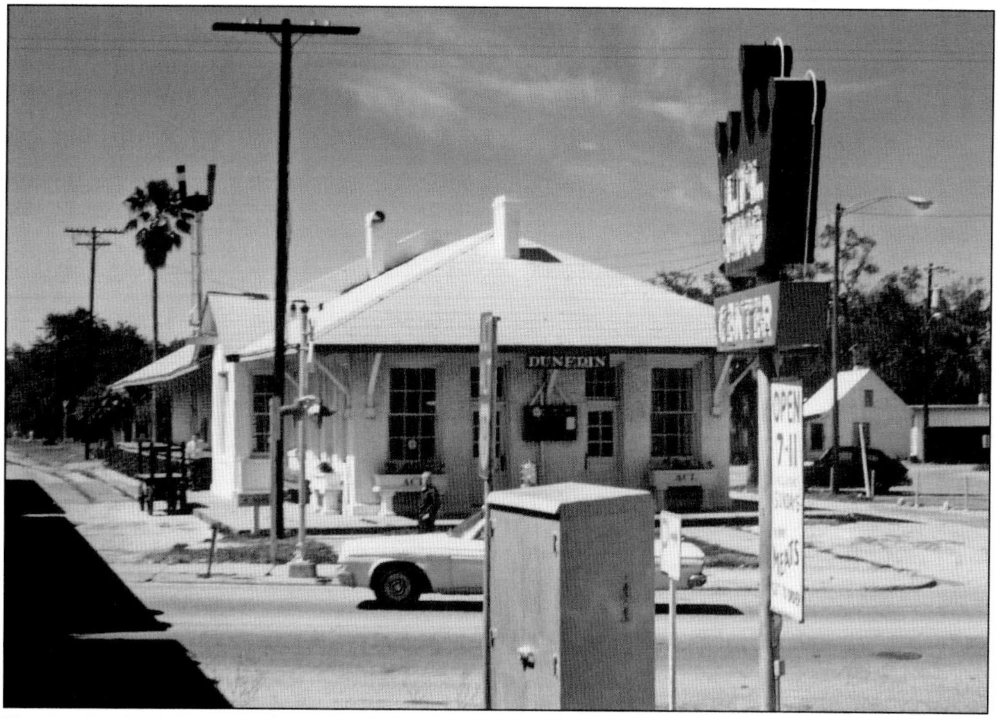

DUNEDIN. A passenger rail car vestibule serves as the platform for this May 1969 image. Regularly scheduled passenger trains would only serve Dunedin for another two years. The rail line was abandoned in 1986 but converted to a recreational trail by Pinellas County. The brick depot built in 1922 still serves the community as home to the local historical society and museum. (Courtesy of Paul Coe.)

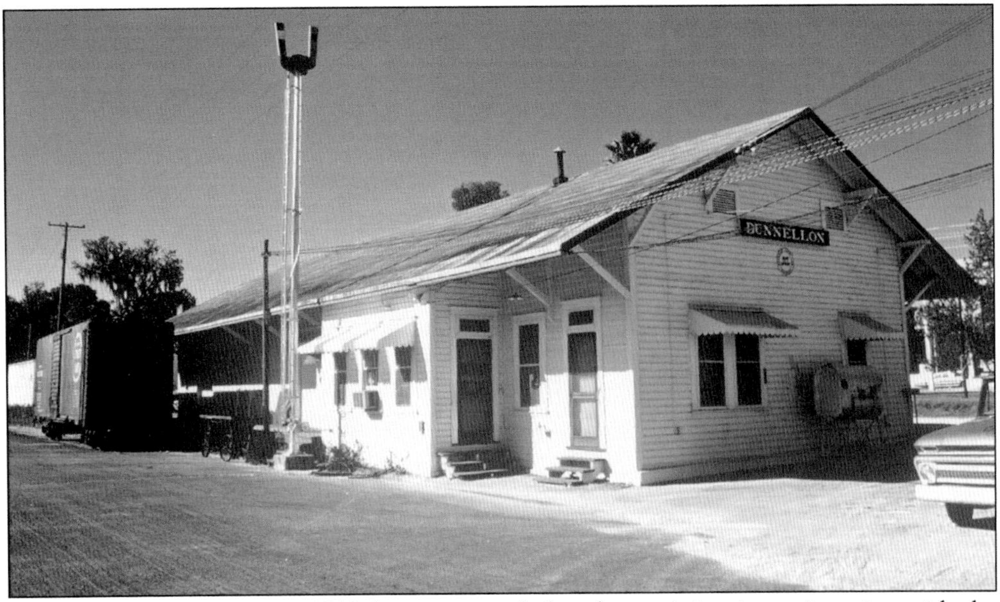

DUNNELLON. Beginning in 1889, limestone and phosphate mining in conjunction with the arrival of the railroad brought prosperity to Dunnellon. The boom years lasted until 1920 and are commemorated now with a designated "Boomtown Historic District" that includes 70 structures. The 1908 depot seen here in December 1968 is included. It is now home to the Greater Dunnellon Historical Society. (Courtesy of R. Randolph Stevens.)

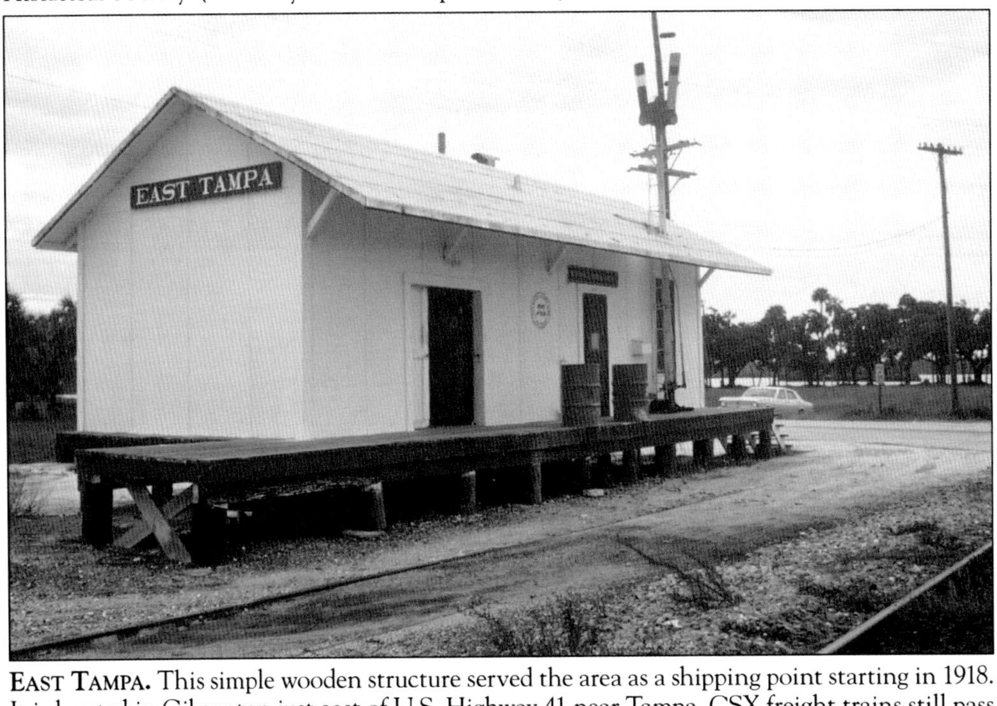

EAST TAMPA. This simple wooden structure served the area as a shipping point starting in 1918. It is located in Gibsonton just east of U.S. Highway 41 near Tampa. CSX freight trains still pass by regularly, including the famous Tropicana Juice train on its way to and from the plant in Bradenton. CSX Transportation, East Tampa Engineering-Fertilizer Business Unit was using the building as of March 2004. (Courtesy of R. Randolph Stevens.)

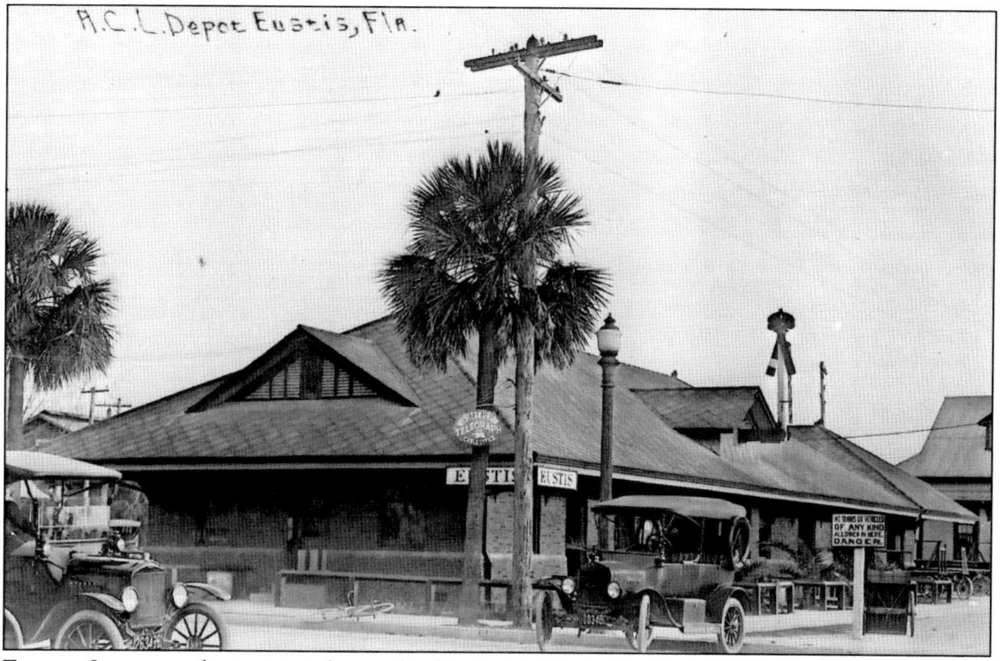

EUSTIS. Lying on the eastern shore of Lake Eustis, the city of Eustis is a popular tourist town. In the early years of the last century, it formed the northern apex of the "Golden Triangle," a prosperous citrus-growing area, with Mount Dora and Tavares. Built in 1913, the impressive station served the needs of the city through the years of World War II. It was taken down a few years later. (Courtesy of Clayton Bishop Jr. Collection.)

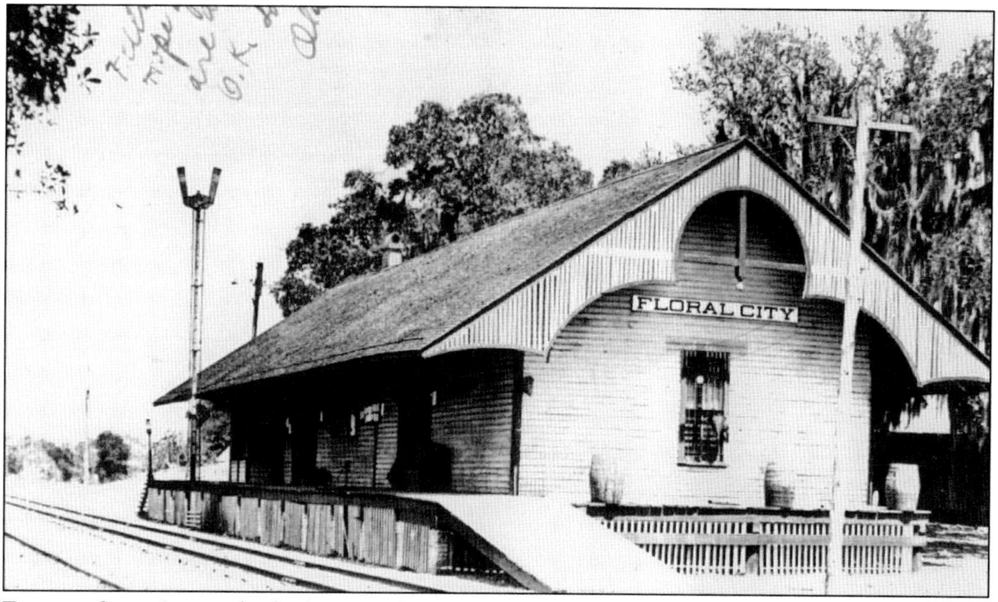

FLORAL CITY. Located a little more than six miles south of Inverness, Floral City was once a prosperous phosphate-mining town. At one time, it was believed to be the largest city in Florida. The depot, located just north of Orange Avenue, was a bustling place whenever the passenger trains arrived. The wooden depot has been gone for many years. The rails were removed in the mid- to late 1980s. (Courtesy of Old Courthouse Heritage Museum.)

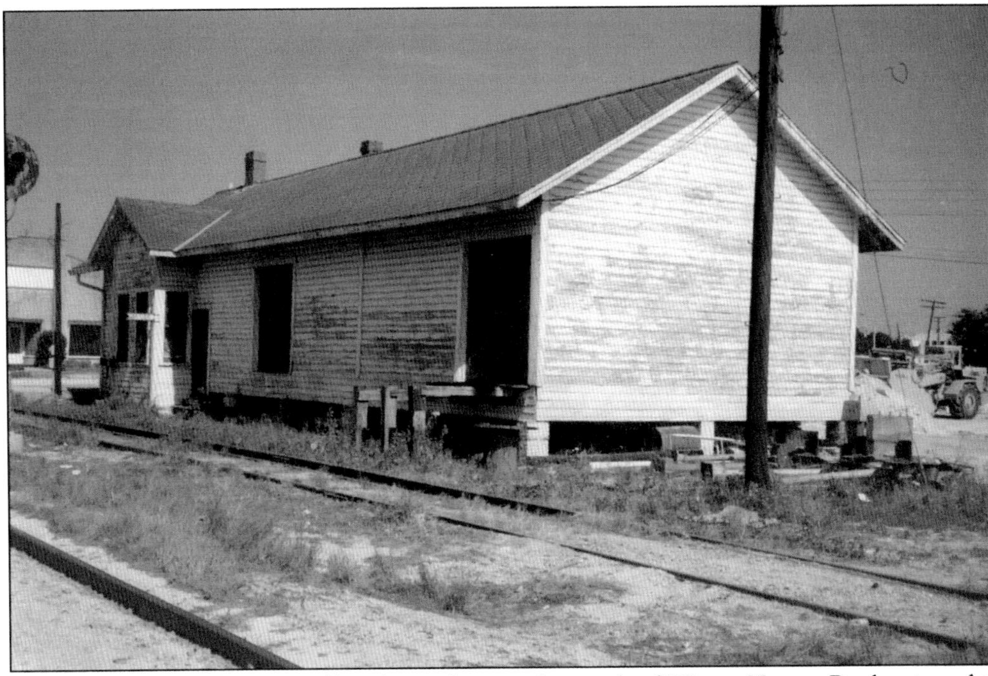

FLORENCE VILLA. Florence Villa is located two miles north of Winter Haven. By the time this photograph was taken, the depot appears to be no longer in railroad company service. Florence Villa was located on the Bartow Branch, constructed in 1885. The depot dates to around 1900. The relatively modern earth-moving machine in the background would date this image to around 1960. (Courtesy of Polk County Historical Museum.)

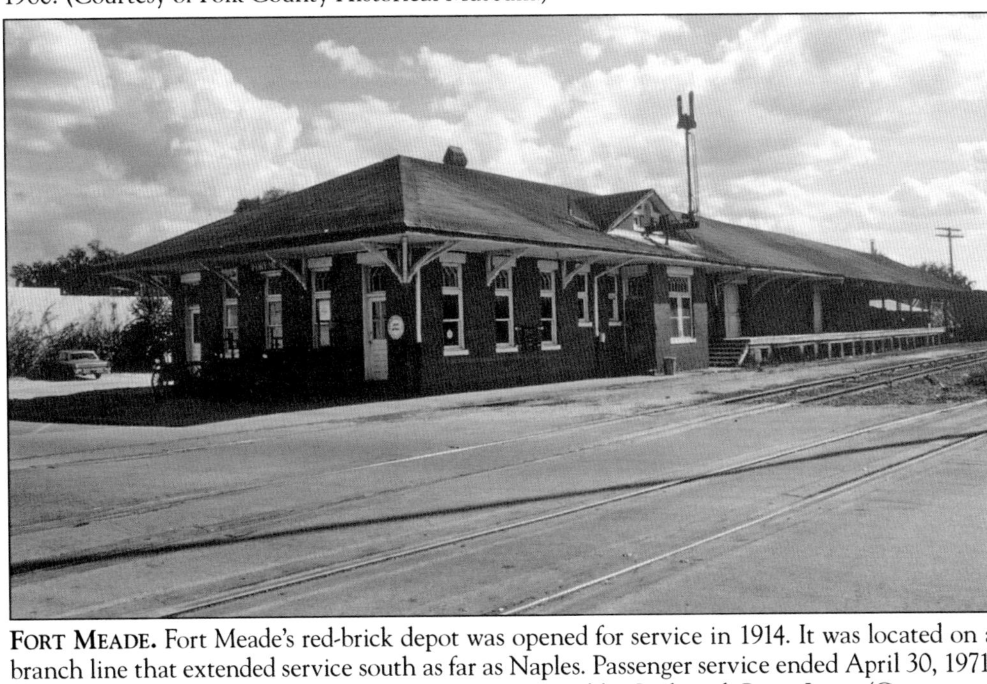

FORT MEADE. Fort Meade's red-brick depot was opened for service in 1914. It was located on a branch line that extended service south as far as Naples. Passenger service ended April 30, 1971. It is seen here as it looked in early 1969, when operated by Seaboard Coast Line. (Courtesy of R. Randolph Stevens.)

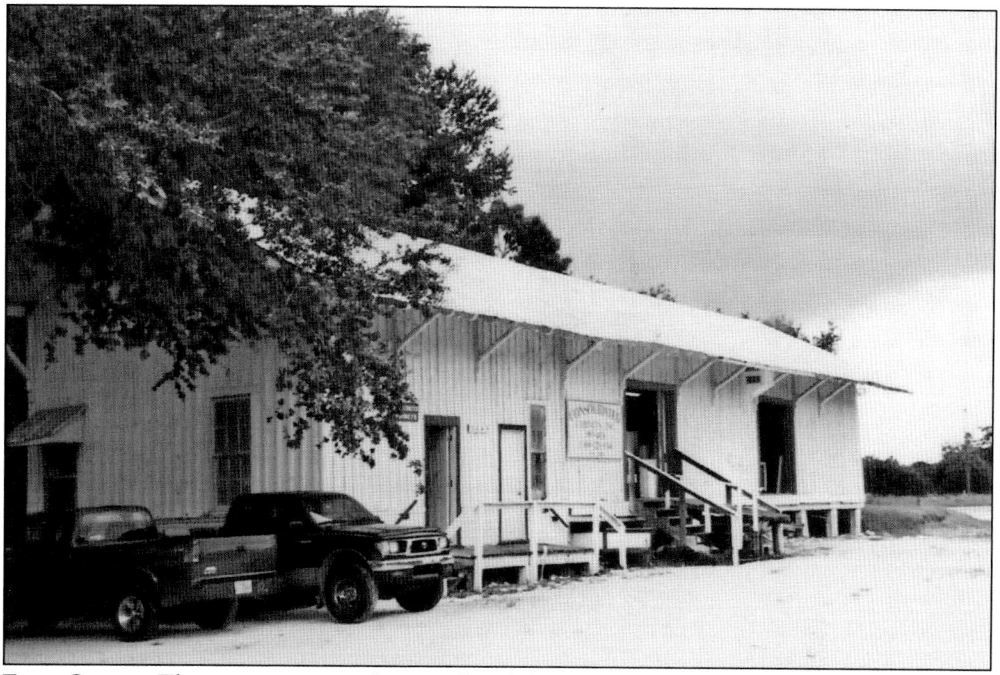

Fort Ogden. This structure served as a railroad depot, post office, and cabinet shop for about 100 years, but Hurricane Charley destroyed it in a matter of hours on August 13, 2004. The building had been moved a short distance south after the conclusion of its railroad service. This photograph captures the building in 2000. (Courtesy of Jeanne Hickam.)

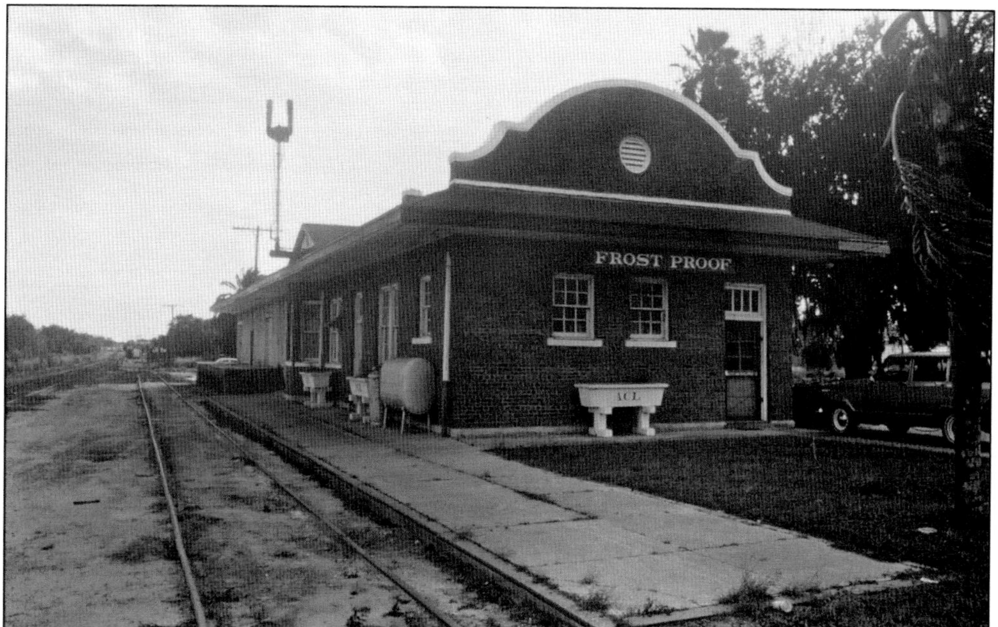

Frostproof. The tracks still run alongside the Frostproof depot, but the building is no longer used for railroad purposes. When this image was made in early 1969, the station was still manned by a freight agent. Built in 1912, it currently serves as the home of the chamber of commerce. (Courtesy of R. Randolph Stevens.)

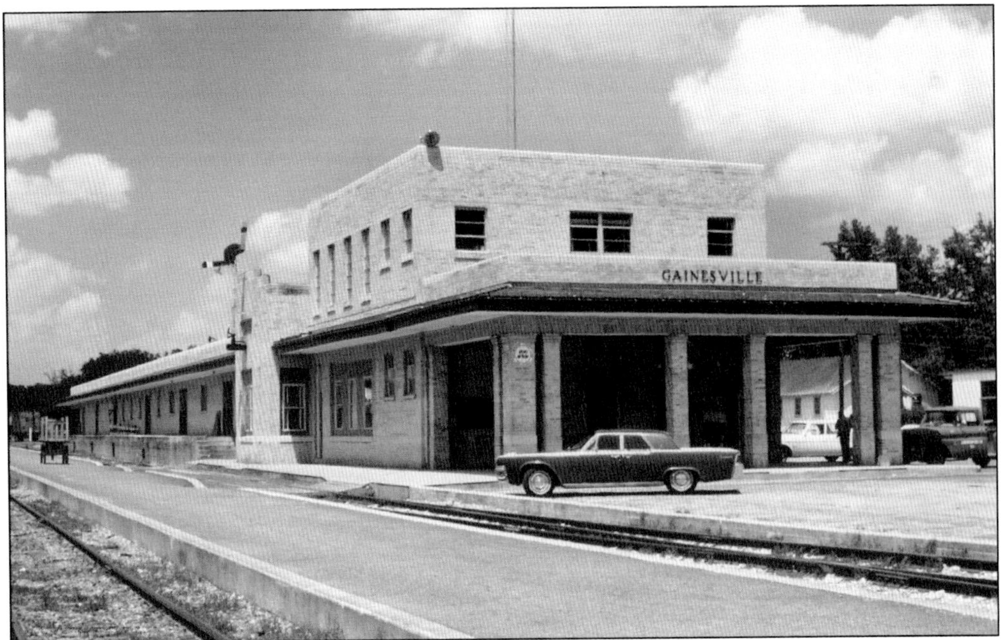

GAINESVILLE. On September 15, 1881, Florida Southern Railway commenced service to Gainesville. The tracks and depot were located in the center of Main Street. The city grew, the automobile came along, and this arrangement caused problems. Finally a new station was built on the northwestern side of the city in 1948, serving passengers until 1971. Seen here in 1971, it has been renovated for use by Santa Fe Community College. (Courtesy of R. Randolph Stevens.)

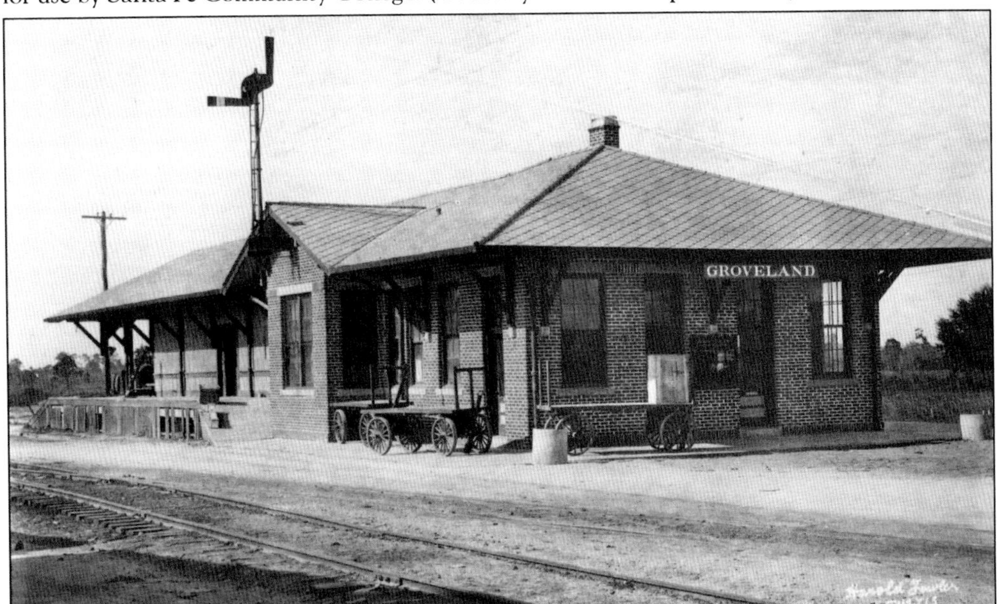

GROVELAND. Groveland's population was just over 400 at the time of incorporation in 1922. In 1925, a brick railroad depot was placed in service. This area was a producer of citrus and watermelons. Over the years, the station lost the wooden freight section, and tracks through Groveland were pulled out by 1984. Afterward, the remaining structure was used by an adjacent citrus-processing plant. It survived as of late 2005. (Courtesy of Florida State Archives.)

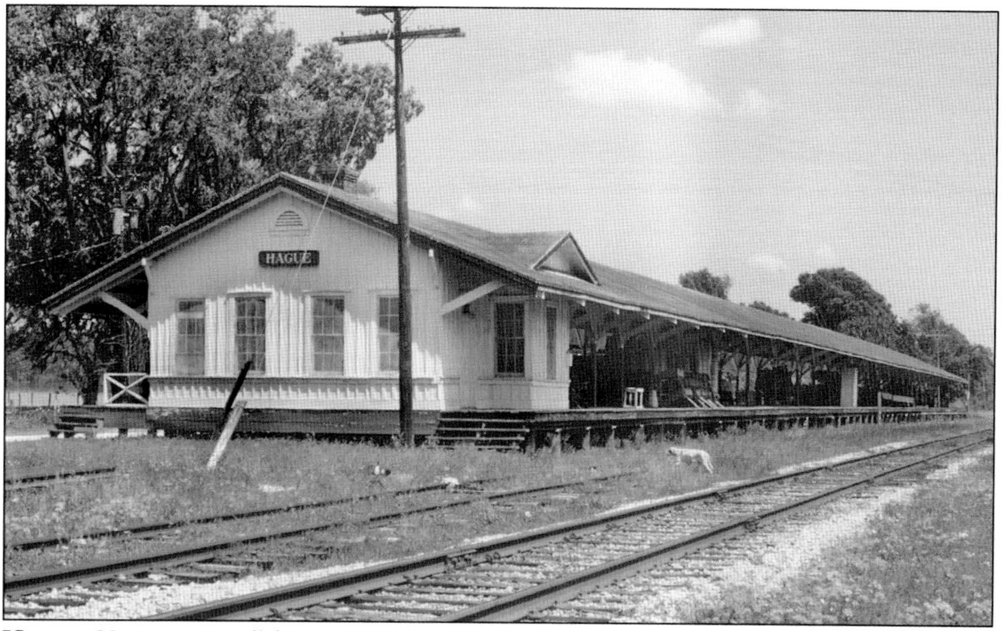

HAGUE. Hague is a small farming community located north of Gainesville in Alachua County. Vast quantities of produce were shipped from the large freight shed. Things are quiet at the depot on this spring day in 1971. (Courtesy of R. Randolph Stevens.)

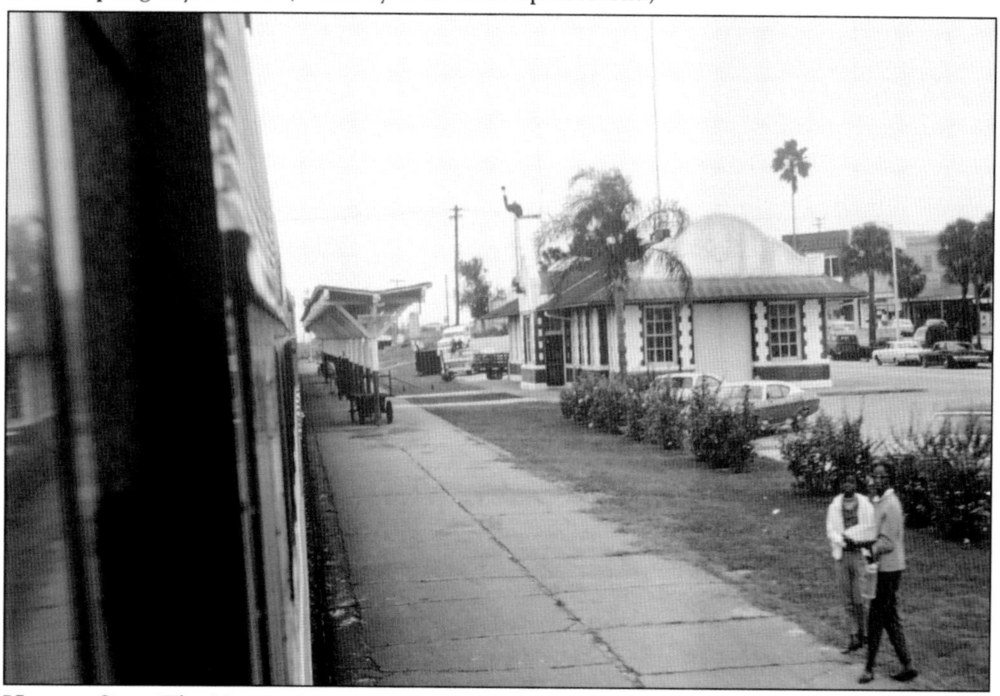

HAINES CITY. The Haines City station is seen as it appeared from a passenger car vestibule in November 1968. A local story suggests the town was named after Henry Haines, an official with the South Florida Railroad, so that he might use his influence to secure trains stopping here. He did, and service continued until April 30, 1971. The 1920-era depot survives and was recently (in 2007) used as an antiques shop. (Courtesy of R. Randolph Stevens.)

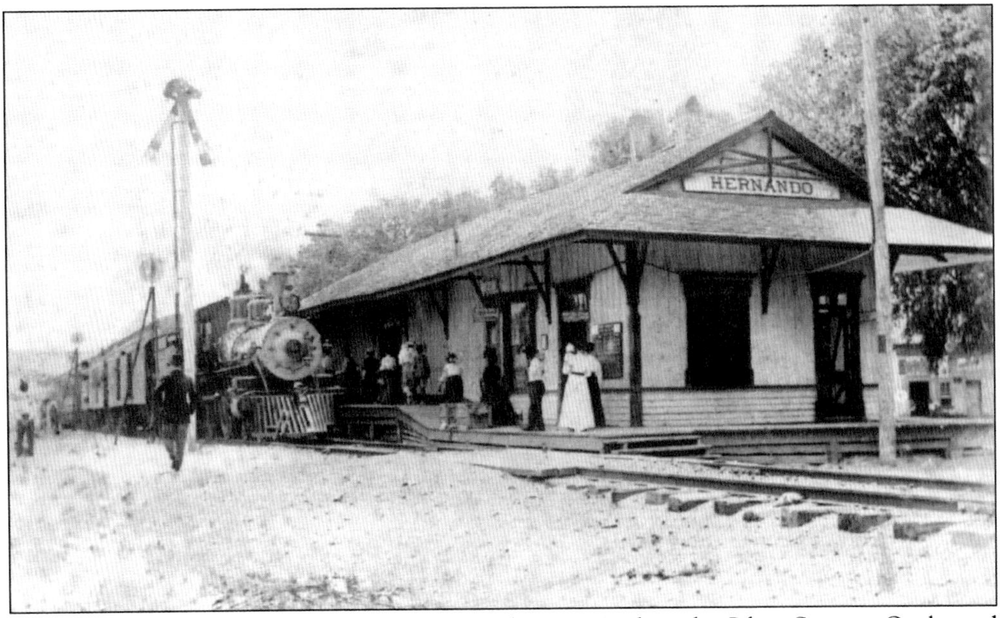

HERNANDO. The railroad first came to Hernando in 1892 when the Silver Springs, Ocala, and Gulf Railroad built a 16-mile extension south to Inverness. A wooden depot was built to serve the community and is seen here around 1900. The line was abandoned in the mid-1980s and the right-of-way is now part of the 46-mile-long Withlacoochee State Trail. (Courtesy of Old Courthouse Heritage Museum.)

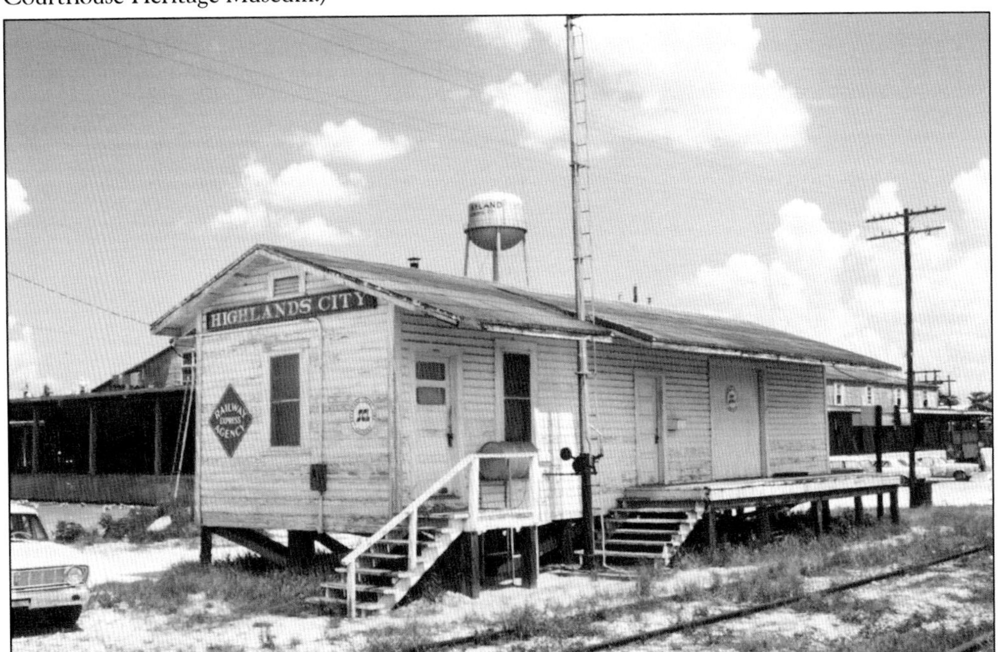

HIGHLANDS CITY. The tracks that serve Highlands City are rusty, and weeds are filling in the right-of-way in this July 1968 view. The simple wood-frame depot and the tracks are long gone. The right-of-way was recently opened as a trail stretching 7.75 miles and connecting Lakeland and Bartow. Highlands City is about halfway between those cities. (Courtesy of R. Randolph Stevens.)

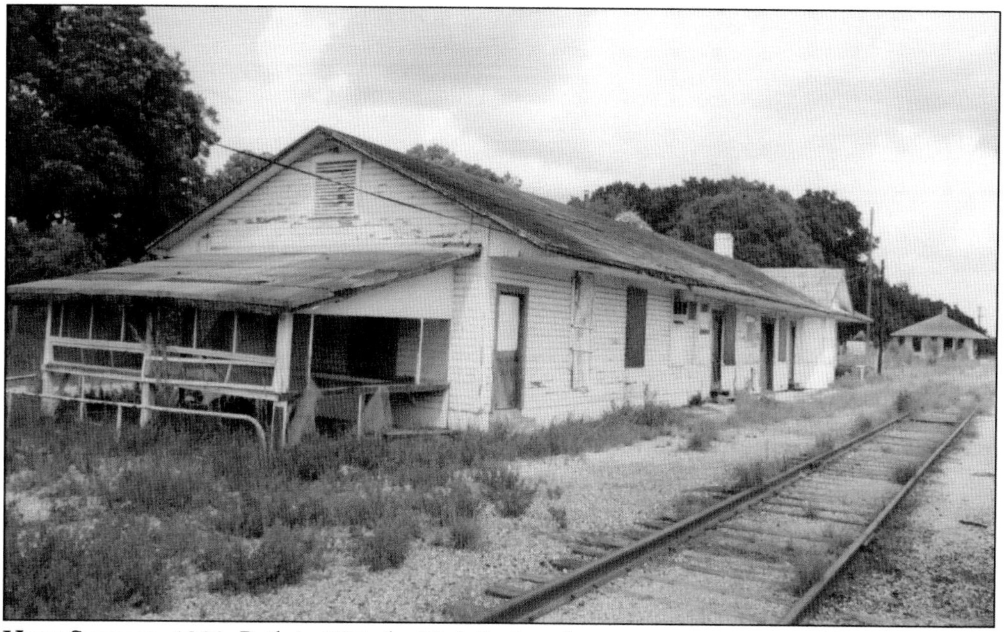

HIGH SPRINGS, 1992. Built in 1910, the High Springs depot is seen at its original location on July 25, 1992. The partially torn down freight house lies just down the tracks. The railroad employed many people at their large yard, servicing center, repair shops, and divisional headquarter offices. The depot was moved to downtown and renovated in 1994 and operated as a railroad museum. (Courtesy of Mike Mulligan.)

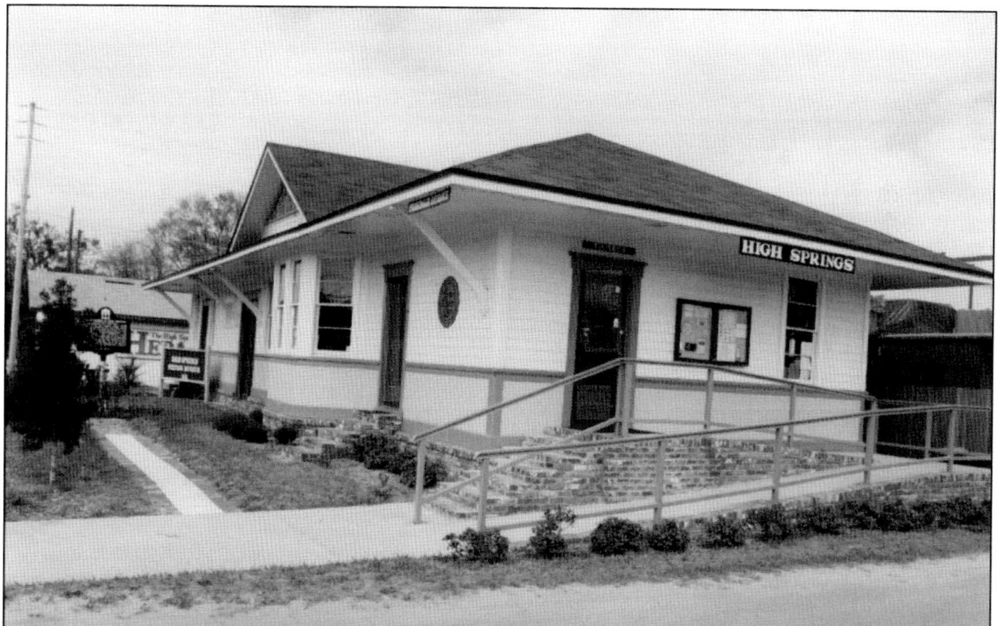

HIGH SPRINGS, 1996. The High Springs depot is seen in March 1996 as it appeared after its relocation to the business district, renovation, and conversion to a railroad museum. The railroad museum would be short-lived, closing in 1998. A bakery/restaurant appropriately named Station Bakery now occupies the building. (Courtesy of Mike Mulligan.)

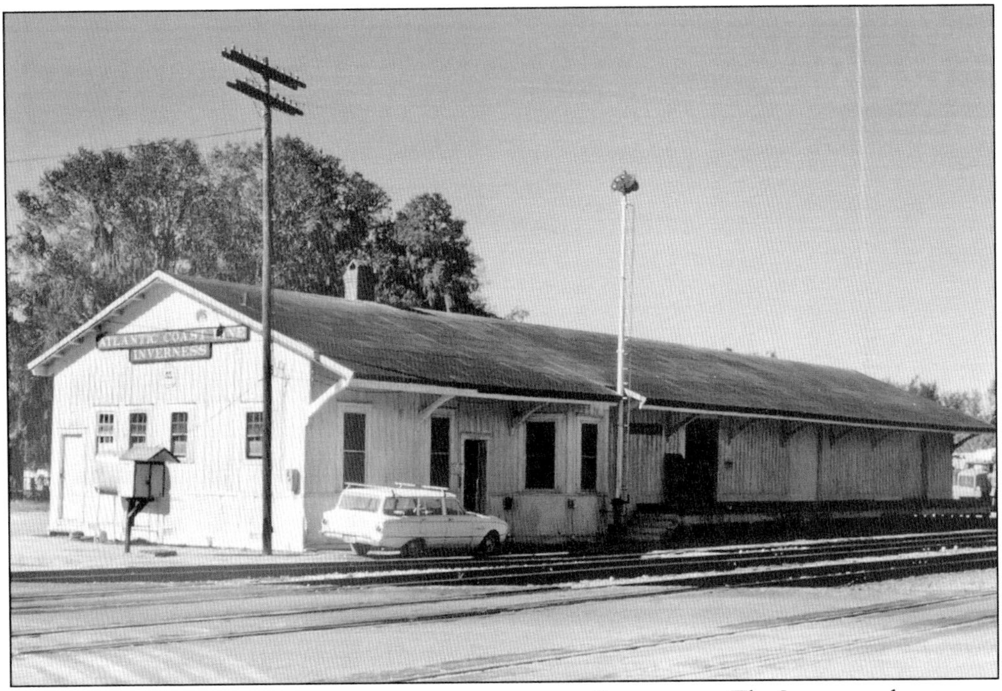

INVERNESS. The Inverness depot no longer sits alongside a rumbling rail corridor, but activity goes on as recreational trail users pass by on the Withlacoochee State Trail. In 1989, the city's last link to the national rail system was lost when the branch to Gulf Junction was abandoned. Built in 1900, the depot is shown as it appeared in late 1968. (Courtesy of R. Randolph Stevens.)

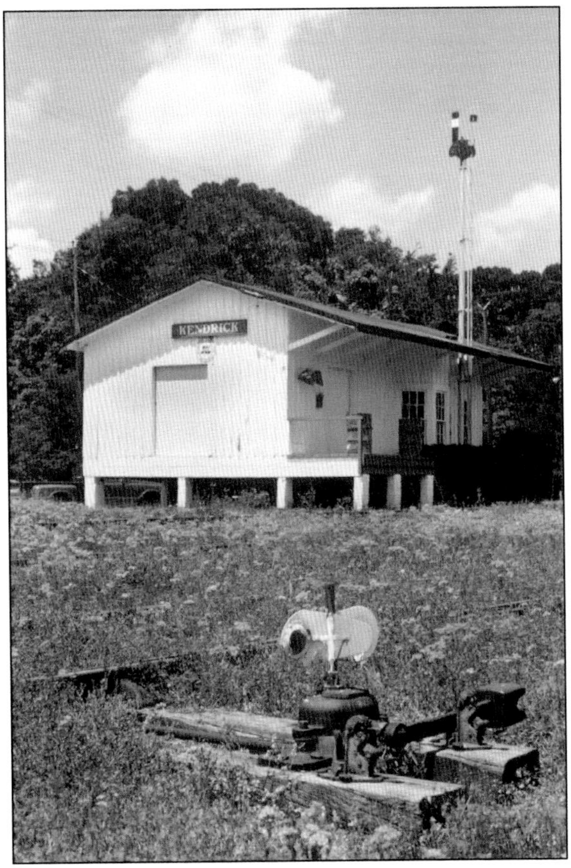

KENDRICK. Florida Southern Railway brought rail service to Kendrick, a small community north of Ocala in 1882. A simple wooden depot served the community for many years, and after its railroad service ended, it was converted to a private residence. It appears well maintained in April 1971. (Courtesy of R. Randolph Stevens.)

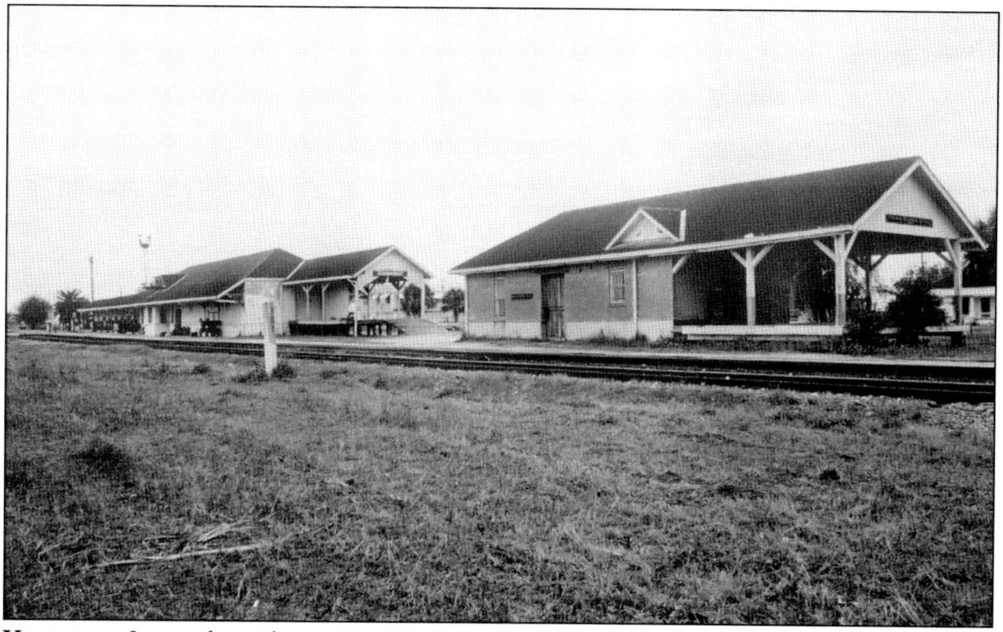

KISSIMMEE. Located at milepost No. 808, Kissimmee's Union Depot and Railway Express Agency (REA) are located on the former South Florida Railroad, built in 1883. Union Depot is somewhat of a misnomer, as the ACL owned all railroads that served the station. Currently Amtrak serves the station, built in 1910, with four trains per day. The REA building was removed prior to 1990. Both buildings were photographed in November 1968. (Courtesy of R. Randolph Stevens.)

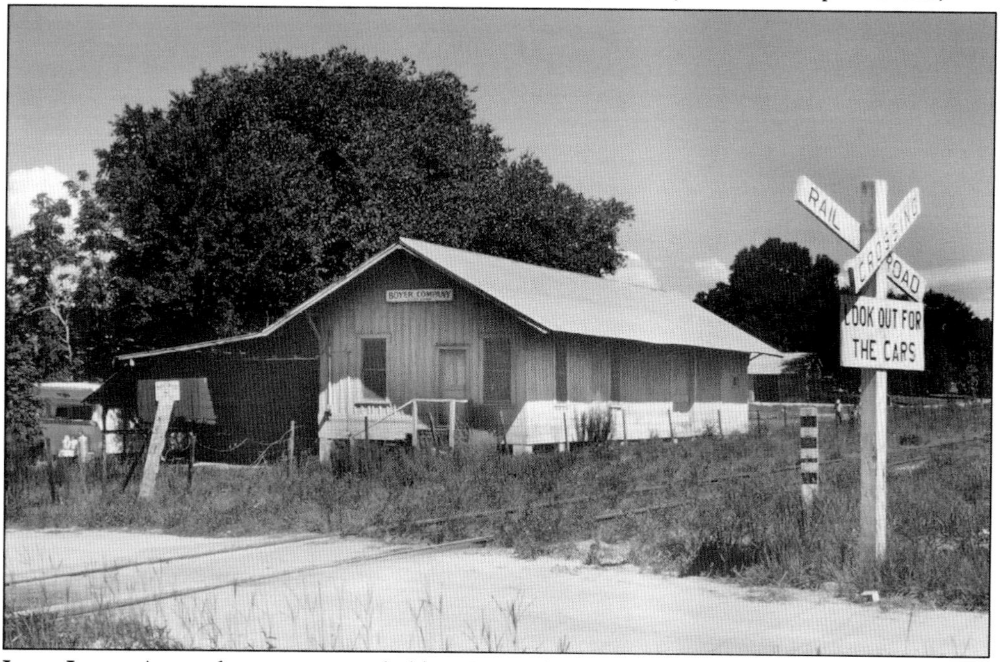

LADY LAKE. A grand reopening was held on September 22, 2007, as the former Lady Lake depot assumed its new role as the Lady Lake Historical Society Museum. The building was constructed around 1900 and served the railroad into the 1960s. It was used by the Boyer Company, as seen here early in 1971. Line abandonment occurred in 1979. (Courtesy of R. Randolph Stevens.)

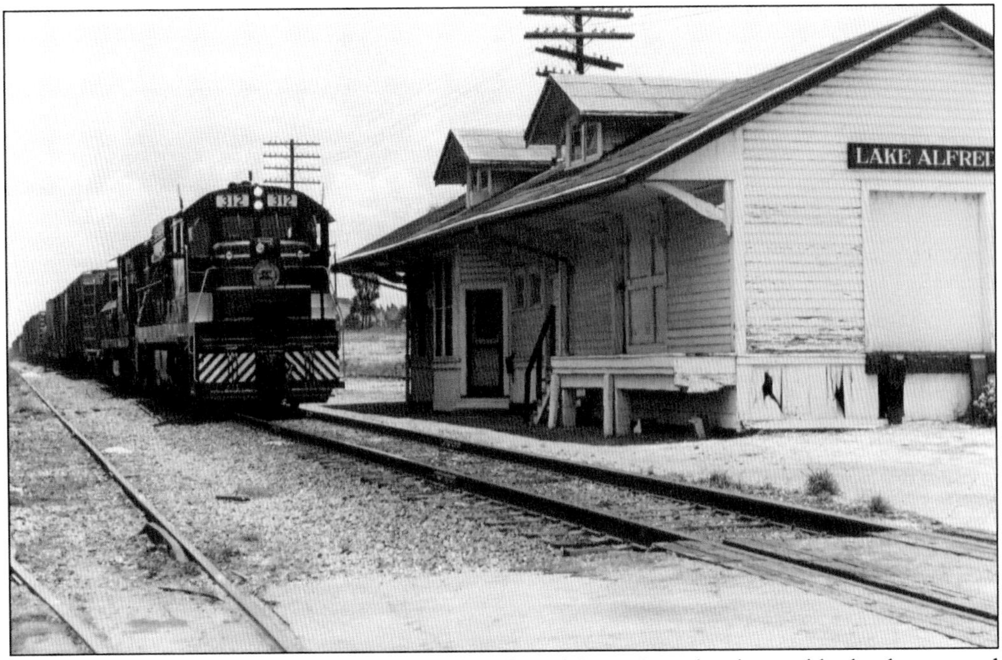

LAKE ALFRED. On June 9, 1973, a westbound Seaboard Coast Line freight rumbles by the vacated depot. Times are changing as passenger trains and manned stations are becoming fewer and farther between. The depot, built around 1920, would be removed later in the decade. (Courtesy of Fred Clark Jr.)

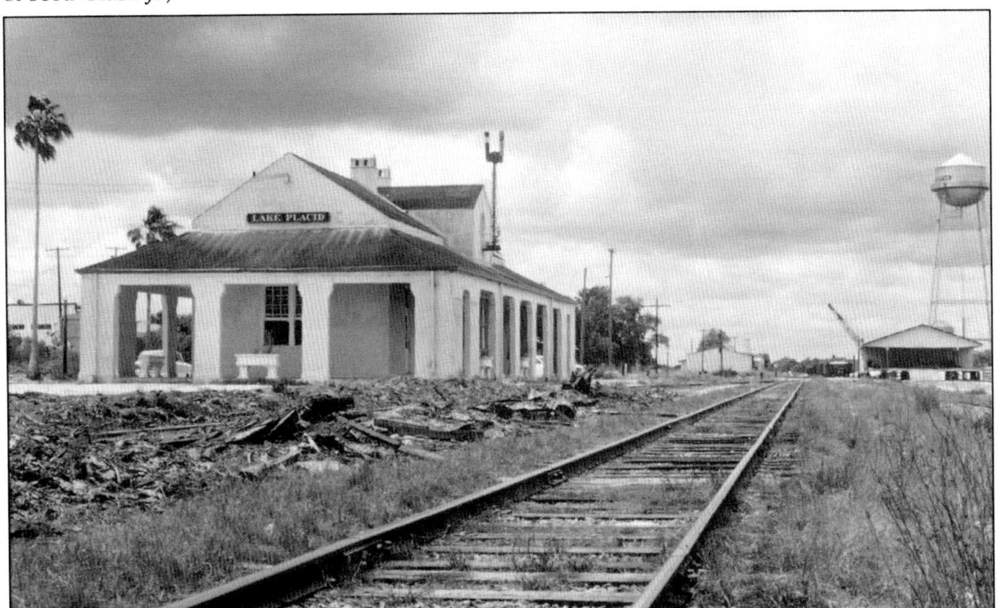

LAKE PLACID. Passenger trains stopped serving Lake Placid in the mid-1950s. The freight agency would continue until the 1970s. The masonry vernacular building was constructed in 1926 and captured here on a spring day in 1970. The depot is now home to the Lake Placid Historical Society and operated as a local history museum. In early 1997, excursion trains were operated over consecutive weekends, drawing large crowds to the station. (Courtesy of R. Randolph Stevens.)

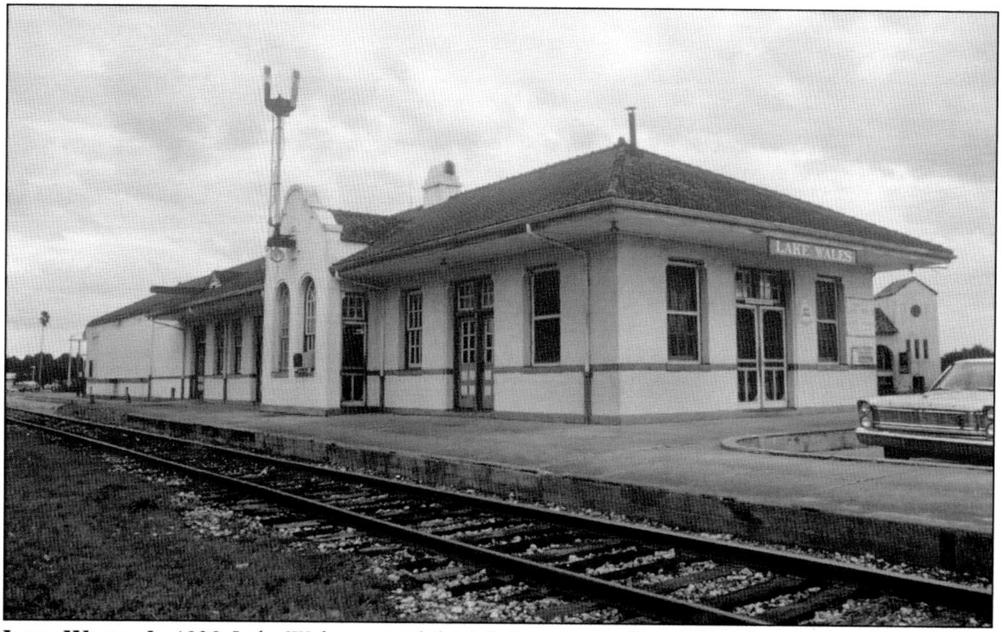

LAKE WALES. In 1928, Lake Wales opened this Mediterranean Revival brick station with a barreled-tile roof, which cost approximately $51,000. Ten years later, a loading platform and freight room were added. The last passenger train left the depot in 1954. Freight service would continue until the 1970s. In 1976, the building was reopened as a museum and cultural center, a role it continues to perform. This view is from January 1969. (Courtesy of R. Randolph Stevens.)

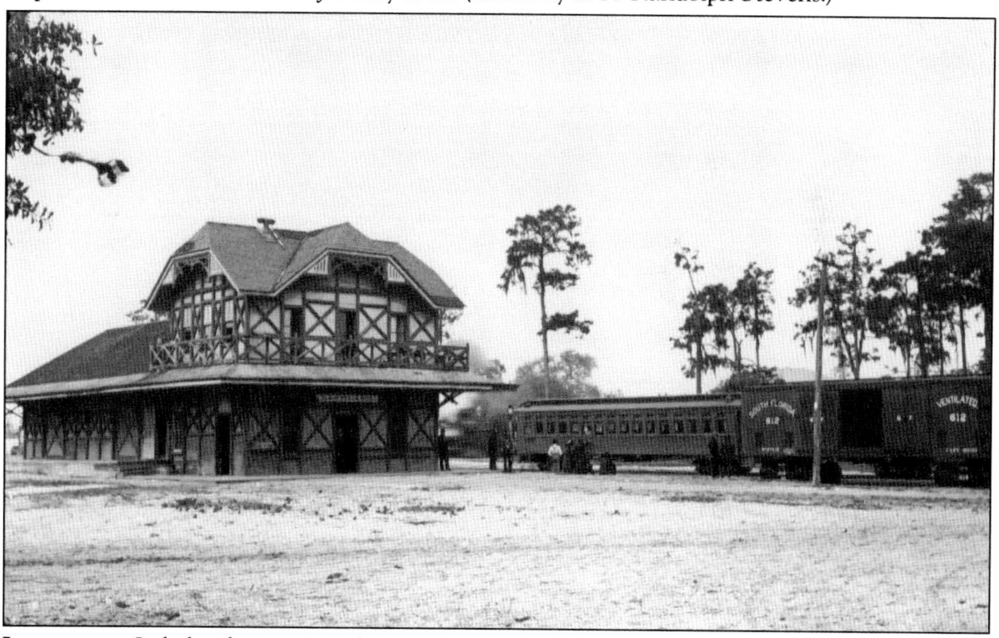

LAKELAND. Lakeland was created when the South Florida Railroad extended their line from Kissimmee to Tampa in 1884. Lakeland founder Abraham Munn financed a two-story wooden depot that cost $2,500. The building opened in 1886. It was consumed by fire in 1901. A replacement one-story wooden building was constructed a short time later. Within 10 years, the replacement would be inadequate to meet the needs of the city. (Courtesy of Polk County Historical Museum.)

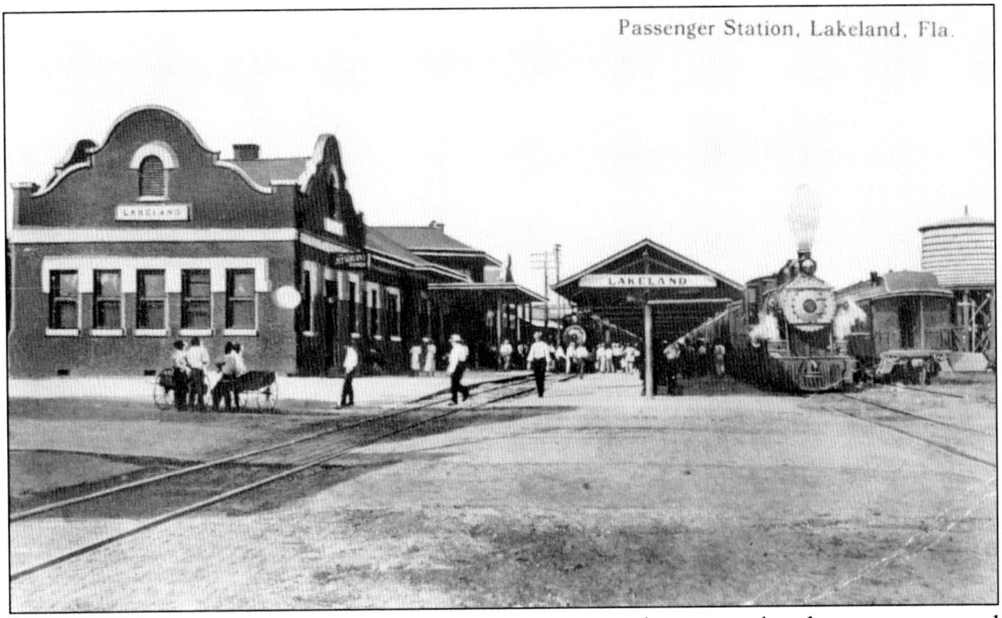

LAKELAND, 1913 AND 1919. In 1910, city representatives, the state railroad commission, and the ACL Railroad agreed a modern new depot was needed to replace the inadequate facility constructed in 1902. A single-floor brick station was opened with over 1,000 citizens turning out for the festivities on March 14, 1912. The community took great pride in the new building, with the mayor proclaiming it "a credit to a city many times larger." In February 1918, tragedy would strike the building when a fire broke out, causing $25,000 in damage. The brick construction allowed it to be repaired and improved. With a second-floor addition, the station reopened for business on January 31, 1919. The building accommodated the growing city for over 40 years. (Above courtesy of Florida State Archives; below courtesy of Polk County Historical Museum.)

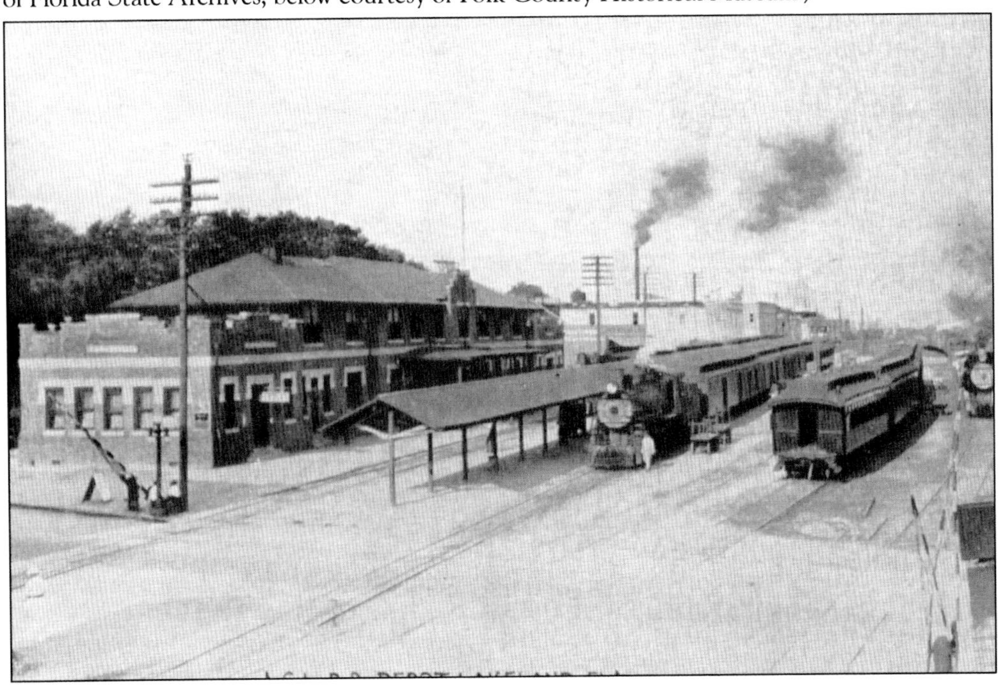

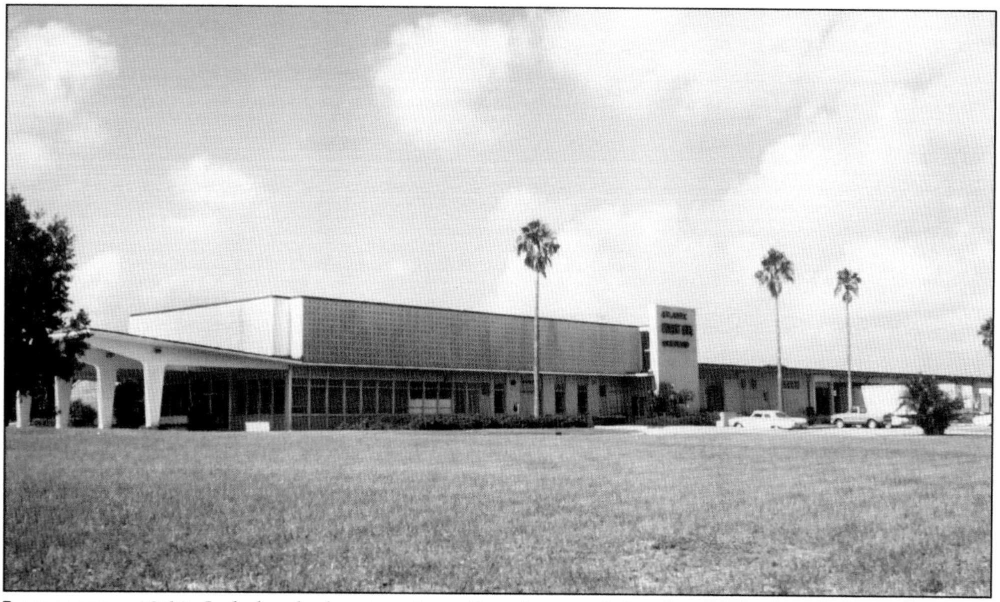

LAKELAND, 1960. Lakeland, the city the railroad created, by the 1950s found the railroad an impediment to downtown development. The city arranged for the construction of this new, million-dollar building, which opened in 1960. It was located a mile west of the old brick station, razed soon afterward. Seen in this July 1968 view, the building was used until 1998. It is now derelict and has an uncertain future. (Courtesy of R. Randolph Stevens.)

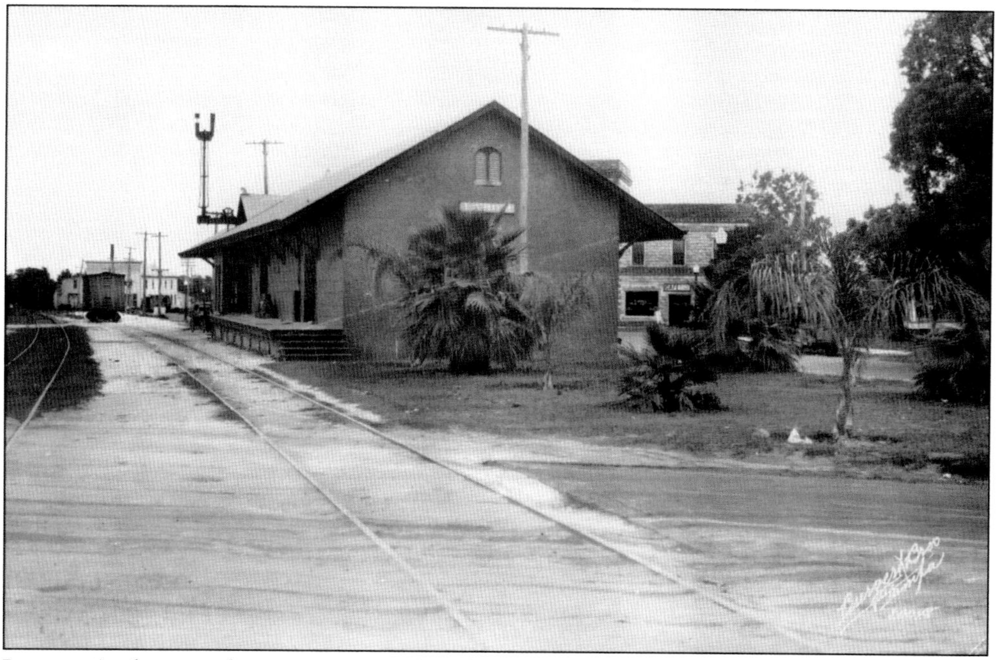

LARGO. At the time this image was made in June 1926, Largo had less than 1,000 people living in the community. Back then, an almost continuous stretch of small truck farms and orange and grapefruit groves existed between here and St. Petersburg. The depot built in 1915 would survive until 1966. It was torn down to facilitate the widening of U.S. Highway 19. (Courtesy of Tampa-Hillsborough Public Library.)

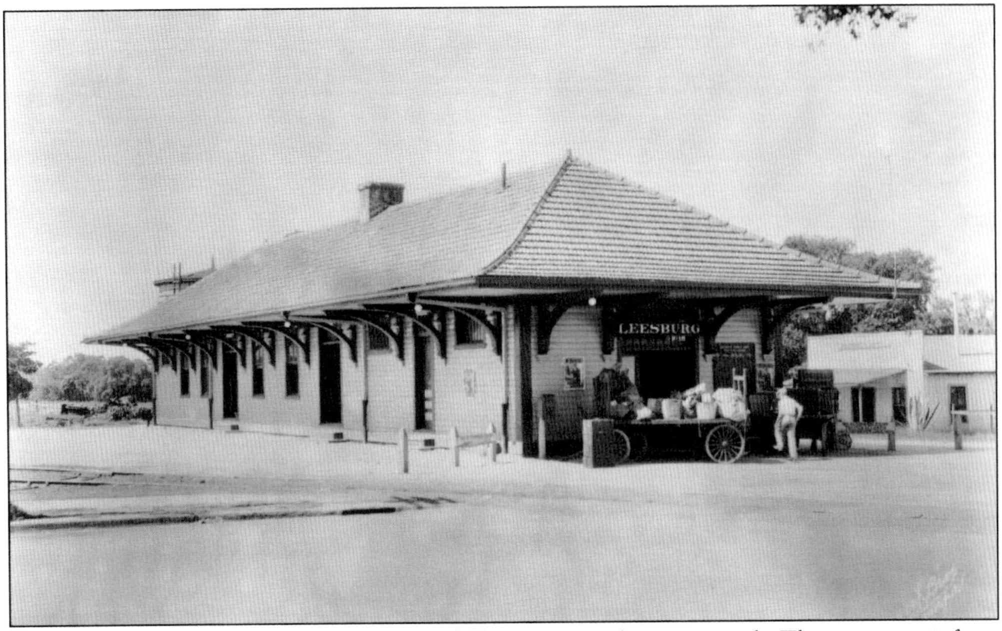

LEESBURG. Two views of Leesburg are from different eras and opposite ends. The top scene is from June 1926 in the heyday of railroading. Three posters posted on the building urge pedestrians to "Cross Crossings, Cautiously." The small wooden signs off either side declare automobile and trucks are prohibited on depot grounds. The baggage cart is loaded with items for shipping. Contrast the above image with the one below, made in 1975, four years after the last passenger train pulled out. Seaboard Coast Line is making use of the building for maintenance purposes; perhaps it is manned by a freight agent. Aside from that, the station is quiet. The Plant System constructed the building around 1900, and it would just miss turning 100 years old, coming down in the 1990s. (Above courtesy of Tampa-Hillsborough Public Library; below courtesy of Fred Clark Jr.)

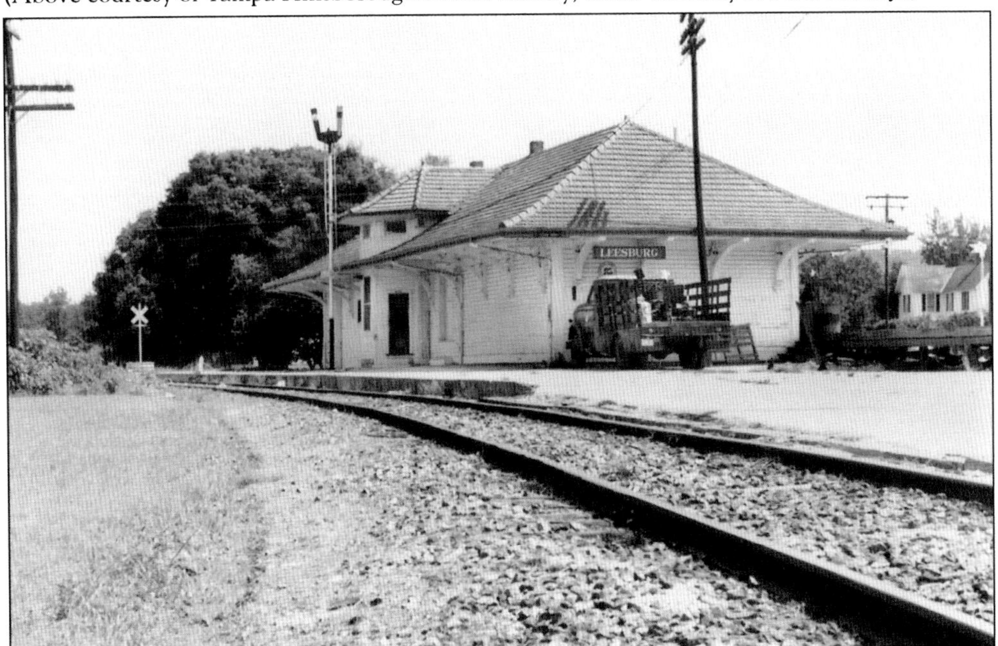

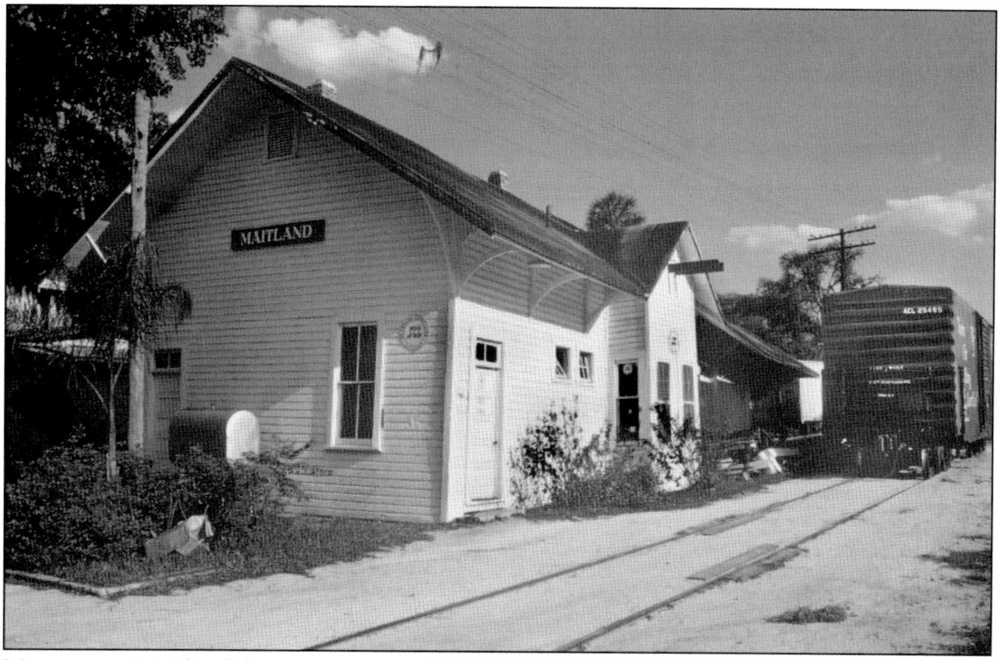

MAITLAND. Maitland depot is seen as it appeared in April 1969. A storm severely damaged the building a short time later. The remnants were dismantled and removed by May 5. South Florida Railroad built its line through Maitland in 1882. It was a stop on ACL up to the merger on July 1, 1967. (Courtesy of R. Randolph Stevens.)

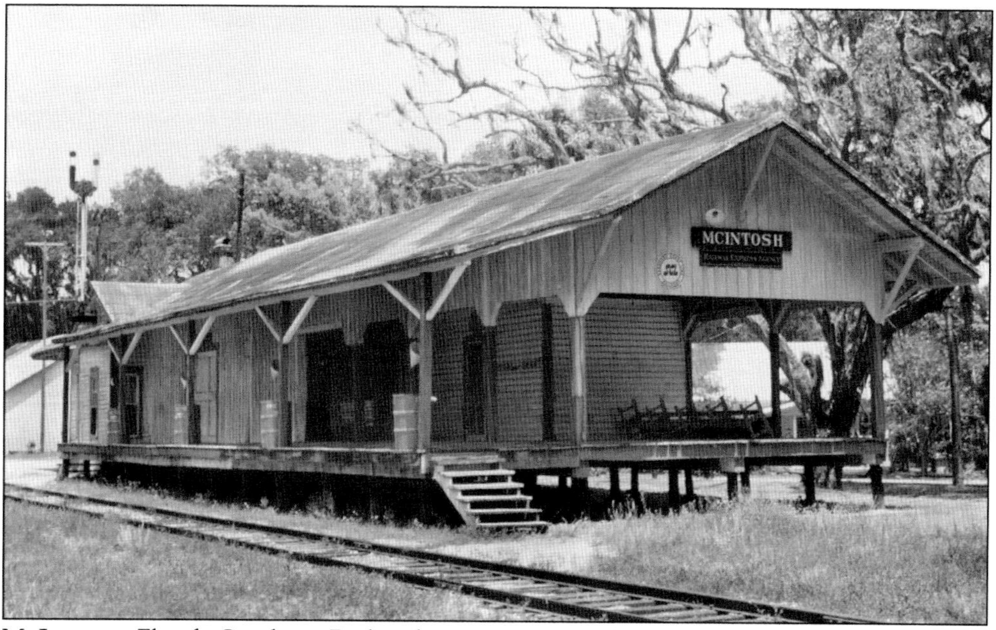

MCINTOSH. Florida Southern Railroad came to McIntosh in 1892, when the main line was extended from Rochelle, located nine miles east of Gainesville south to Ocala. A wooden depot was built around 1895. It appears here in early 1971 in the service of Seaboard Coast Line. A few years later, it was obtained by Friends of McIntosh and moved off the railroad right-of-way, which by 1984 was abandoned. (Courtesy of R. Randolph Stevens.)

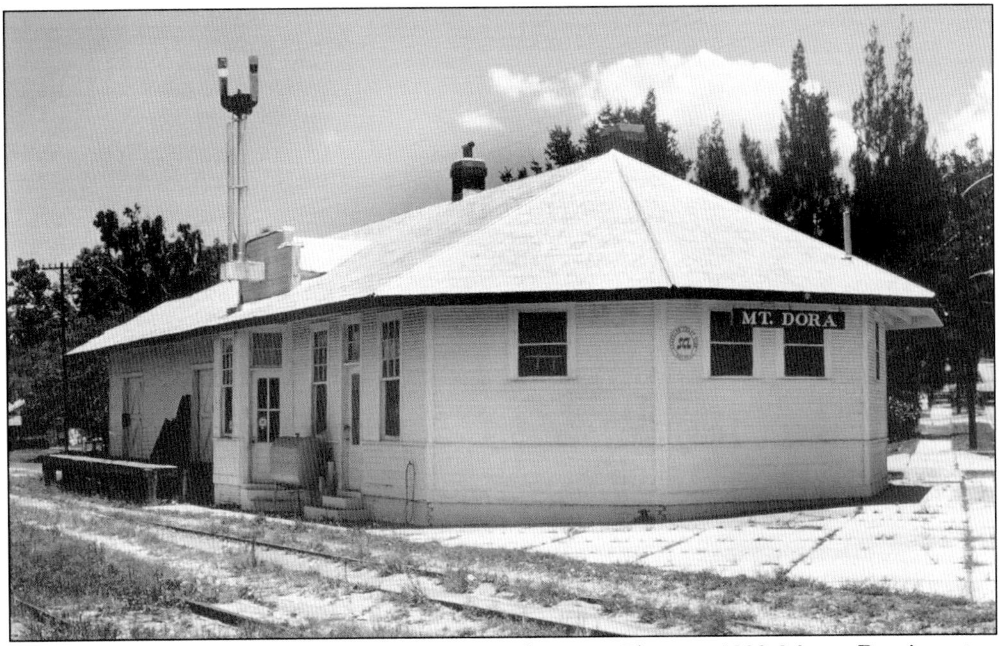

MOUNT DORA. Placed on the National Register of Historic Places in 1992, Mount Dora's station was built in 1915 at a cost of $8,223. Passenger train service ended in 1950, and freight activity in 1973. Mount Dora Chamber of Commerce moved in a short time later. The depot appears well maintained in this summer 1969 scene. (Courtesy of R. Randolph Stevens.)

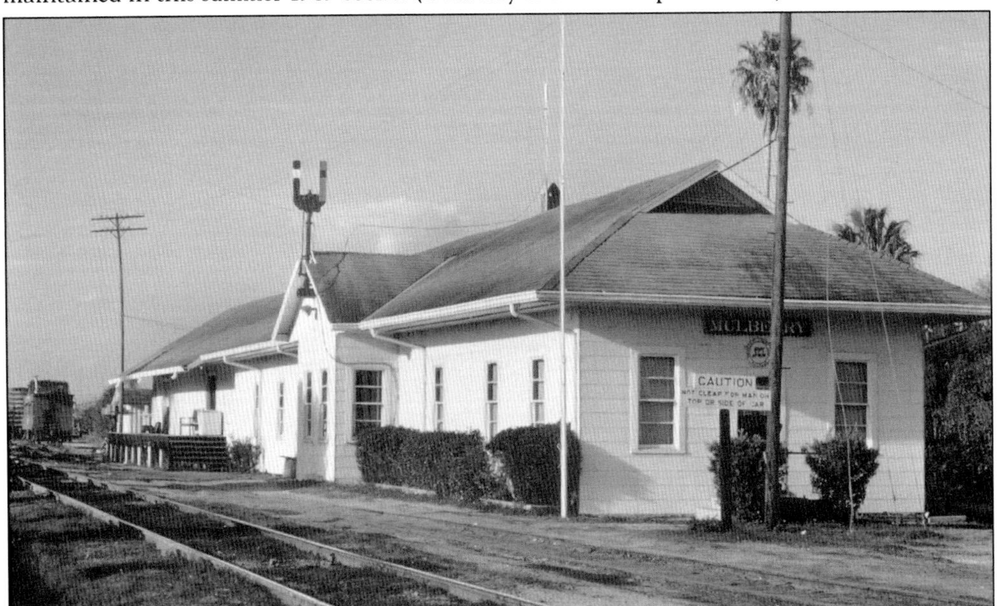

MULBERRY. Winston and Bone Valley Railroad came to Mulberry in 1892. Vast quantities of phosphate lay throughout the surrounding area waiting to be mined. The town incorporated in 1901. The year 1919 would bring violence as miners demanded reduced work hours and better pay from management. By 1929, the town had slightly less than 1,500 inhabitants and was serviced by two railroads. Shown here in 1968, the depot has been gone for many years. (Courtesy of R. Randolph Stevens.)

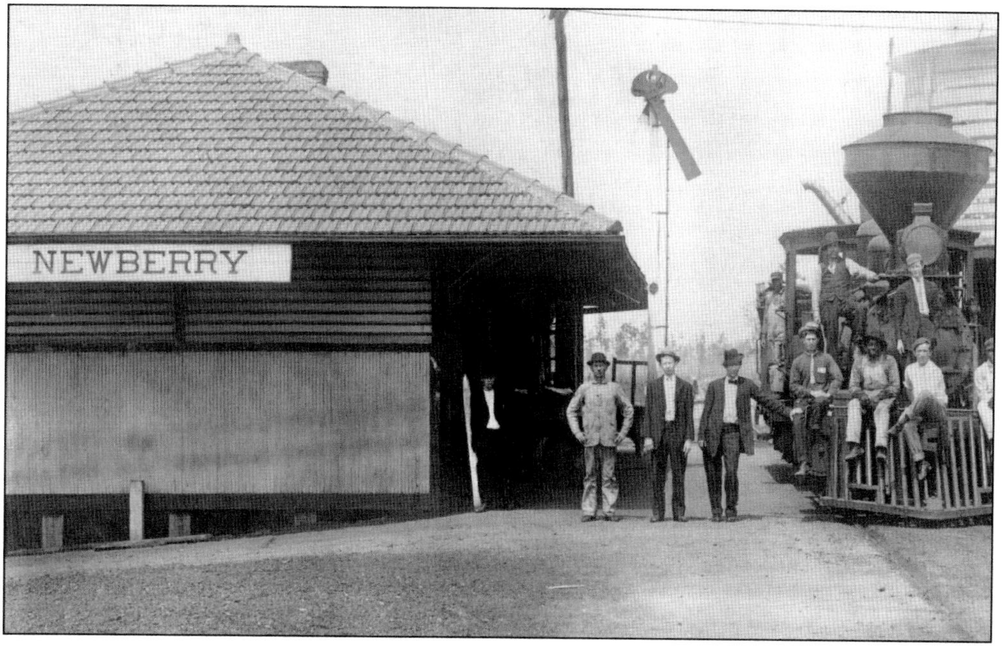

NEWBERRY. The above image captures train crew and other railroad men proudly posing around 1900. Newberry began as a phosphate-mining town and later became a production center for rough pine lumber. Railroad tracks still run through Newberry, but only a modern concrete block structure exists for railroad use, shown below in early 1971. (Above courtesy of Florida State Archives; below courtesy of R. Randolph Stevens.)

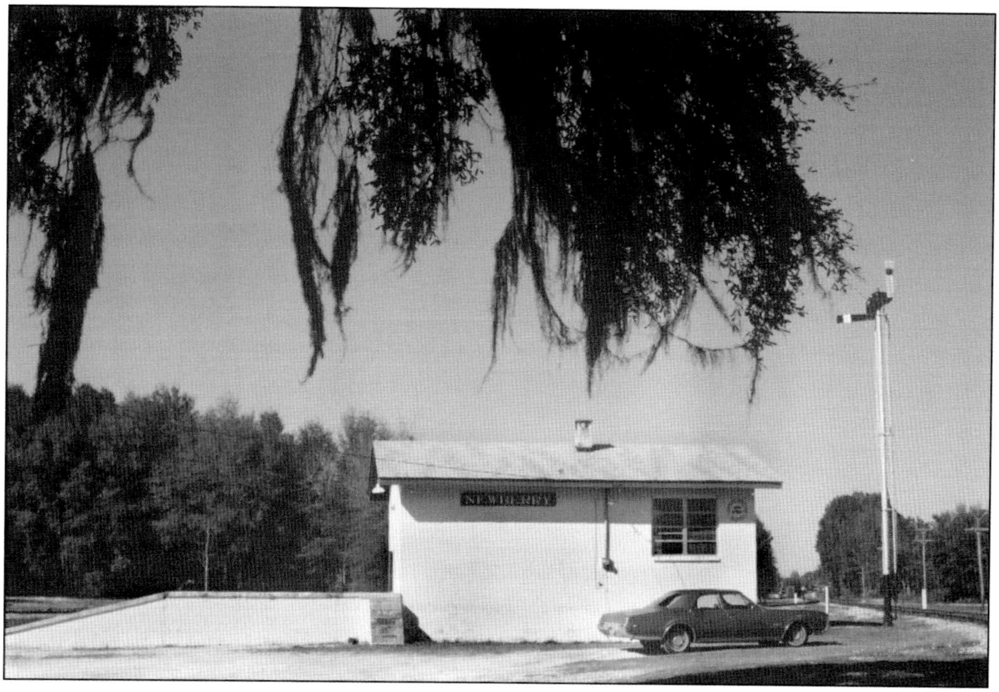

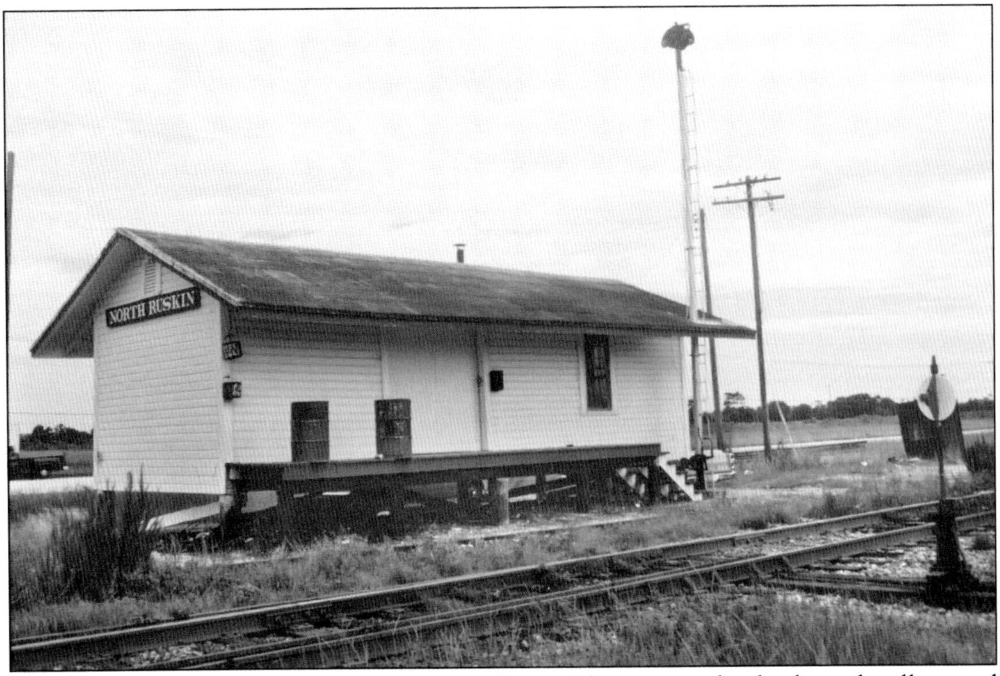

NORTH RUSKIN. Fire caused the loss of many depots. The concern for this hazard is illustrated in this view from the summer of 1968. Fire buckets are in position to be used quickly. The Ruskin area is famous for tomato production and the annual event that celebrates it. A vintage image of the Ruskin depot hangs framed at the Ruskin Hardee's Restaurant on U.S. 41. Unfortunately, it couldn't be used for this book. (Courtesy of R. Randolph Stevens.)

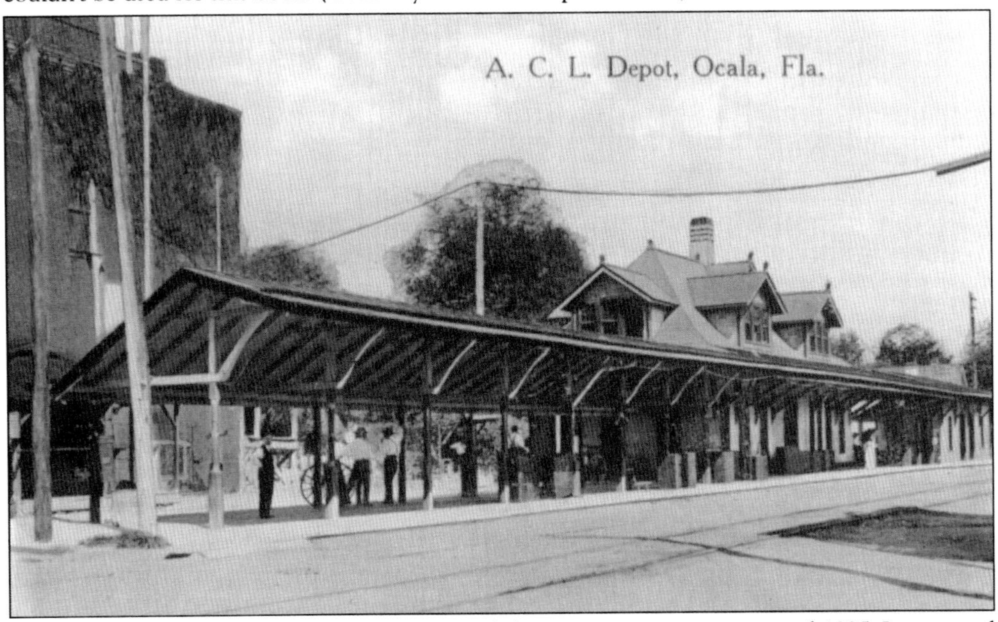

OCALA. Florida Southern Railroad constructed this impressive station around 1895. It was used until the opening of the new Union Station in 1917. It was located on the southwest corner of Fourth Street and Osceola Avenue and afterward was used as the district office of the rail system. The building was demolished in the 1960s. (Courtesy of Florida State Archives.)

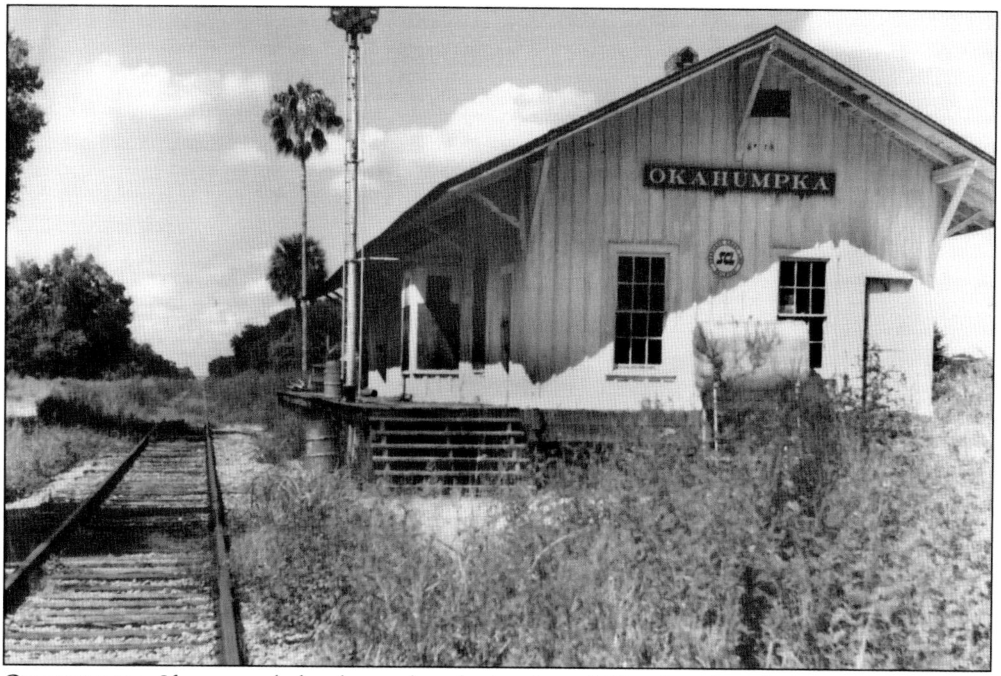

OKAHUMPKA. If one needed a depot that depicted rural Florida railroading, it is hard to beat Okahumpka. Seen above in 1976, the depot served a community that numbered around 200 people located just south of Leesburg. Seaboard Coast Line donated the 1898 period building to the Florida State Fairground's Cracker Country exhibit. The exhibit features rural Florida living from 1870 to 1912. The building now houses a model railroad layout depicting Central Florida around 1900. It appears in this new role below in 2005. (Above courtesy of Fred Clark Jr.; below courtesy of Mike Mulligan.)

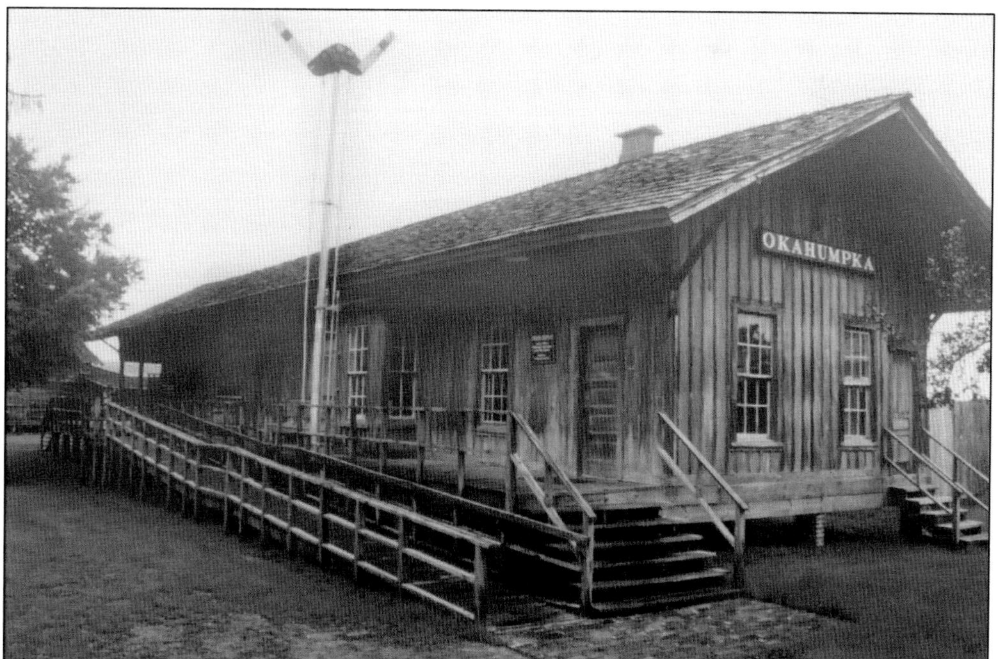

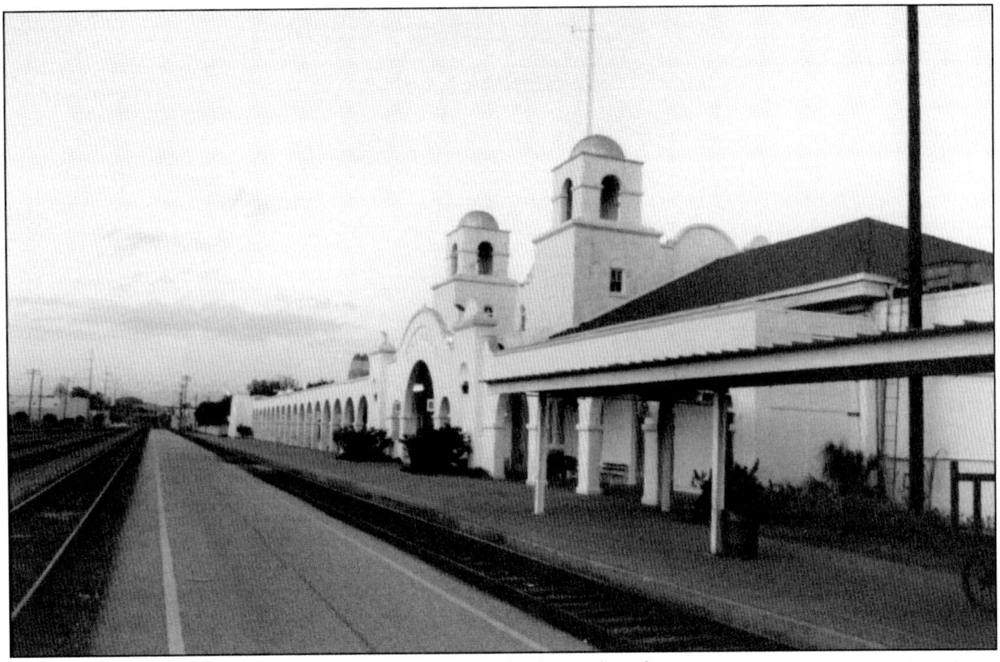

ORLANDO. The Spanish Mission–style Orlando depot has been in continuous service since January 11, 1927. Final construction cost was $500,000. Originally an arched arcade, just like the northern one shown in this January 30, 1994, view, extended to the south. It was removed in 1963 and replaced with a freight warehouse. Currently Amtrak's *Silver Meteor* and *Silver Star* make four stops per day. (Courtesy of Mike Mulligan.)

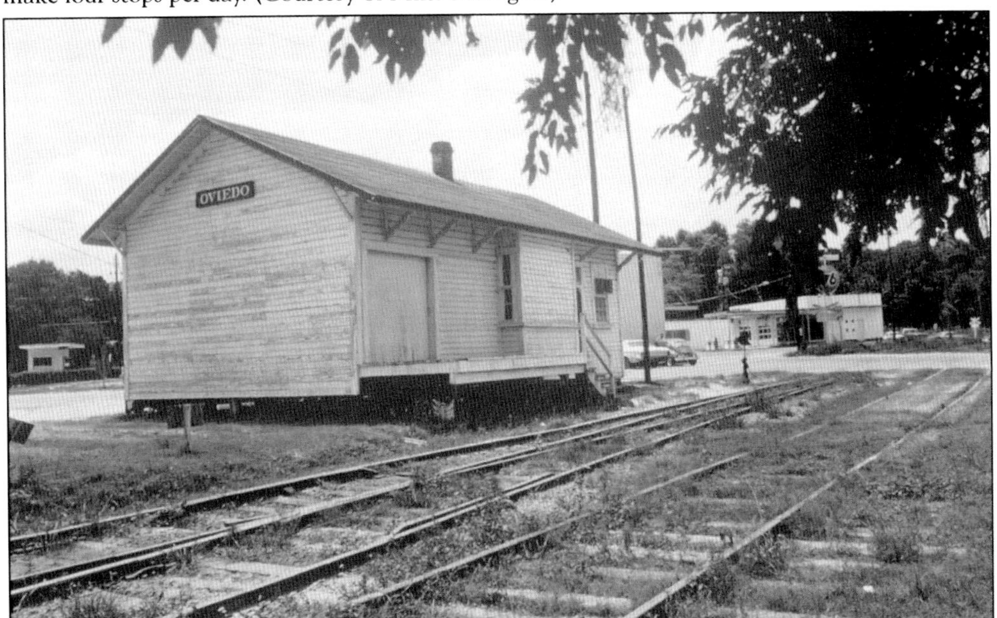

OVIEDO. South Florida Railroad built this depot in 1887 when the community numbered around 50. Oviedo incorporated in 1925 with a population of 800. The building was moved about a mile from the original location in the early 1970s and remodeled into a guesthouse. This trackside image is from early 1970. (Courtesy of R. Randolph Stevens.)

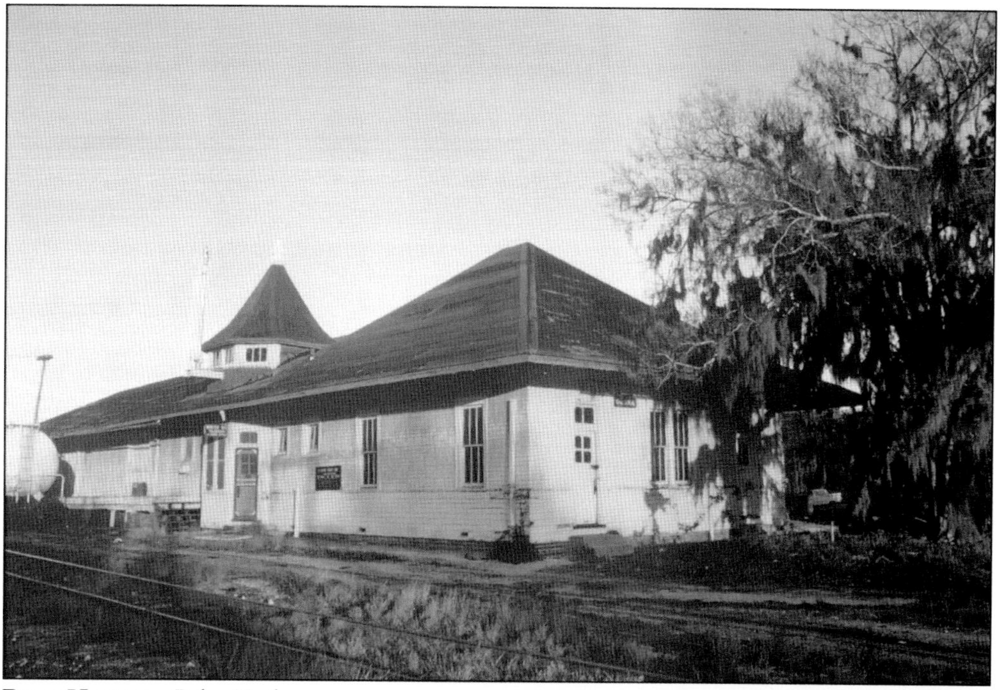

Palm Harbor. Palm Harbor was called Sutherland up to 1925. At that time, the community numbered around 400 people. The Orange Belt Railroad had come along in 1888 and built a wooden depot. Two views of the second depot, which came on the scene around 1914, and was photographed around the first of the year in 1969. The train bulletin board is still in place sometime after passenger service concluded. It carded two trains per day, one going to New York, the other to St. Petersburg. Demolition of the building occurred a short time later. (Both courtesy of R. Randolph Stevens.)

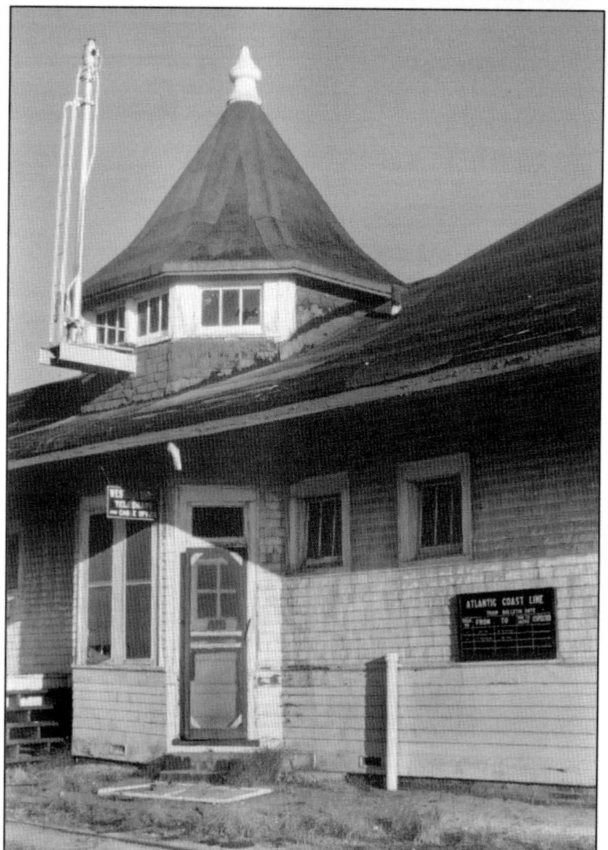

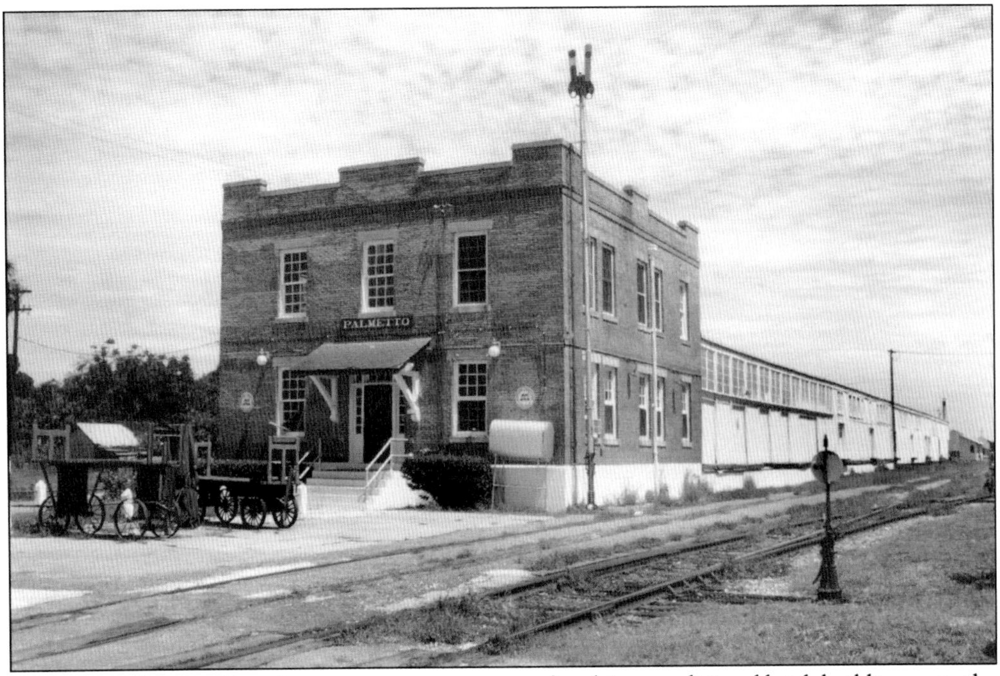

PALMETTO. Atlantic Coast Line passengers were served at this untraditional brick building up to the July 1, 1967, merger. This view is post-merger from mid-1968. The long freight house suggests many carloads were handled here. Railroad use stopped in the early 1970s. A tomato-packing company operated there afterward. It was torn down before 1998. (Courtesy of R. Randolph Stevens.)

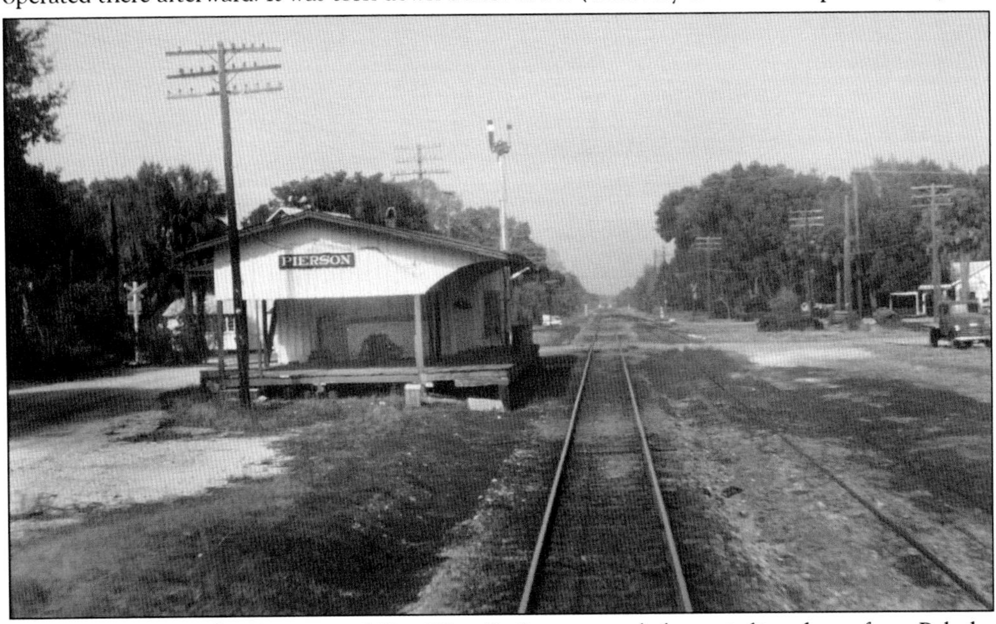

PIERSON. Jacksonville, Tampa, and Key West Railway extended a mainline down from Palatka through Pierson to Sanford in 1885. A wood-frame depot was built on the east side of the tracks. The depot was relocated to the west side in 1915. By the time of this early-1970 scene, it was no longer a station stop. The building was moved to the Pioneer Settlement for Creative Arts in 1982. (Courtesy of R. Randolph Stevens.)

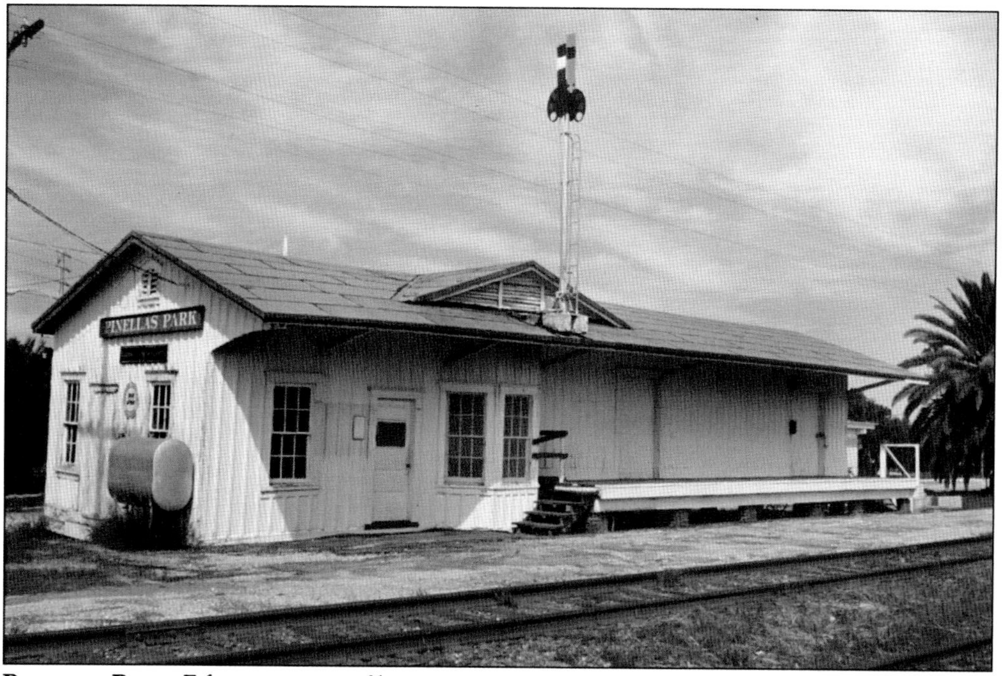

PINELLAS PARK. Fifty-nine years of history came to an end on April 9, 1971, when the Pinellas Park depot was knocked down by a demolition crew. Freight service had been terminated, and passenger service ended around 1960. The old building was considered an eyesore. However, on a summer day in 1968, it appears to be in good order. The old right-of-way is now part of the Pinellas Trail. (Courtesy of R. Randolph Stevens.)

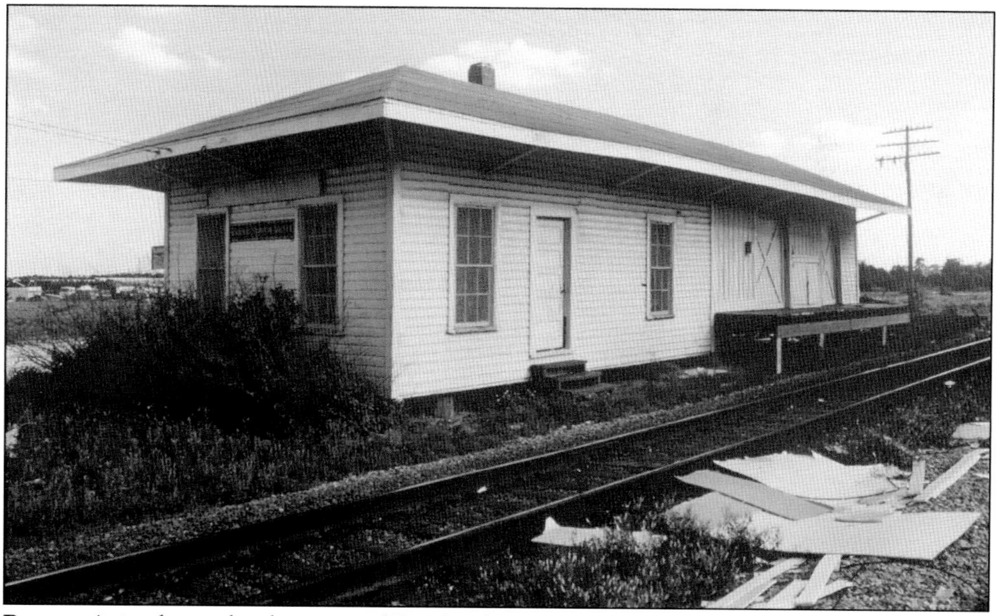

RANDS. A simple wooden depot served Rands, where some years back vast quantities of watermelons and cantaloupes were shipped. Rands is located near Sanford at the site of a freight yard. It was taken down some years back, but it looked like this in the spring of 1969. (Courtesy of R. Randolph Stevens.)

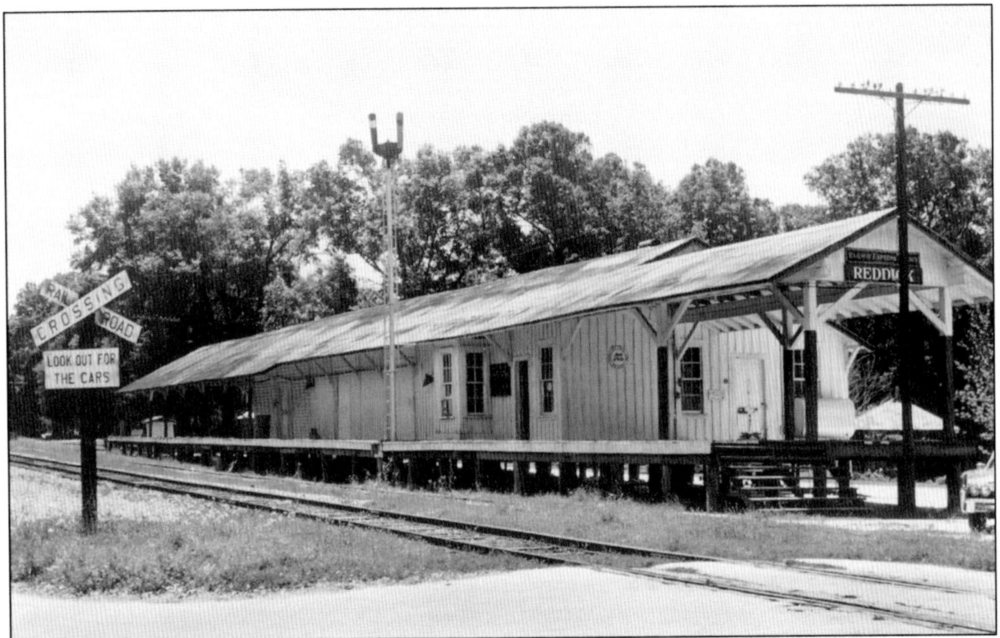

REDDICK. Florida Southern Railroad came to Reddick in 1882, when a line was extended south from Rochelle to Ocala. A wooden depot with a large freight shed was built to accommodate vast amounts of agricultural products produced in the area. Little railroad activity is taking place on this early-1971 day. After railroad service ended, it was moved to McIntosh on U.S. 441 and is used as an antiques shop. (Courtesy of R. Randolph Stevens.)

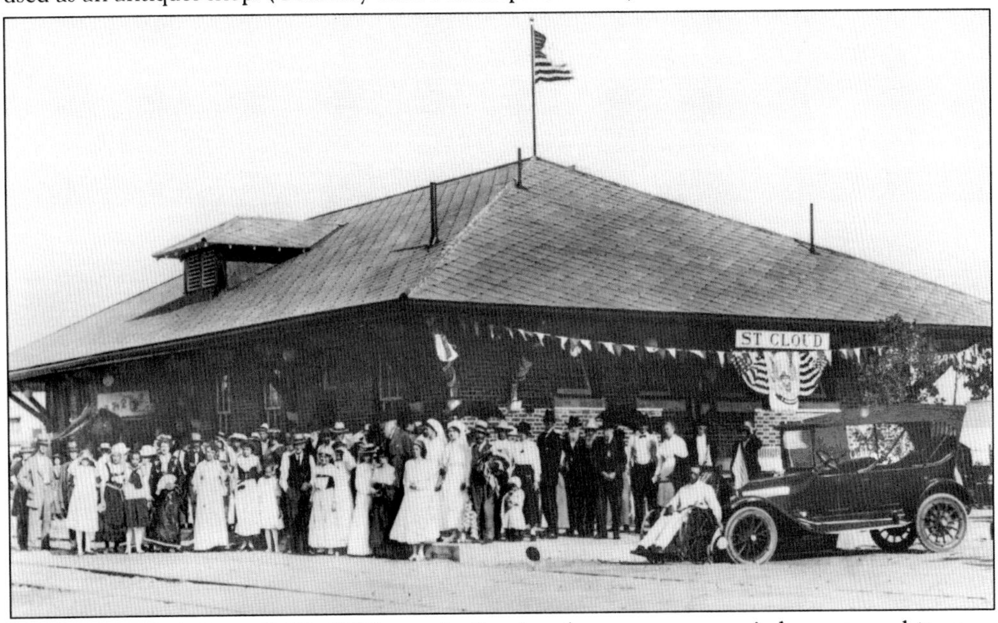

ST. CLOUD. Ida A. Ryan (1873–1950) was the first female to earn a master's degree in architecture in the United States. She designed the St. Cloud depot in 1917. The building opened in 1918, and this image may capture that celebration, including a parade. Rail service ended in 1943. Veterans of Foreign Wars Post No. 3227 has owned the property since the 1970s. (Courtesy of Florida State Archives.)

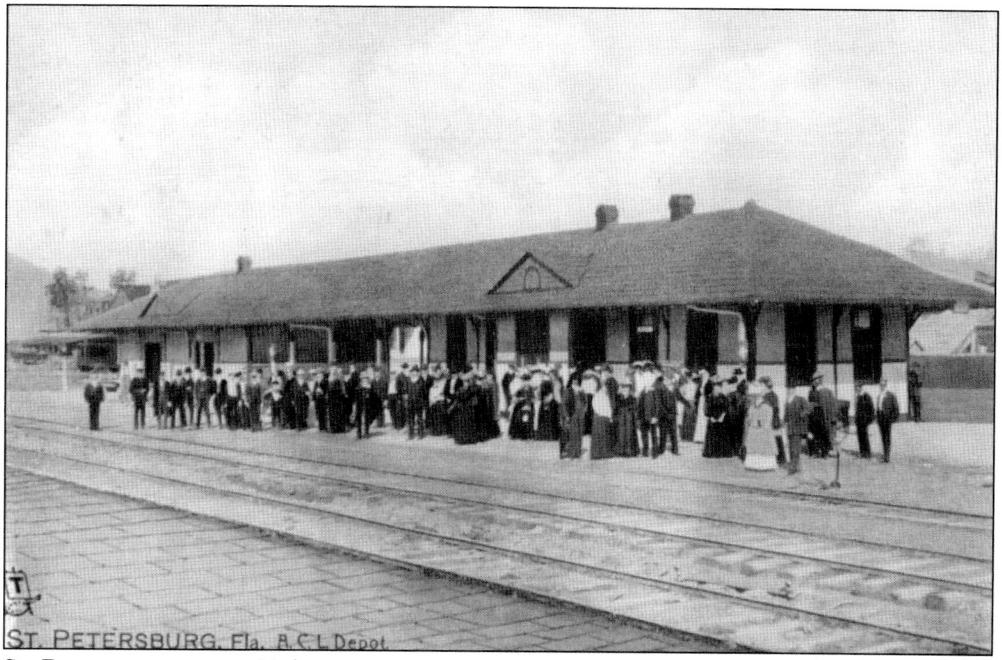

ST. PETERSBURG, 1906. Unhappy St. Petersburg citizens shouted, "We deserve better than this!" after reviewing plans proposed by the Atlantic Coast Line for a new depot (above) in 1905. The *St. Petersburg Times* editorialized on the plans with "the building will be—just plain wood—with probably a tin roof—which will be a great disappointment to the people of Saint Petersburg." Nevertheless, the ACL constructed the building, finishing it January 27, 1906. Business conditions warranted improved accommodations, with a new depot (below) opened in 1913. This impressive station served until 1963, when the city's request to relocate rail service away from downtown was satisfied. It was razed soon afterward. (Courtesy of Florida State Archives.)

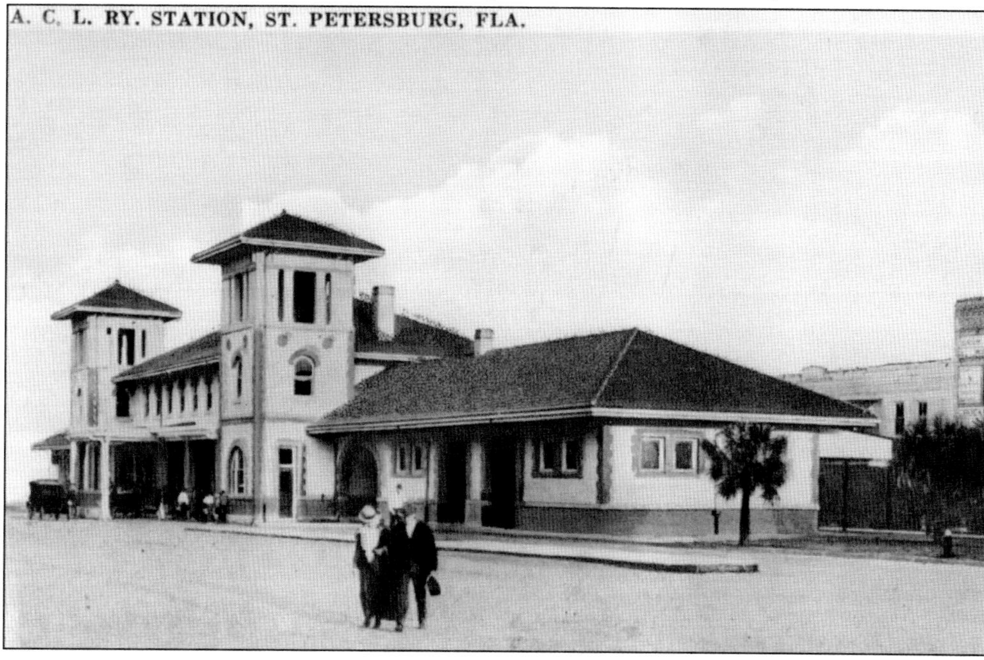

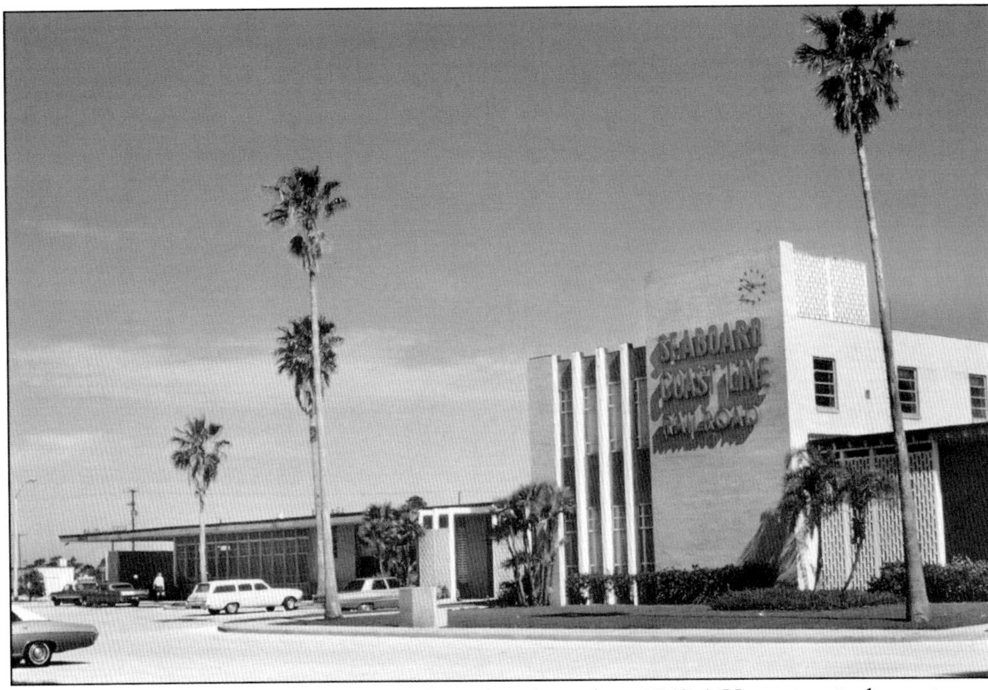

St. Petersburg, 1969 and 1968. St. Petersburg's modern 1963 ACL station is shown in two views from early 1969 (above) and 1968 (below). From 1969, a street-side shot suggests the ACL still felt passenger rail service was going to be around for many years to come. Clearly, at this date, it is in the service of the merged company. Note the clock above the railroad name appears to indicate 10:16 a.m. A May 1968 track-side view shows the three station tracks with the main line to the far left. The building would serve Amtrak rail passengers to 1984 and then as motor-coach boarding site to the 1990s. It has been substantially altered for use by a pharmaceutical company. (Above courtesy of R. Randolph Stevens; below courtesy of Paul Coe.)

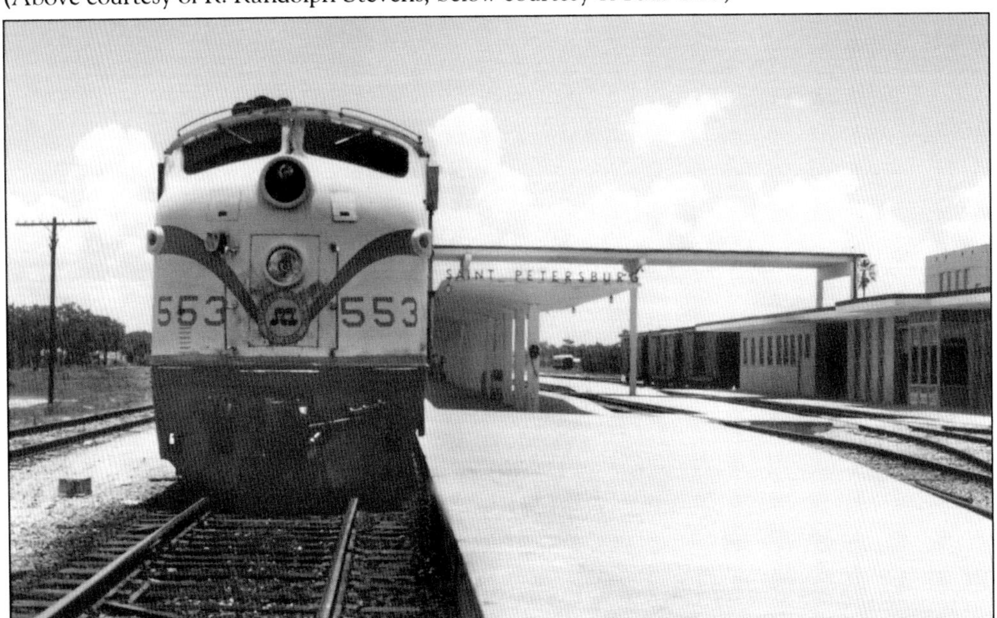

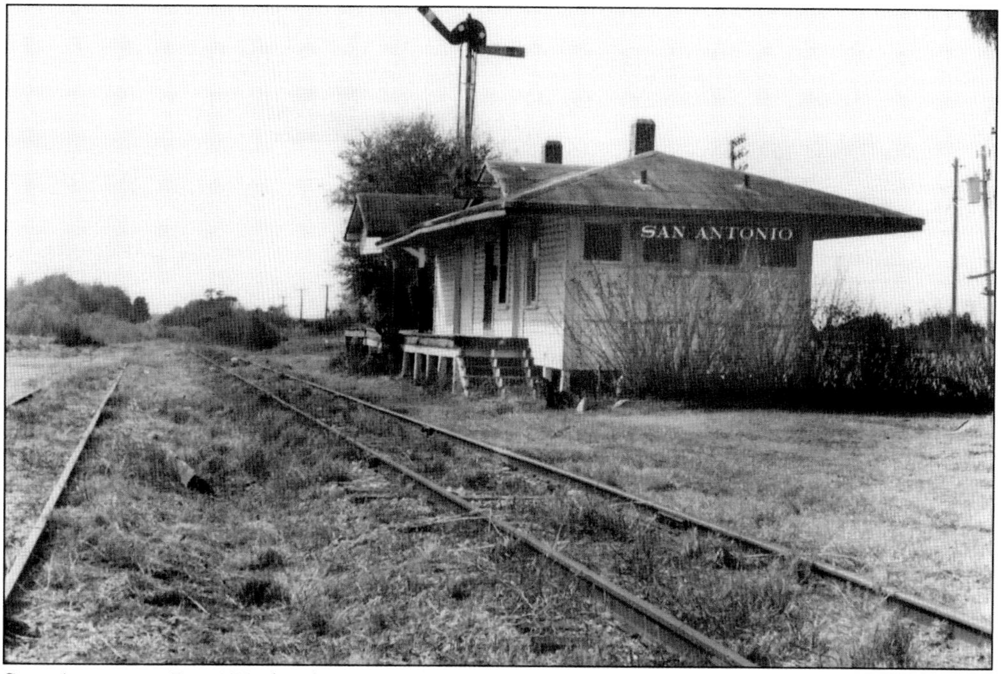

SAN ANTONIO. By 1975, this former main line of the Atlantic Coast Line was overgrowing with vegetation. The tracks were pulled out in 1978 except a short segment used by the short-lived Orange Belt Rail Road excursion train. San Antonio's depot, built in 1948, was a station stop until April 30, 1971. Freight activity carried on for another year or so. The restored depot serves the community for meetings and social gatherings. (Courtesy of Fred Clark Jr.)

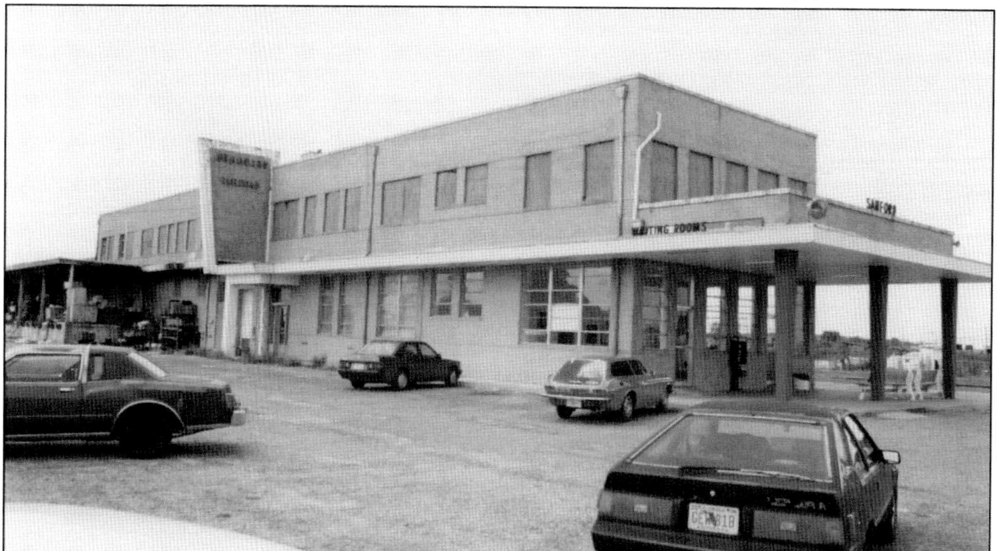

SANFORD. In 1953, a new station was opened on the main line to serve Sanford. This relocation allowed for more efficient train operations and replaced the previous depot from 1913. Amtrak used the station until August 2005 and vacated, citing the rundown condition. CSX Transportation owns the property. Currently the building sits derelict with an uncertain future. This view is from September 1992. (Courtesy of Mike Mulligan.)

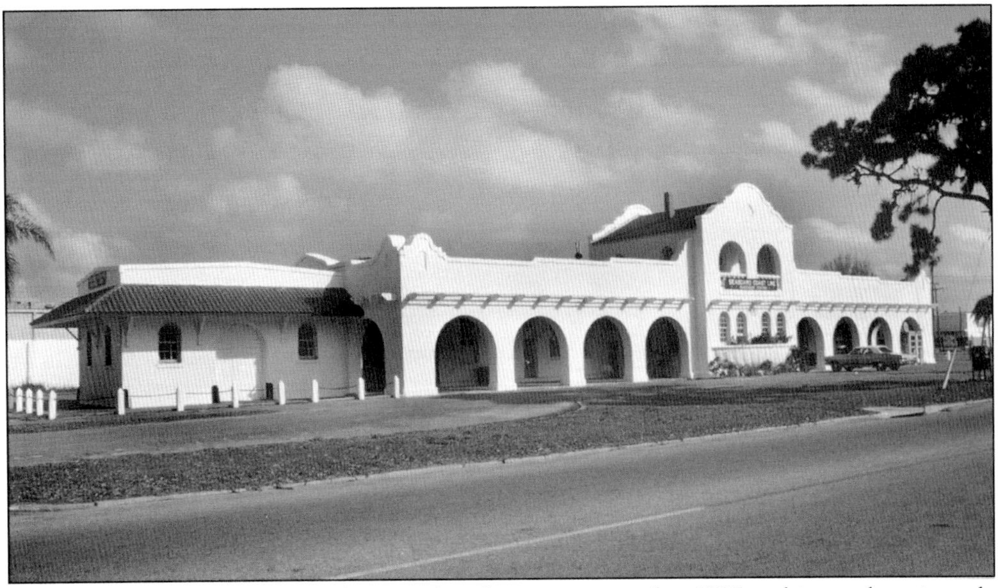

SARASOTA. This Mission/Spanish Revival–style station opened in 1925 and is seen here in early 1969. Railroad use ended upon Amtrak's takeover of passenger trains on May 1, 1971. Later a portion of the building was used for a restaurant and offices. It was placed on the National Register of Historic Places in 1984, and then was demolished a few years later. A virtual twin survives in Fort Myers, used as a history museum. (Courtesy of R. Randolph Stevens.)

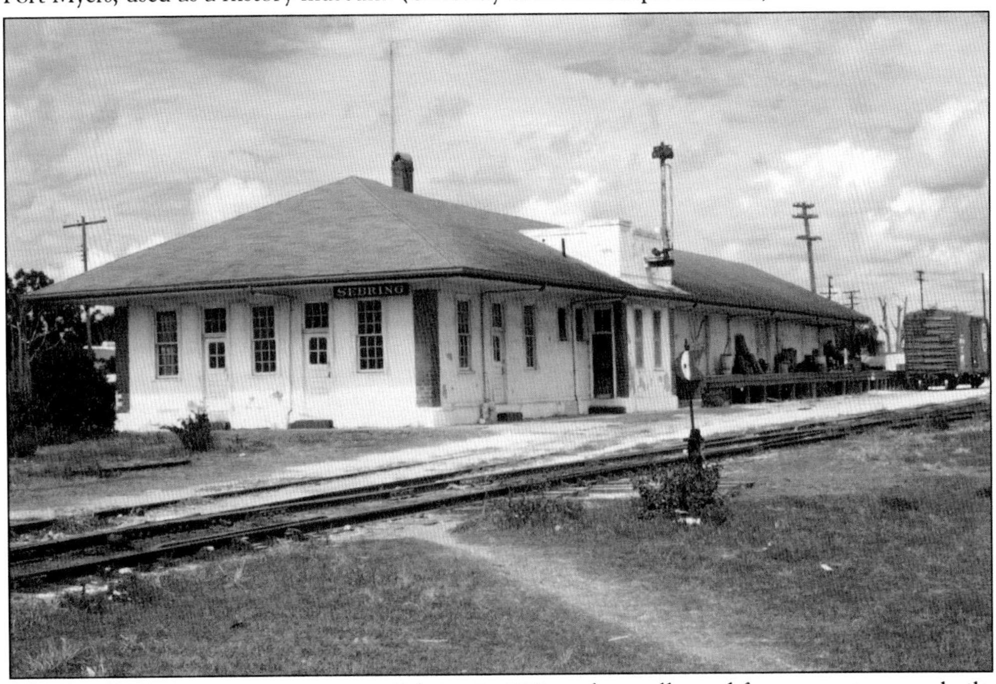

SEBRING. Rail transportation came to Sebring in 1912, and a small wood-frame structure was built. This soon would be outdated, and town leaders lobbied the railroad for a larger, more substantial building. In 1917, a combination brick and wood-frame depot was constructed. It served passengers until the mid-1950s and freight to the 1970s. Railroad activity appears in this view from early 1970. The building came down around 2000. (Courtesy of R. Randolph Stevens.)

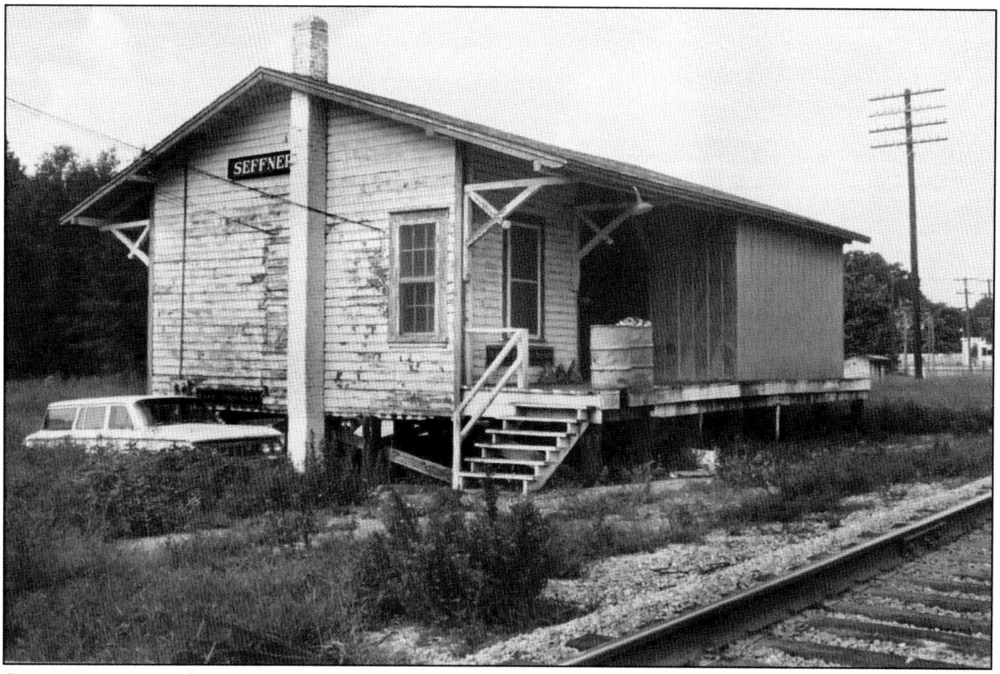

SEFFNER. Located 11 rail miles east of Tampa Union station is Seffner. In 1927, fewer than 300 people resided in Seffner, but Tampa was just a 32-minute train ride away. The depot housed a telegraph and express office. It appeared to be used by the railroad on this summer 1968 day. The building no longer exists. (Courtesy of R. Randolph Stevens.)

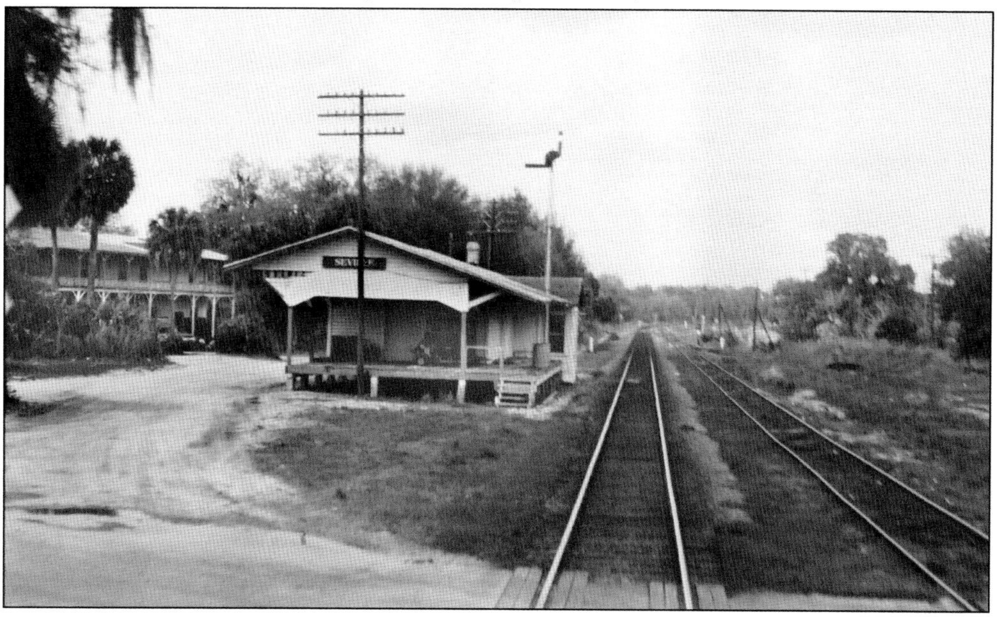

SEVILLE. Seville is located in Volusia County, 83 rail miles south of Jacksonville. The Jacksonville, Tampa, and Key West Railway pushed a main line south from Palatka to Sanford, passing through the area in 1886. The depot was a station stop on the ACL until the 1967 merger. Six years later, the photographer caught this image from the rear car on a passing train. The depot has passed on to history. (Courtesy of R. Randolph Stevens.)

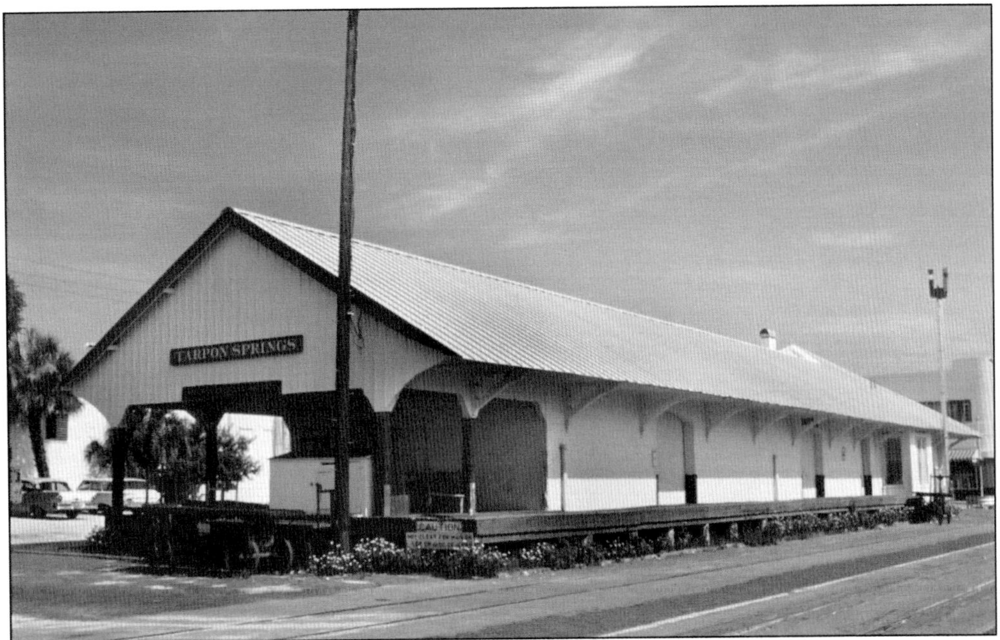

Tarpon Springs. Built in 1909, this structure replaced the original Tarpon Springs depot, which burned in 1908. The well-kept structure presented an appealing subject for the camera on a 1968 summer day. Passenger service ended April 30, 1971. Freight lingered on until the 1980s. Tarpons Springs Area Historical Society first obtained use of a few rooms and later the rest of the building. Their mission is carried on here today. (Courtesy of R. Randolph Stevens.)

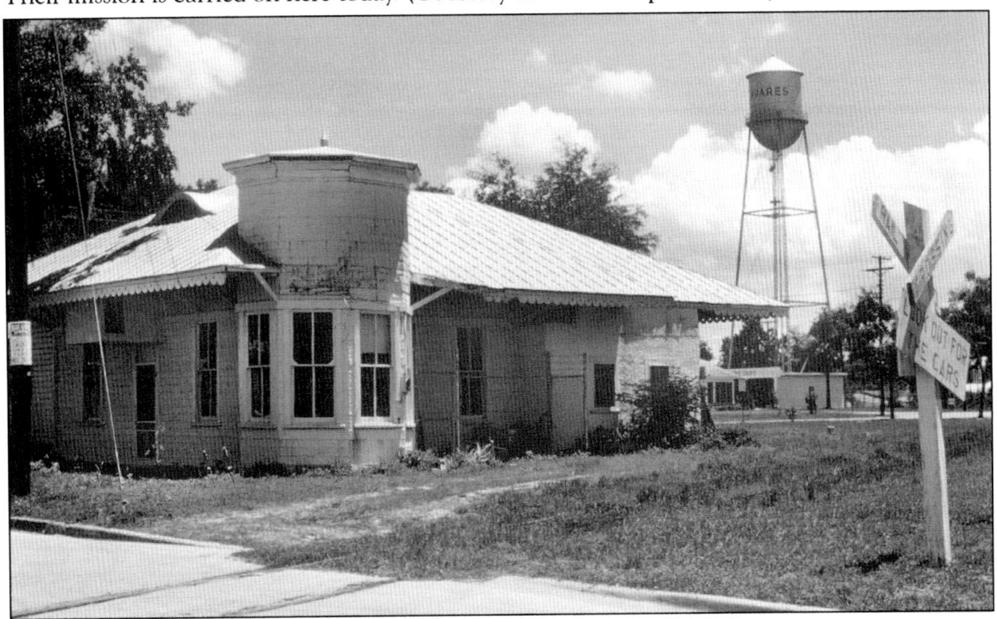

Tavares. Jacksonville, Tampa, and Key West Railway opened this depot in 1886 to accommodate the needs of Tavares. By 1927, the facility was no longer capable of providing adequate service. The railroad traded the property for another better suited for expansion. Later it became the home of American Legion Post No. 76. The end of the line came soon after this 1969 image. (Courtesy of R. Randolph Stevens.)

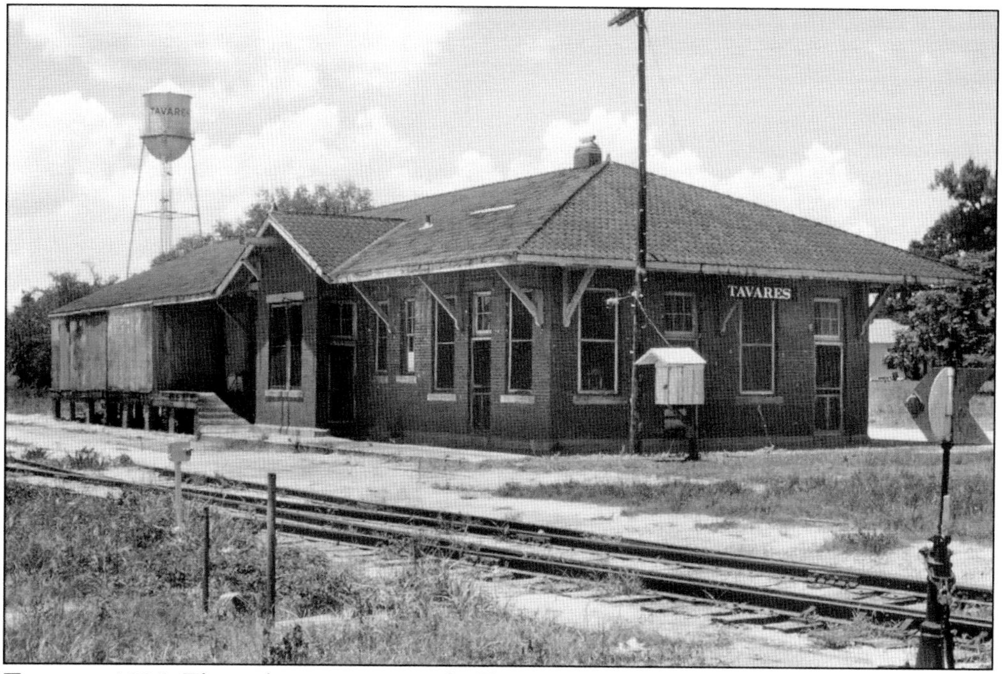

TAVARES, 1926. The replacement station for Tavares was constructed in 1926 with a large yard area to handle increased freight business. Red brick was used to build the structure, which handled business up to the July 1, 1967, merger. With many depots in the vicinity, the Tavares station was redundant to the company and closed. Seen here in 1969, the building was converted to a fire station in 1975, a role it plays today. (Courtesy of R. Randolph Stevens.)

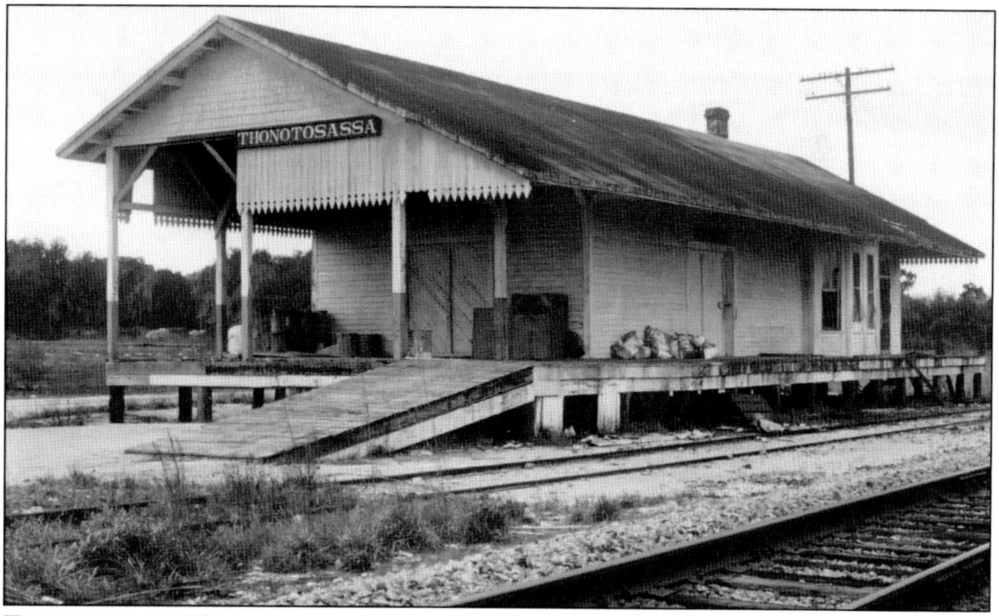

THONOTOSASSA. Thonotosassa is a community 13 miles northeast of Tampa. In 1893, a rail line was built from Tampa. A standard wooden depot was provided to conduct business. ACL Railroad purple paint is still evident in the trim in this 1969 scene. The depot and track would be gone by the 1980s. (Courtesy of R. Randolph Stevens.)

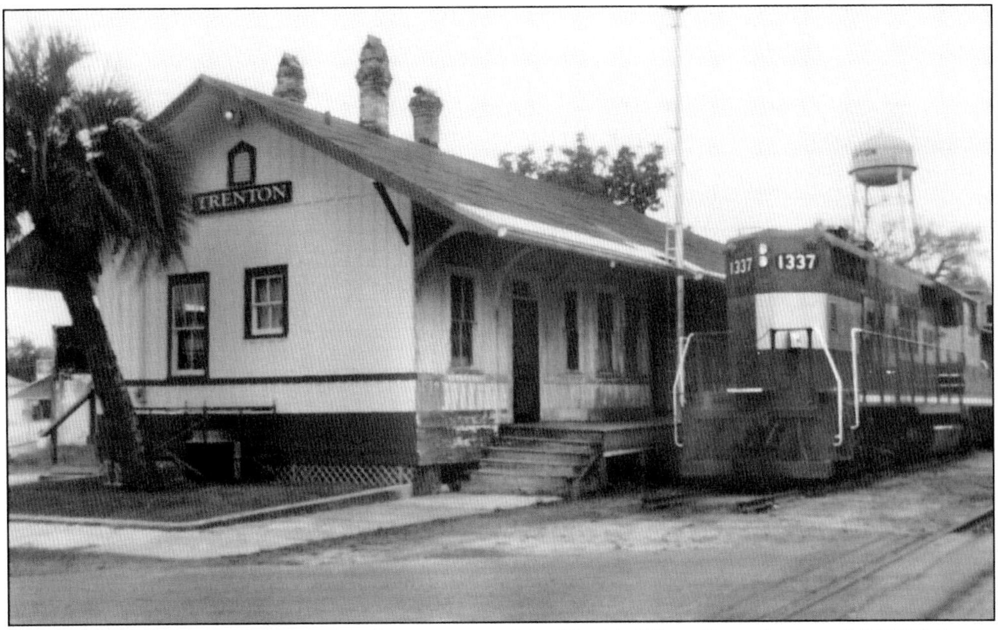

TRENTON. In later years, Trenton's depot was used by Florida West Coast Railroad (FWC) for its general offices. Built in 1909, it is now a trailhead for Nature Coast Trail State Park. FWC began operations in December 1987, continuing until abandonment of their last line from Newberry to Trenton in 2004. A previous abandonment provided the right-of-way for the trail in the mid-1990s. Locomotive No. 1337 sits alongside the building on October 30, 1988. (Courtesy of Jeanne Hickam.)

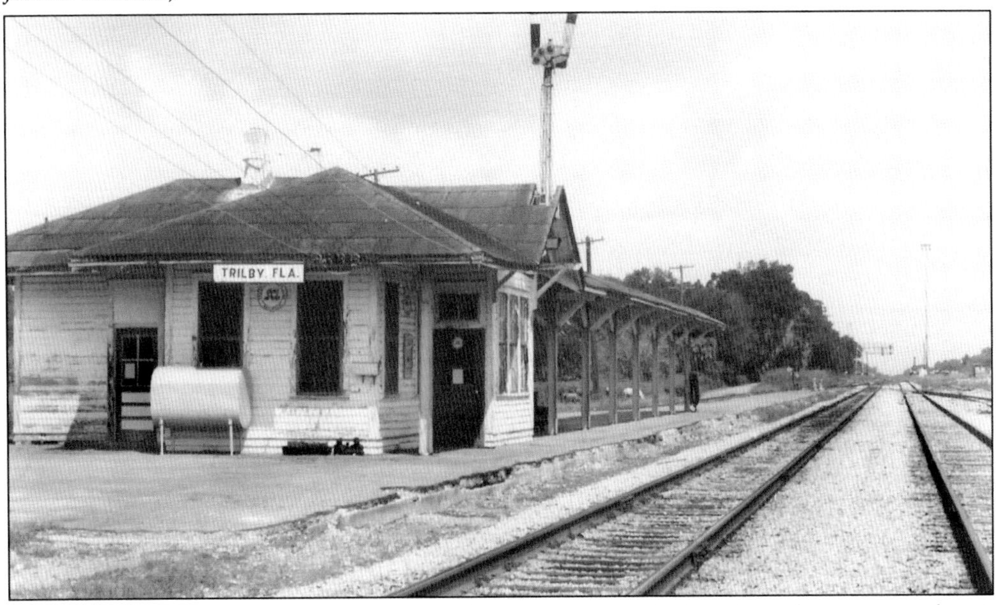

TRILBY. Trilby was once a railroad junction where the Savannah, Florida, and Western Railway's west coast route met the Sanford and St. Petersburg Railway. A larger depot built in 1896 was converted to a smaller structure in 1927. The depot was moved in 1978 to Dade City, becoming part of the Pioneer Florida Museum. In this 1975 scene, the railroad is prominent, but the right-of-way is all that is left today. (Courtesy of Fred Clark Jr.)

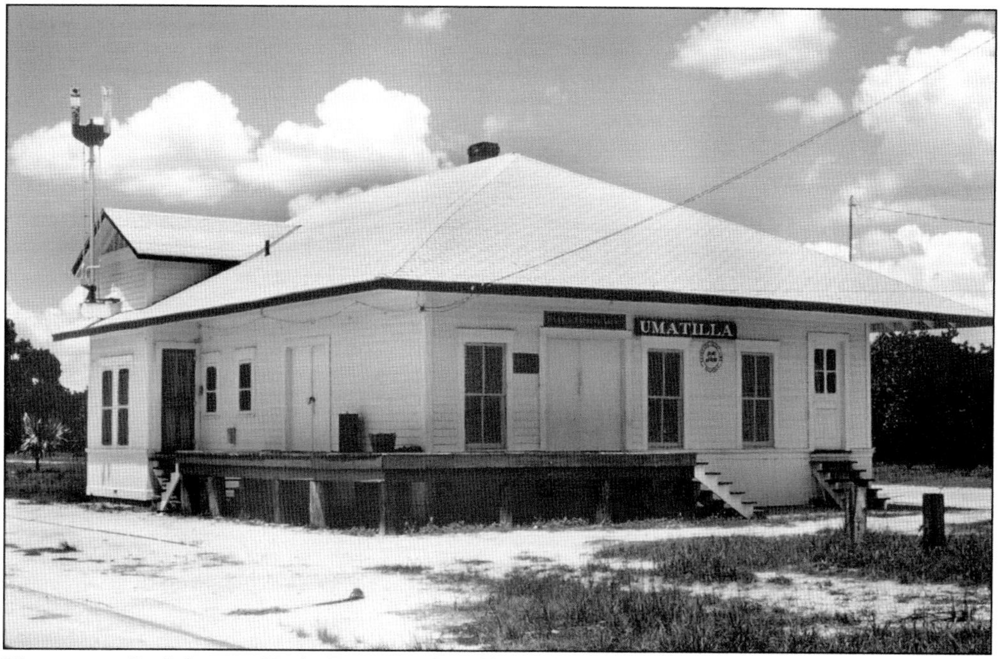

UMATILLA. St. Johns and Lake Eustis Railroad brought rail service to the Umatilla area in 1884. In 1915, this depot was built and used by the railroad until the 1970s. In the summer of 1969, it appears well maintained. For some years, the depot sat unused and fell into disrepair. Donated to the city, it was relocated, and the 1,600-square-foot building converted to a library. (Courtesy of R. Randolph Stevens.)

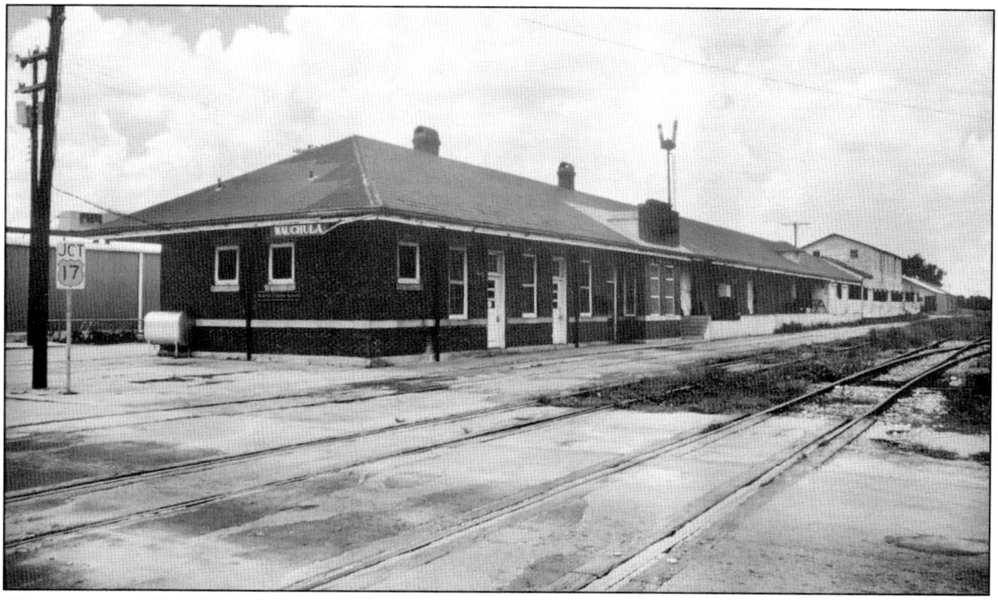

WAUCHULA. Florida Southern Railway built through the Wauchula area in 1886. A new brick station was built to replace a previous wooden building in 1914. Railroad passenger use ceased April 30, 1971, and tracks would come out by 1984. The city-owned building sustained severe damage to the north wall from Hurricane Charley on August 13, 2004. This is how it looked the summer of 1969 when still in regular passenger service. (Courtesy of R. Randolph Stevens.)

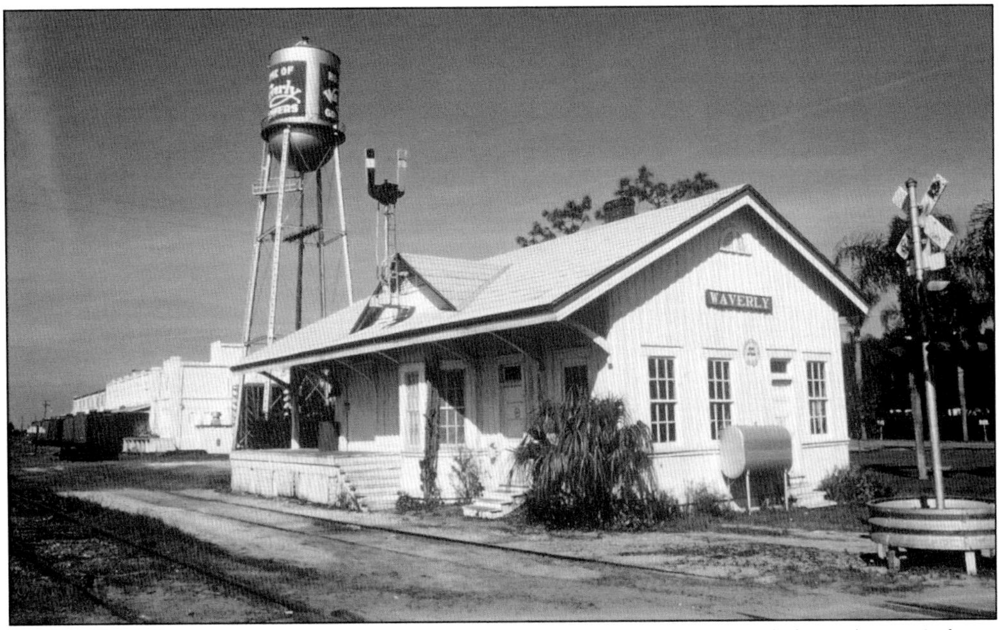

WAVERLY. Railroad service came to Waverly in 1912, when the line was extended to Sebring. A depot was added around 1915. By 1929, the village numbered 51 people with citrus groves in abundance in the surrounding hills. Early in 1969, railroad use of the building is apparent with the Seaboard Coast Line logo proudly displayed. However, abandonment of the line to Sebring would commence in 1969 and conclude through Waverly by 1984. (Courtesy of R. Randolph Stevens.)

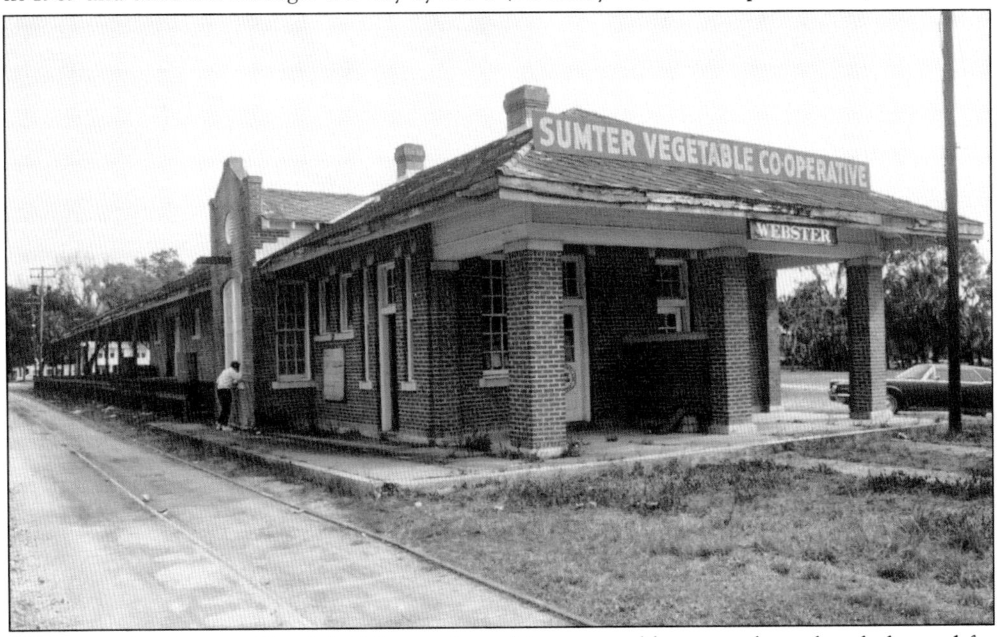

WEBSTER. A substantial brick building such as this one would suggest the railroad planned for many years of revenue from the small community of Webster. Seen in early 1969, the Seaboard Coast Line logo on the door indicates continued railroad use. However, the sign on the roof brings a different conclusion. Perhaps they shared the 1927 building for a time. Tracks came up 1978. The building survived until around 2002. (Courtesy of R. Randolph Stevens.)

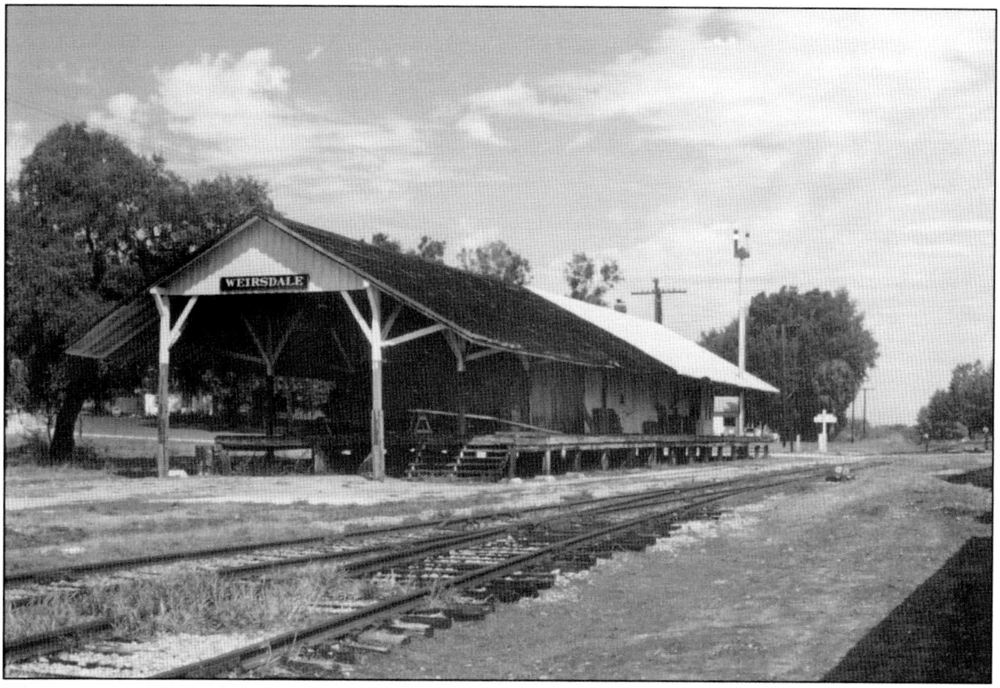

WEIRSDALE. Weirsdale, a resort and community that once had four large citrus packing plants, received rail service in 1883. The depot's appearance is a bit shabby by this early-1971 image. Track was abandoned in 1979. The depot destruction year is unknown. (Courtesy of R. Randolph Stevens.)

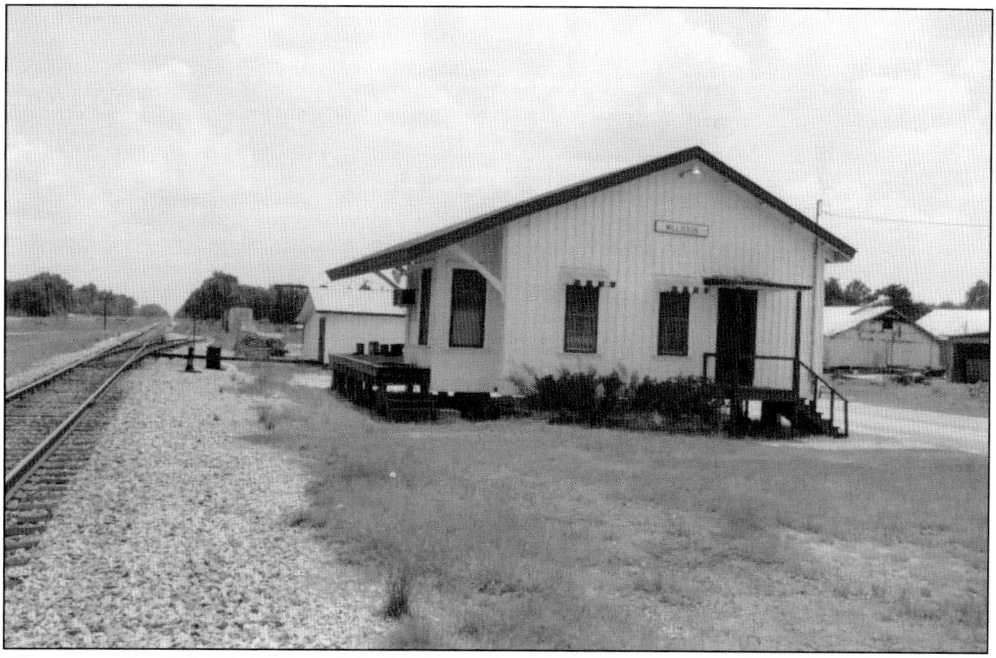

WILLISTON. It is July 25, 1992, and the Williston depot is looking neat and orderly. The building was in railroad use but not for passengers or freight. Currently it is used by Florida Northern Railroad, a short-line operation that took over this line a few years back. (Courtesy of Mike Mulligan.)

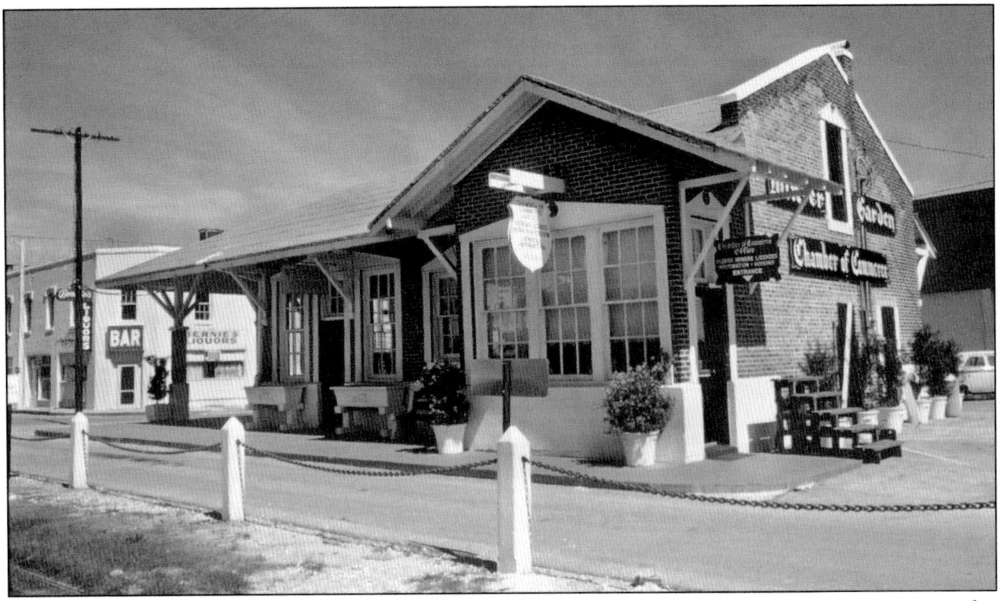

WINTER GARDEN. Winter Garden Heritage Foundation's Heritage Museum now occupies the former depot, built in 1918. Previously the building had hosted a hair salon and before that the chamber of commerce offices (after railroad service ended). It is seen in the chamber role in the summer of 1969. Note the ACL planter boxes. (Courtesy of R. Randolph Stevens.)

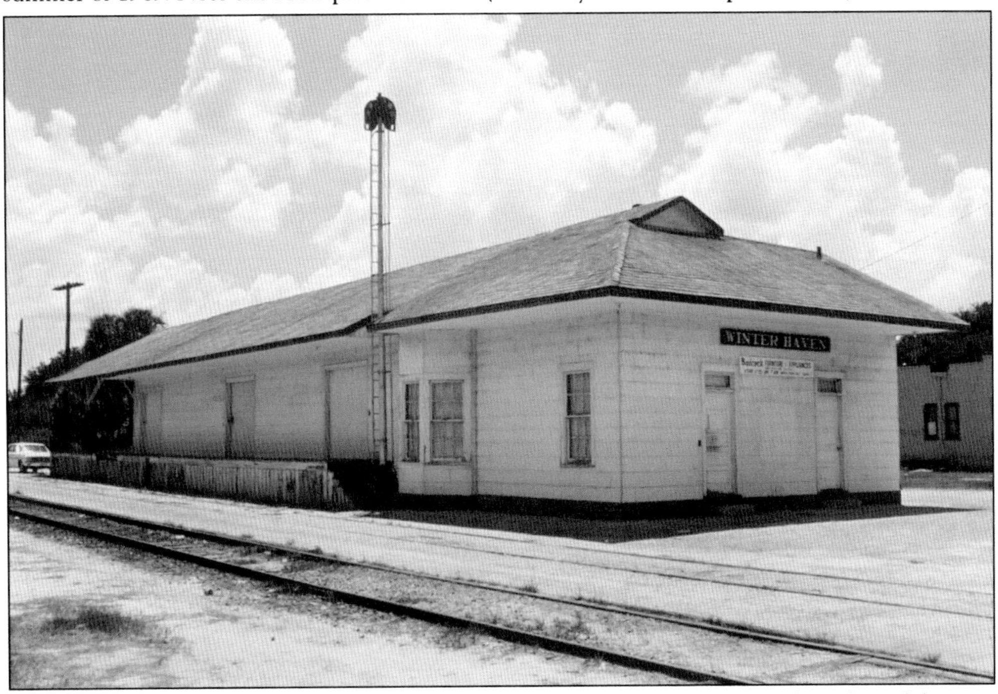

WINTER HAVEN. The resort city of Winter Haven has 97 lakes within a 5-mile radius of the city. The city is home to world-famous Cypress Gardens, Florida's first theme park. ACL operated this station there into the 1960s, but by the time of this photograph in summer of 1968, it was being used by Badcock Furniture and Appliances. It is believed this building was torn down in the 1990s. (Courtesy of R. Randolph Stevens.)

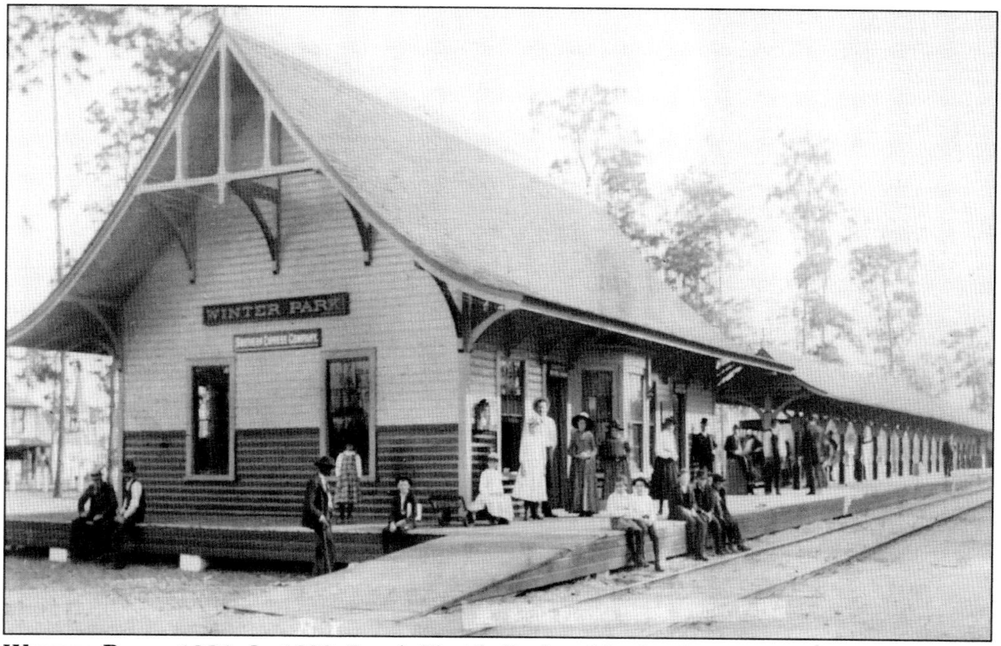

WINTER PARK, 1890. In 1880, South Florida Railroad built a line connecting Sanford and Orlando. Local residents made contributions to convince the railroad to build a depot. It opened in 1882 as the first building in town. This wooden building served until 1913. Many people are at the depot in this 1890 view. A train pulling in was cause for much excitement in those days. (Courtesy of Rollins College.)

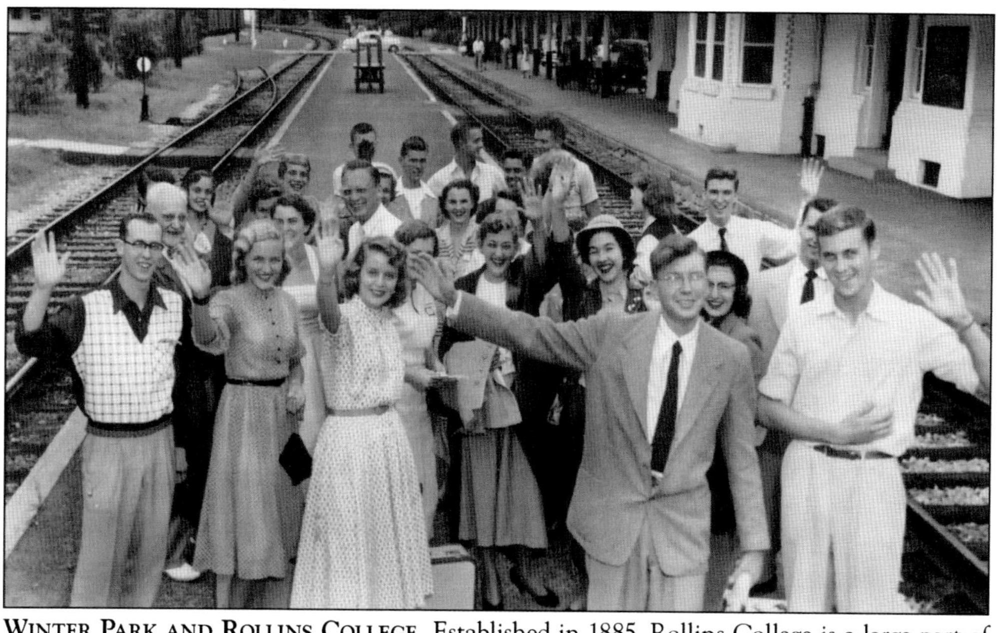

WINTER PARK AND ROLLINS COLLEGE. Established in 1885, Rollins College is a large part of the success and growth of Winter Park. Each year, new students arrive to begin their college education. In years past, the welcoming committee was sent down to the depot to greet arriving students, as depicted in 1952 with the 1913 depot in the background. It would be replaced in 1962. (Courtesy of Rollins College.)

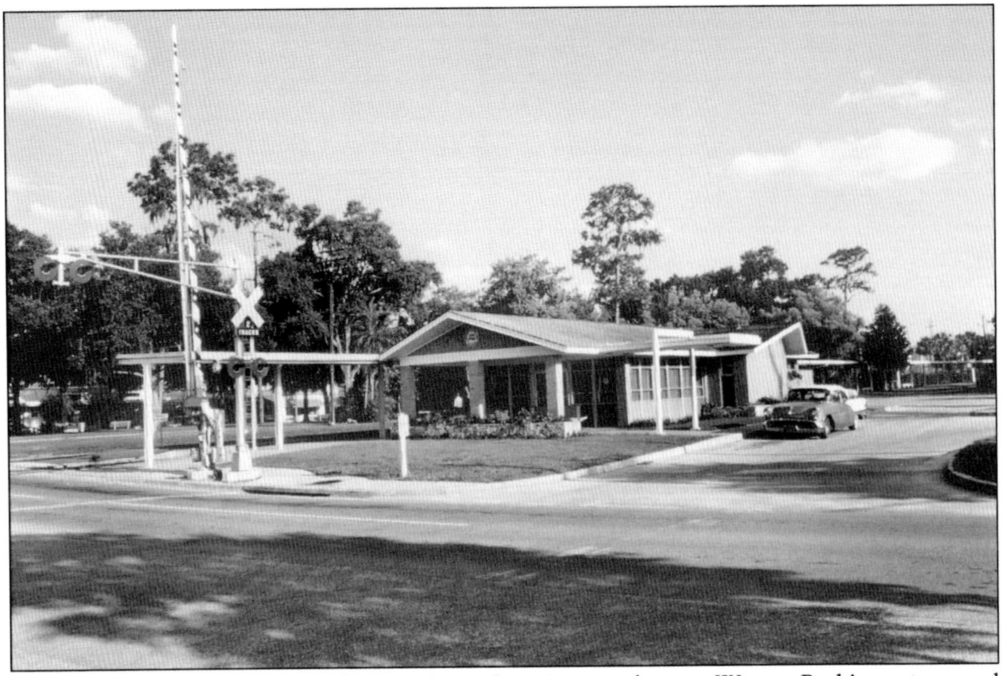

WINTER PARK, 1969. Currently four Amtrak trains per day use Winter Park's station, and commuter rail services are planned for the future. Winter Park's third depot, this brick building, was constructed in 1962 by the ACL with city-provided funding. This street-side scene was recorded on a spring day in 1969. (Courtesy of R. Randolph Stevens.)

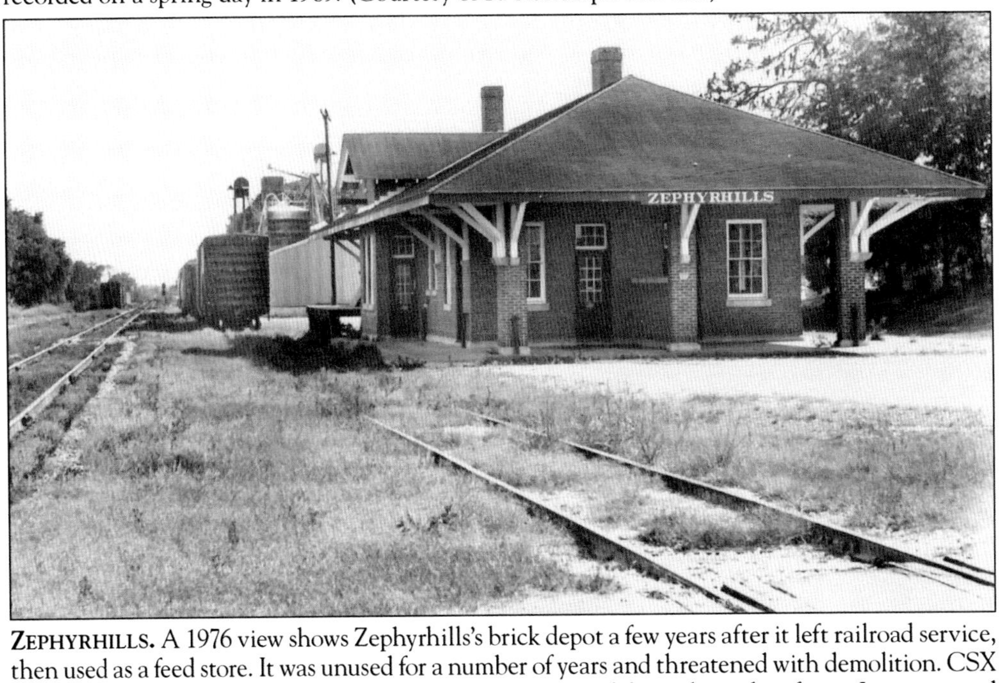

ZEPHYRHILLS. A 1976 view shows Zephyrhills's brick depot a few years after it left railroad service, then used as a feed store. It was unused for a number of years and threatened with demolition. CSX donated the building to the city, stipulating it be removed from the right-of-way. It was moved 200 feet to city property, renovated, and opened as the Zephyrhills Depot Museum. (Courtesy of Fred Clark Jr.)

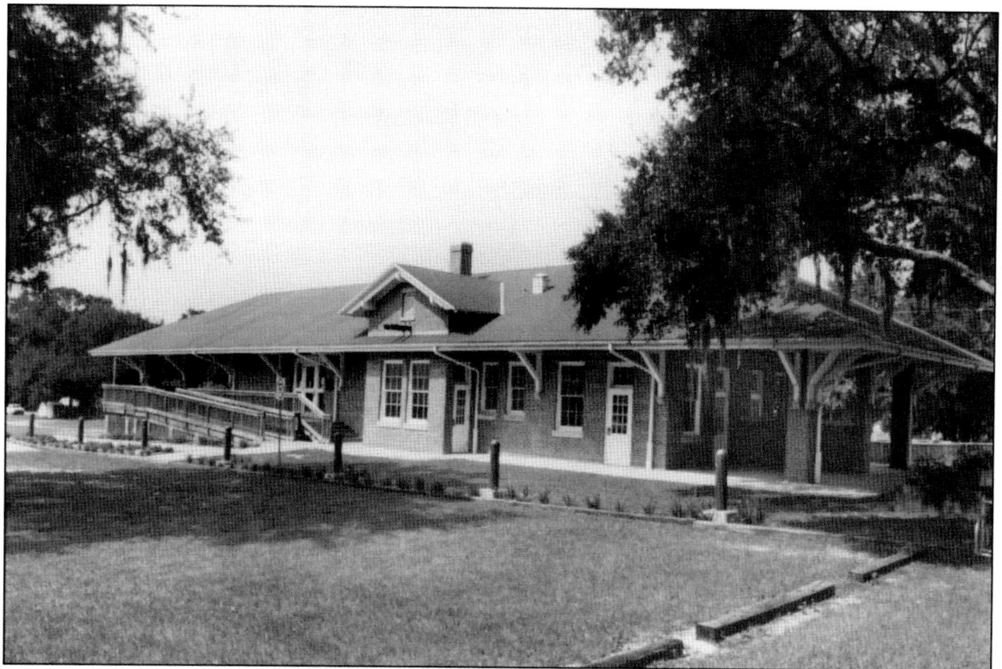

ZEPHYRHILLS. This picture from August 2001 of the Zephyrhills depot clearly shows the excellent restoration work done on the building. In its new role as a museum, it will serve the community for many years to come. (Courtesy of Mike Mulligan.)

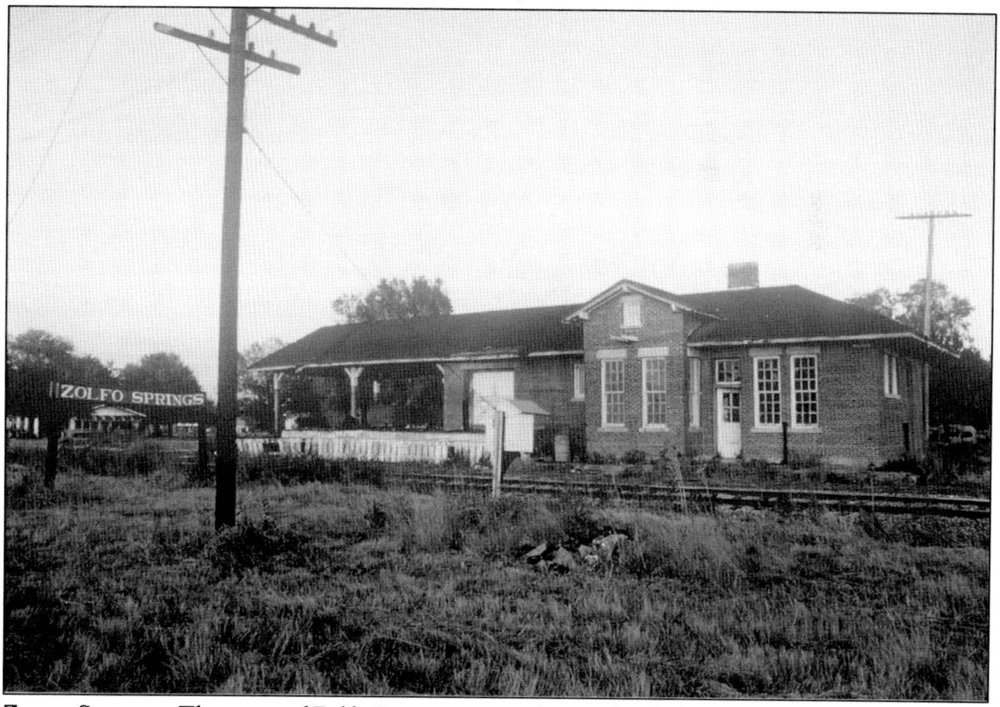

ZOLFO SPRINGS. The town of Zolfo Springs received a new brick depot in 1927. Until the end of 1965, it was passenger flag stop. The vacant building was photographed in early 1969. (Courtesy of R. Randolph Stevens.)

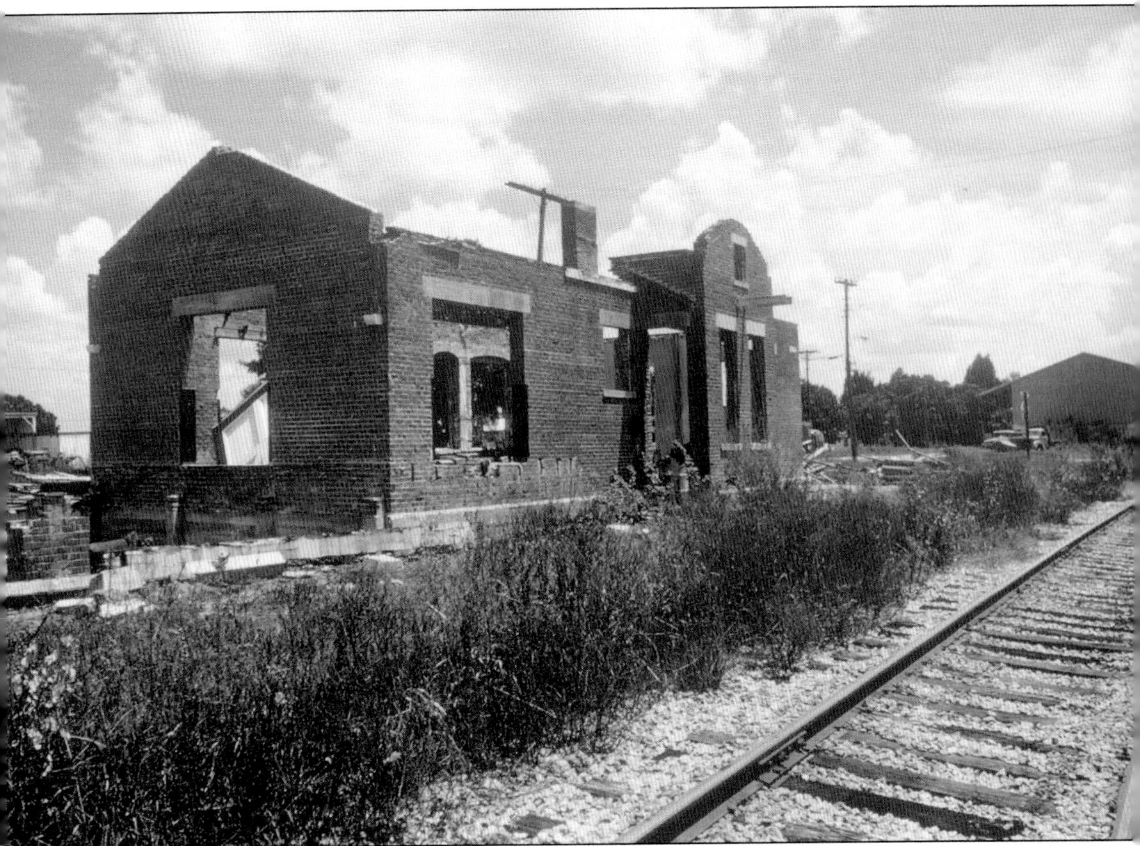

Zolfo Springs—Near the End. Zolfo Springs's depot will soon be gone, as dismantling is well under way in the summer of 1969. Tracks through here were pulled in the early 1980s. Compare this with the previous image. (Courtesy of R. Randolph Stevens.)

Two

Seaboard Air Line Railway and Predecessors

Seaboard Air Line Railway emerged July 1, 1900, when various railroads were tied together by constructing connecting lines. These lines stretched from Virginia to Florida. A large component of the company was the Florida Central and Peninsular Railroad.

Florida Central and Peninsular was formed in 1893. It consisted of 944 miles of track and included the 57-mile subsidiary Suwannee River and Gulf Railway. From 1884 to 1889, the company was known as the Florida Railway and Navigation Company. Predecessor railroads of Florida Central and Peninsular that served the Central Florida region were the Florida Railroad, later known as Atlantic, Gulf, and West India Transit Company, and then Florida Transit Railroad in 1881. Florida Transit operated a line of 156 miles from Fernandina to Cedar Key. It also owned Peninsular Railroad and Tropical Florida Railroad, extending from Waldo to Ocala and eventually reaching Tampa. Florida Transit and Peninsular Railroad was organized to consolidate these three railroads. In 1884, it merged with Florida Central and Western Railroad to form the Florida Railway and Navigation Company. This company constituted the largest rail system in the state in 1884. That same year, the 11-mile Leesburg and Indian River Railroad would be added. In 1888, the largest Florida system was sold at public auction to become Florida Central and Peninsular Railway.

Florida Central and Peninsular Railway acquired Tavares, Orlando, and Atlantic Railroad and the East Florida and Atlantic Railroad. The later road was created by consolidation of Orlando and Winter Park Railway and Osceola and Lake Jessop Railway. Florida Central and Peninsular Railway would become Florida Central and Peninsular Railroad in 1893. Atlantic, Suwannee River, and Gulf Railway's 57 miles of track were added to the system in 1899.

The Seaboard would purchase numerous railroads and expanded lines throughout the state of Florida into the late 1920s. Purchased companies operating in Central Florida included Warnell Lumber and Veneer Company's line (added 1905); Tampa and Gulf Railroad (1912); Tampa Northern (1912); East and West Coast Railway (1915); Charlotte Harbor and Northern (1928); Florida Central and Gulf Railway (previously known as Standard and Hernando Railroad of 1905); and Jacksonville, Gainesville, and Gulf Railway, earlier known as Tampa and Jacksonville Railway (1927). Finally the Tavares and Gulf Railroad came to the Seaboard when purchased in 1926. It operated as a subsidiary and had previously been the Tavares, Apopka, and Gulf Railroad.

Seaboard Air Line merged with Atlantic Coast Line Railroad on July 1, 1967.

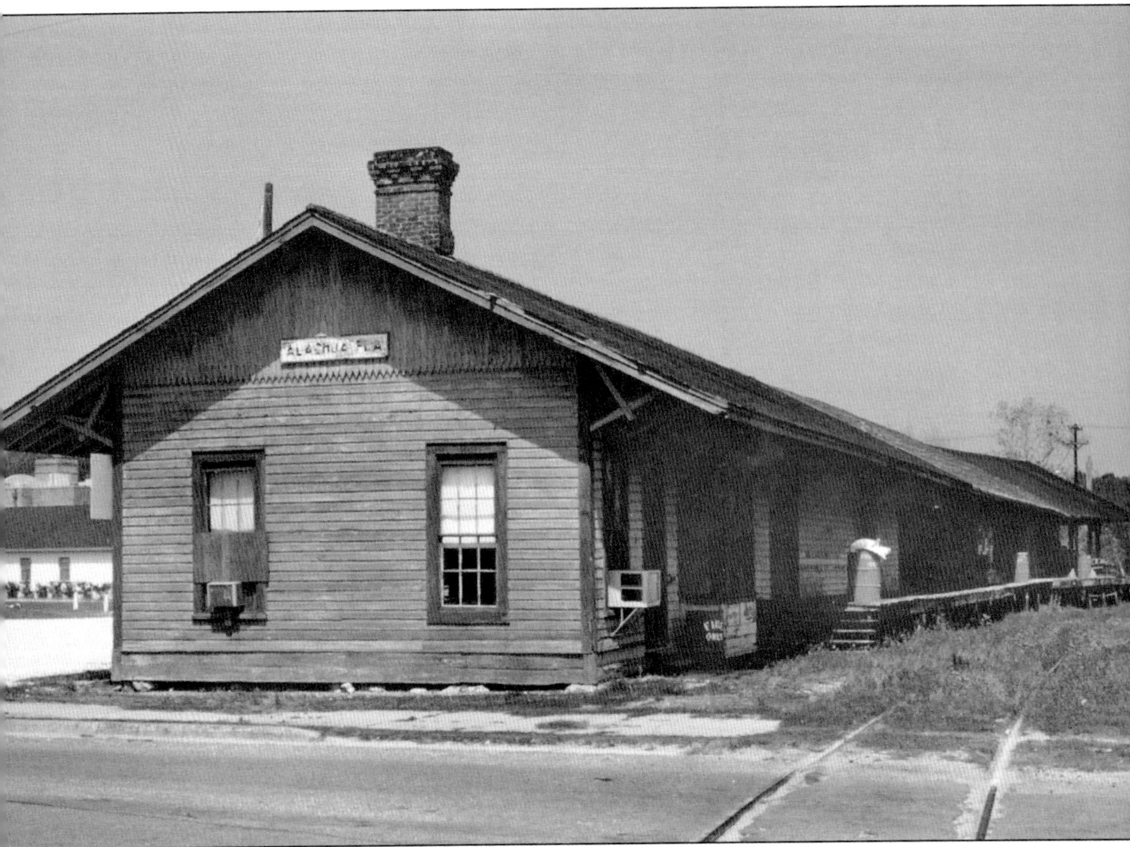

ALACHUA, SPRING 1971. The former Seaboard depot is still ready to serve the needs of the railroad. Predecessor Atlantic, Suwannee River, and Gulf Railway brought a second railroad to Alachua in 1896. This depot was built in 1922. Atlantic Coast Line's depot was located a short distance away. Neither depot survives today. (Courtesy of R. Randolph Stevens.)

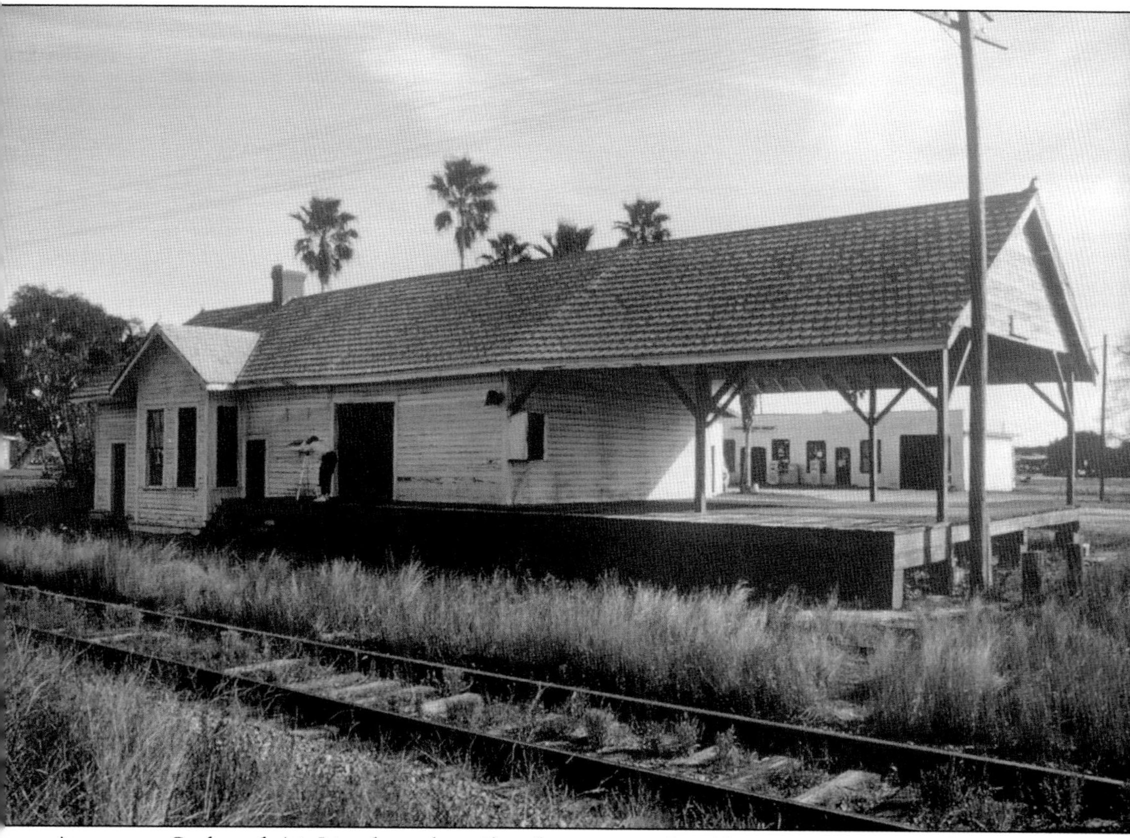

ALTURAS. Seaboard Air Line brought railroad service to the Alturas area in 1915, when they constructed a line from Bartow to Lake Wales. The depot was no longer in railroad use in early 1969, when this photograph was taken. The depot and rails have been removed. (Courtesy of R. Randolph Stevens.)

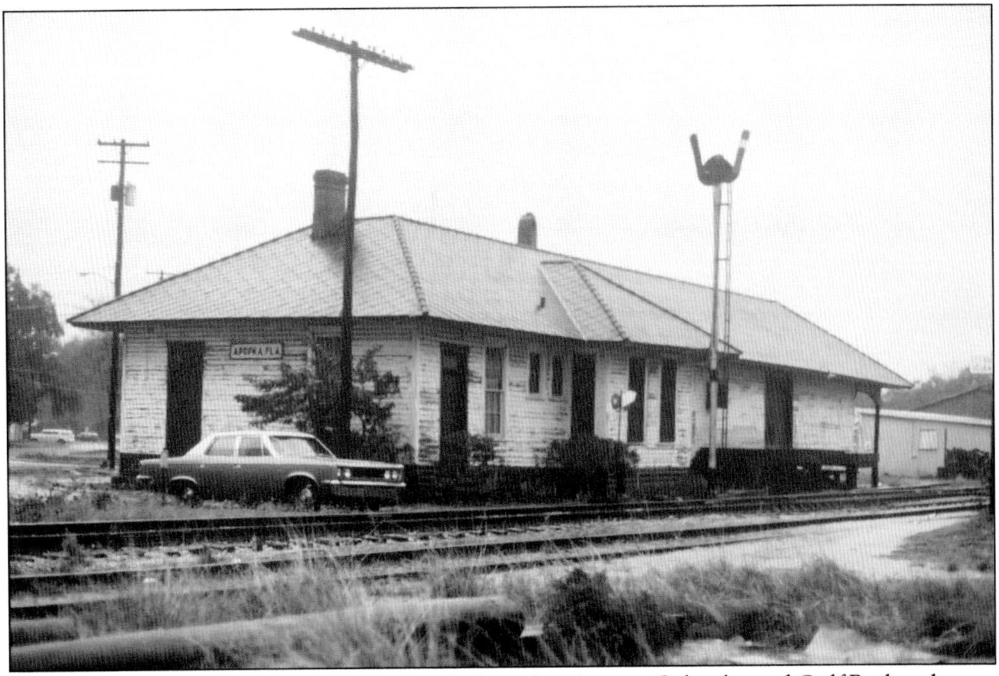

APOPKA. Apopka received a second railroad when the Tavares, Orlando, and Gulf Railroad came to town in 1885. The second depot built for the railroad is seen during the spring of 1971. Built in 1918, the structure was placed on the National Register of Historic Places in 1993. In recent years, it has been used as a warehouse. (Courtesy of R. Randolph Stevens.)

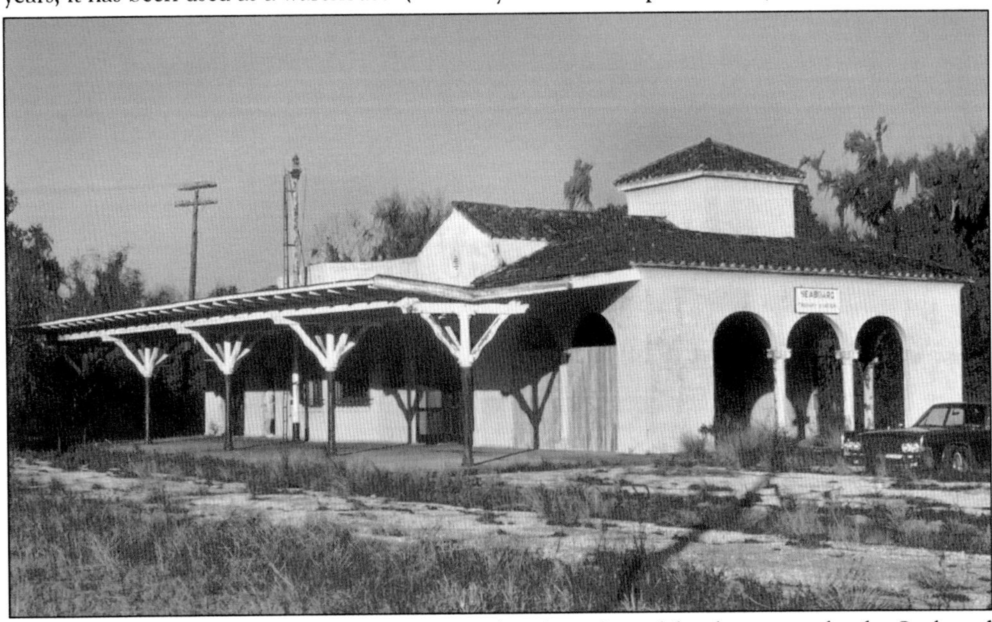

ARCADIA. Charlotte Harbor and Northern Railroad was leased for three years by the Seaboard early in 1925. At the end of the lease, the Seaboard purchased all stock of the Charlotte Harbor and Northern and absorbed its operation. An attractive Mediterranean Revival station was constructed in this time period. Viewed in December 1968, the building lost passenger service in the late 1950s. It was taken down in 1974. (Courtesy of R. Randolph Stevens.)

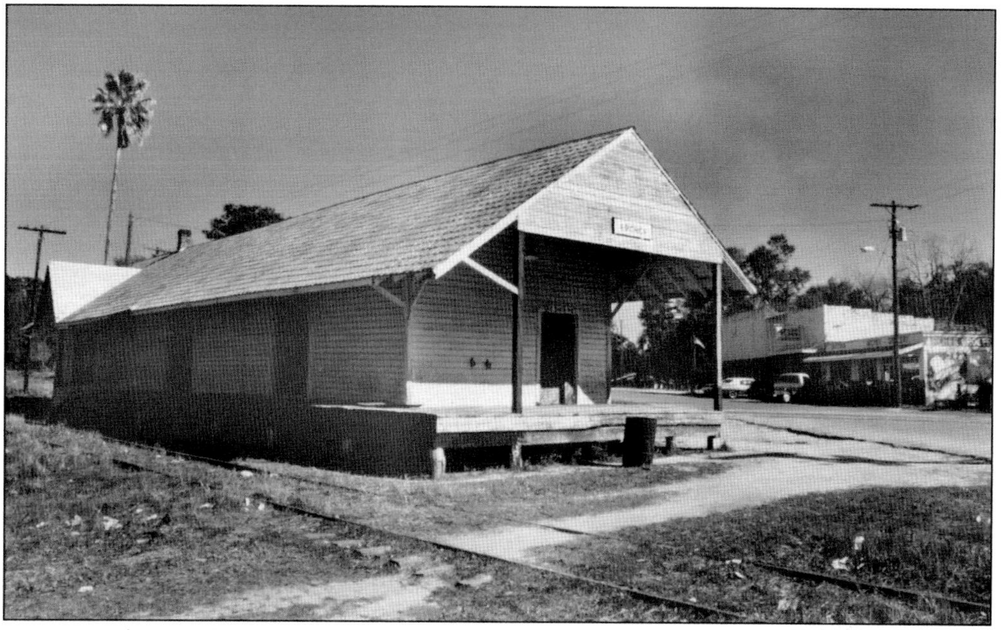

ARCHER. The Florida Railroad came to Archer, then known as Deer Hammock, in 1861. Built prior to 1900, the wooden-frame building appears in this early-1971 scene sometime after railroad use concluded. Tracks have long been removed, but the depot survives and is home to the Archer Historical Society Railroad Museum. (Courtesy of R. Randolph Stevens.)

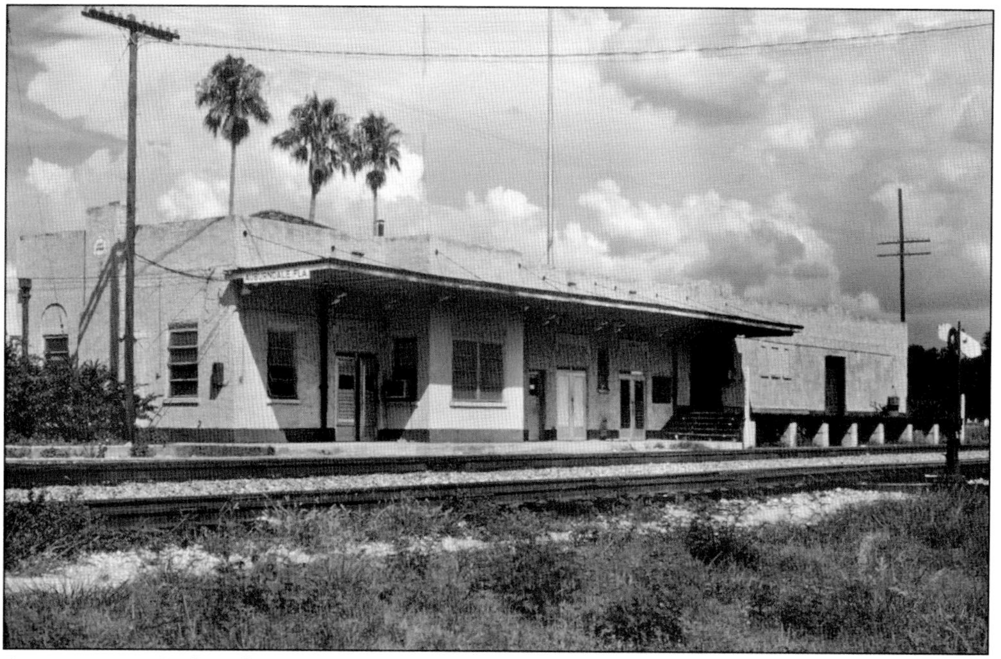

AUBURNDALE. Seaboard Air Line's expansion of the mid-1920s brought the company to Auburndale in 1925. A block and stucco station was built and opened in 1927. It looked like this in 1968, still in railroad use. Sometime after railroad service, the building was moved to the site of the former Atlantic Coast Line depot around 2000. It has been remodeled for use as a community center. (Courtesy of R. Randolph Stevens.)

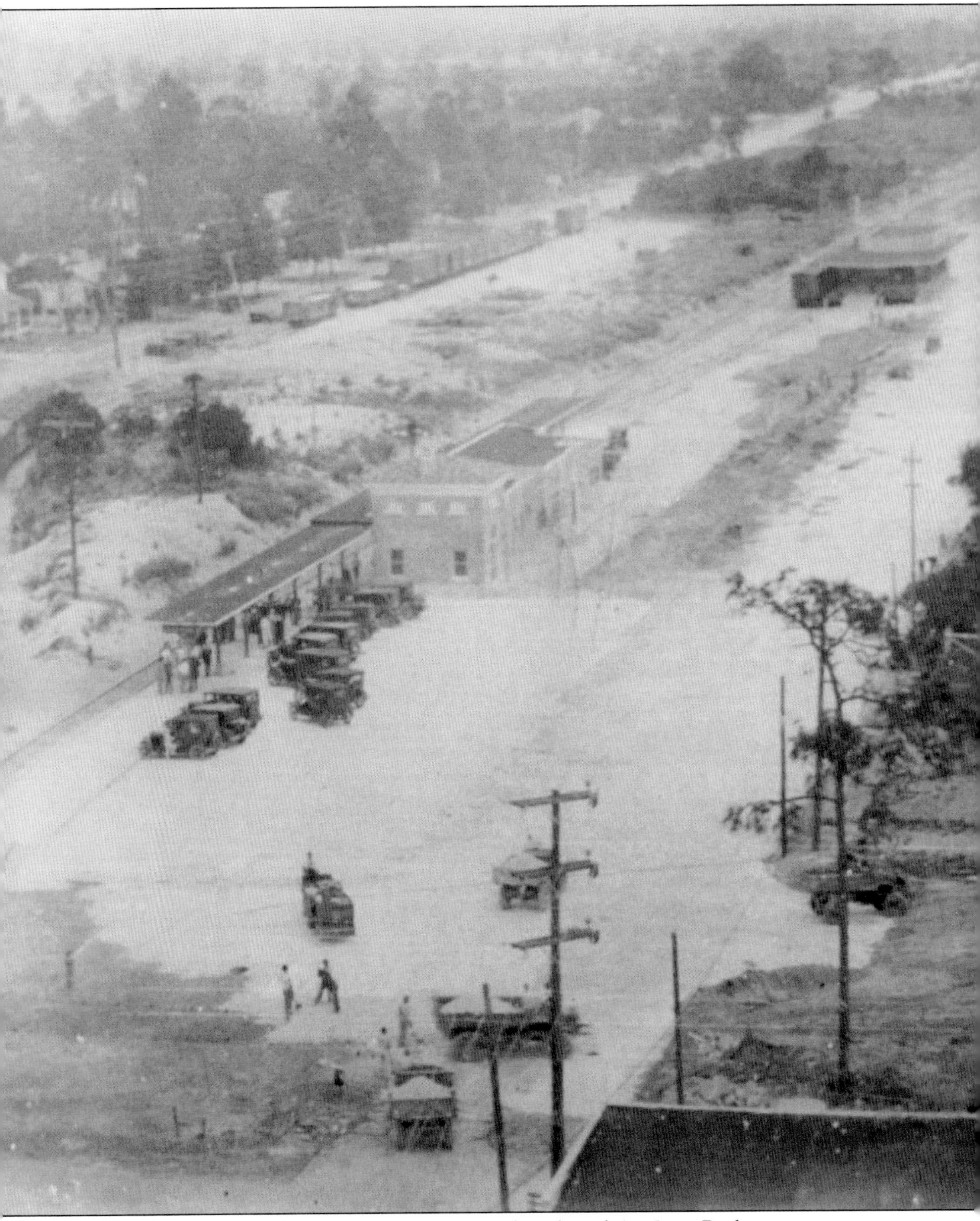

AVON PARK. Atlantic Coast Line Railroad and Seaboard Air Line Railway were competitors throughout many areas of Central Florida. This 1926 bird's-eye view at Avon Park, taken from an adjacent water tower, clearly shows how close rail lines and facilities were located. Looking north, the ACL depot is to the right with boxcars on the depot siding. Seaboard's new station is on the left with automobiles parked and people standing on the track platform. It appears the

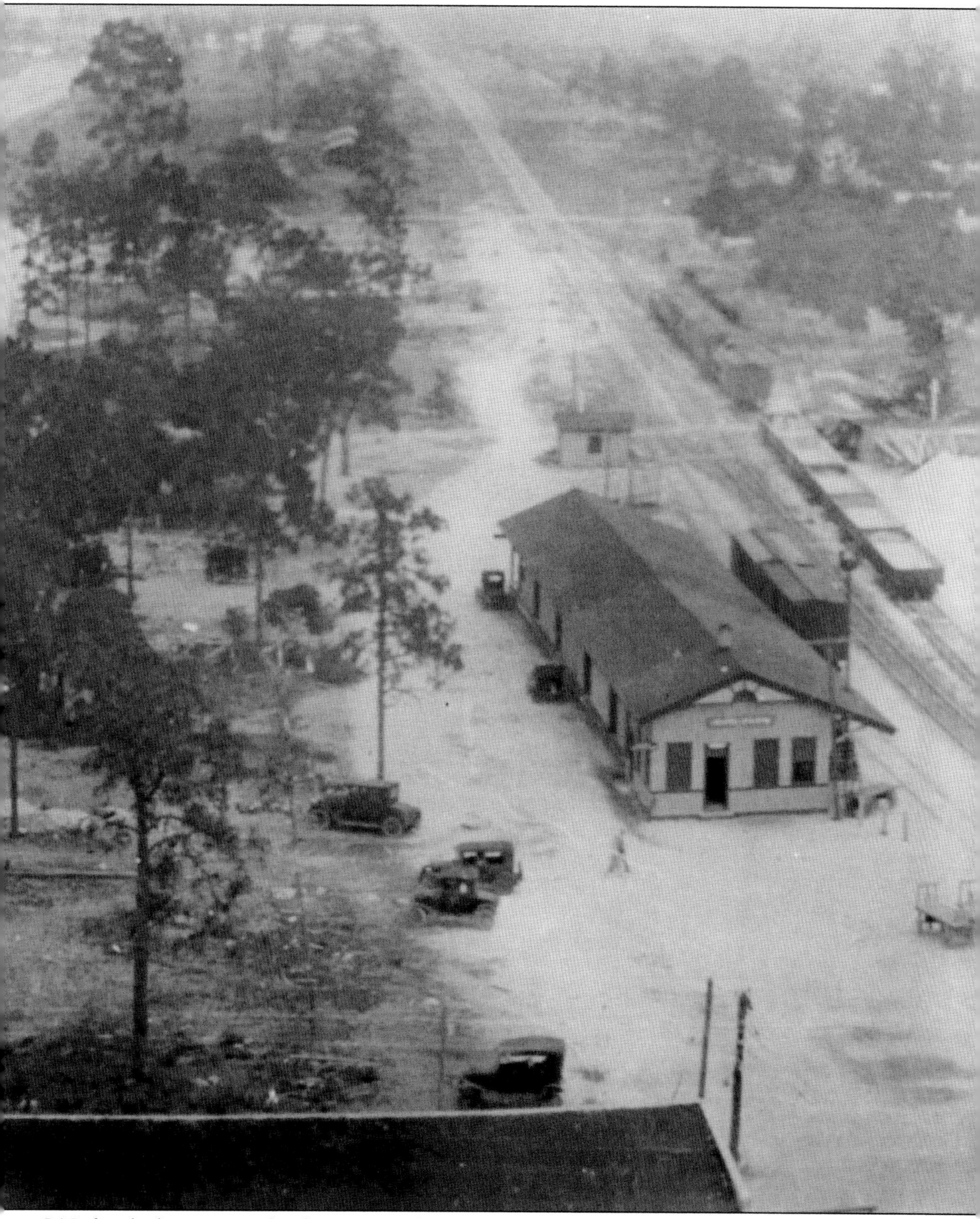

SAL freight house is in the distance up the track. Work is continuing on the parking lot and driveway as dump trucks haul in material for spreading. Shortly after the July 1, 1967, merger between the two companies, a line rationalization program was implemented. The ACL mainline would no longer be a through route, and the ACL depot would come down in 1970. (Courtesy of Avon Park Depot Museum.)

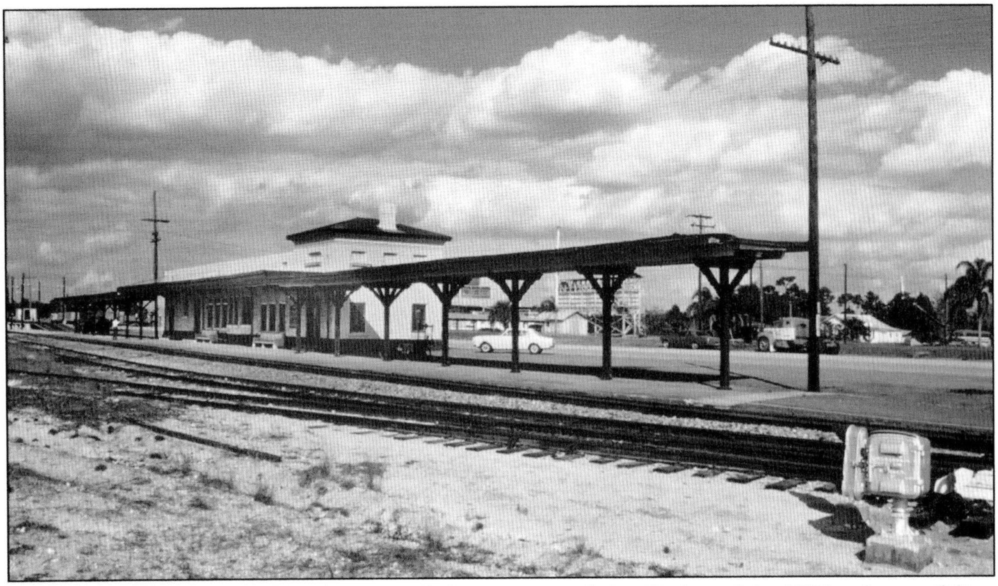

AVON PARK, 1969. Avon Park received the services of the Seaboard in 1926, when rail line expansion from Coleman to West Palm Beach came through town. This Mediterranean Revival building was completed in 1926 and is seen (above) around the first of the year 1969. The Seaboard tracks paralleled the Atlantic Coast Line tracks through town just to the right of the image, as seen in the double-page spread on pages 64–65. Passengers are waiting to board (below) this southbound train coming into the station around 1960. Avon Park lost passenger service on April 30, 1971. The building was donated to the Old Settlers Association on January 4, 1979. It now houses the Depot Museum and Historical Society of Avon Park. (Above courtesy of R. Randolph Stevens; below courtesy of Historical Society of Avon Park.)

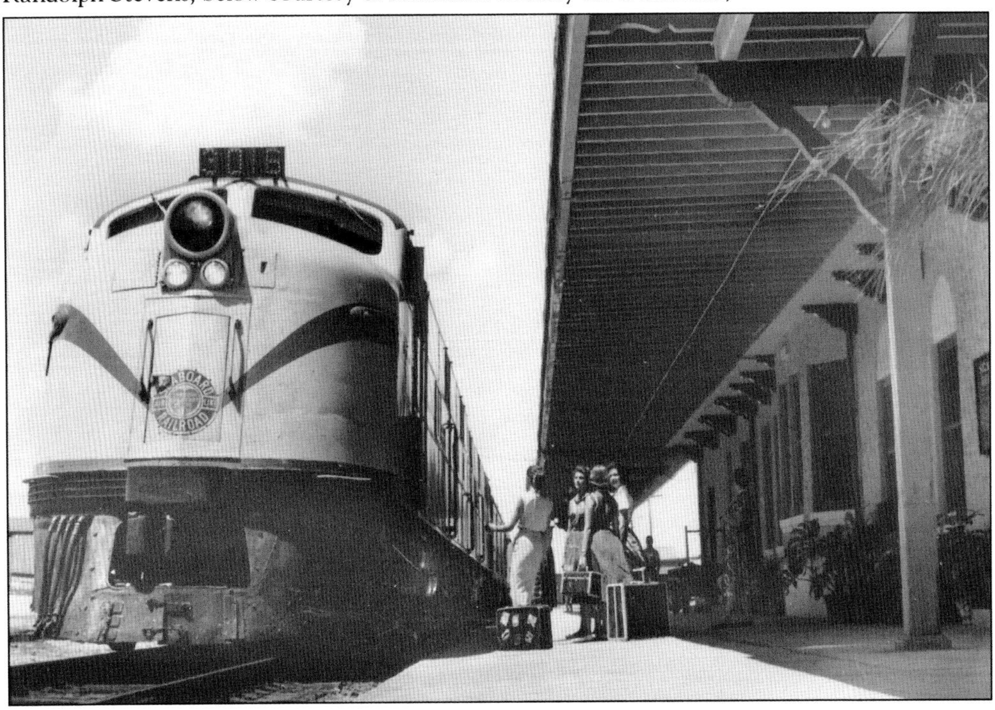

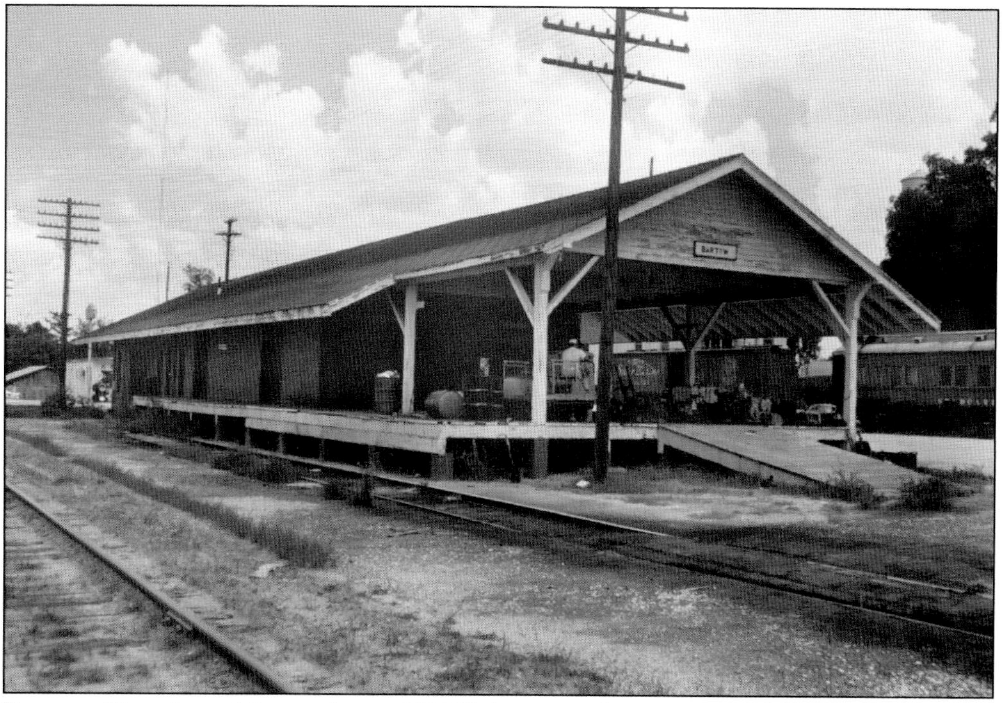

BARTOW. Two views of Bartow from mid-1969 show it in the service of the Seaboard Coast Line Railroad. Passenger services had been discontinued, but it was a base for the freight agent and maintenance-of-way crews. It would continue in railroad use until the mid-1980s. Afterward the property was listed for sale by CSX for $150,000. The building constructed in 1913 was demolished in 1993. (Both courtesy of R. Randolph Stevens.)

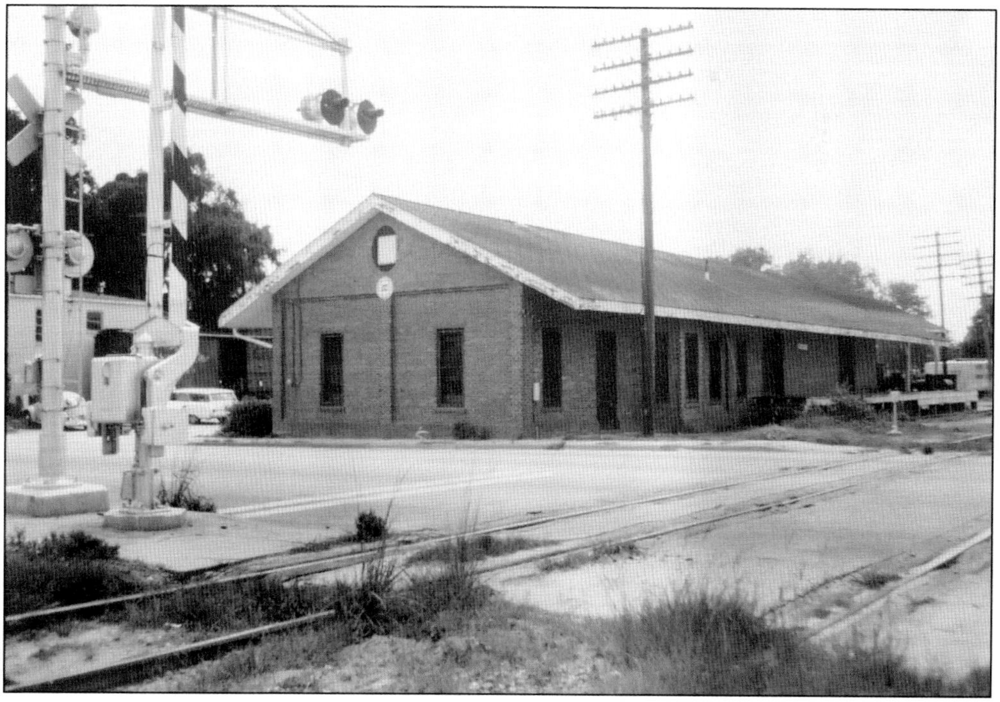

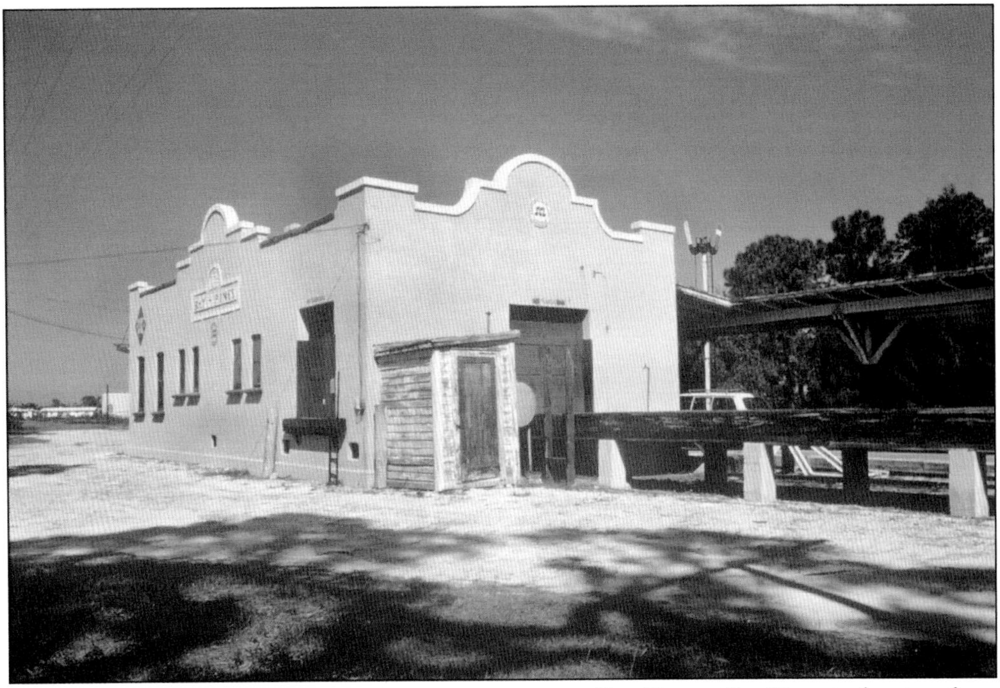

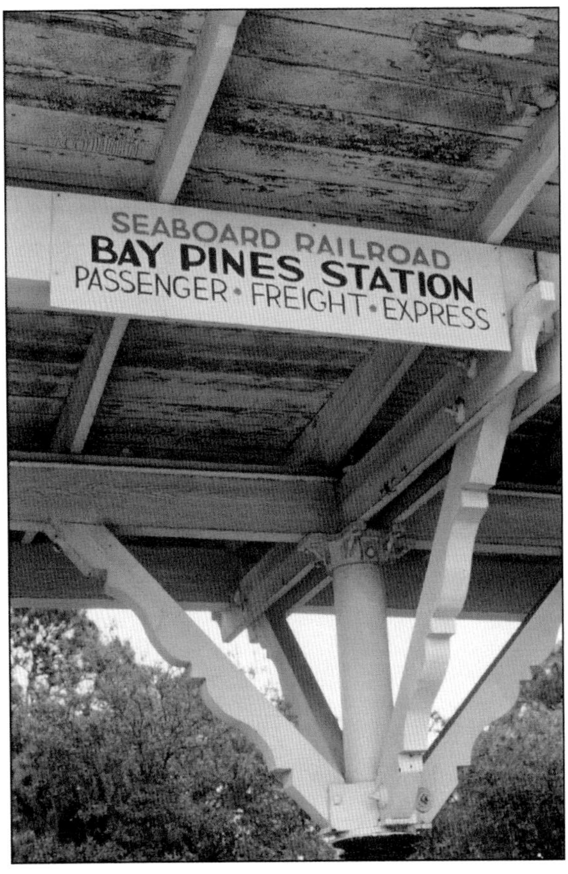

BAY PINES. Bay Pines is the site of a large veterans hospital established in 1933. Seaboard Air Line built an attractive block and stucco building to serve the facility. It was located 11.5 rail miles from St. Petersburg. These scenes are from the beginning of the year in 1969. (Both courtesy of R. Randolph Stevens.)

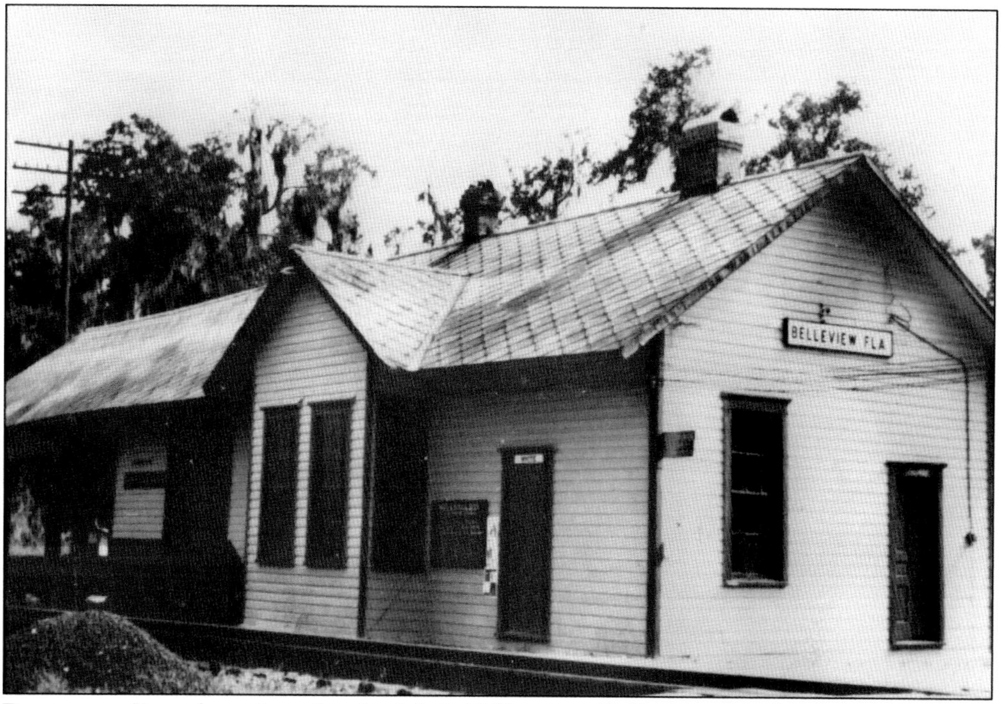

BELLEVIEW. For a short time after the July 1, 1967, merger, Belleview was a flag stop for passenger trains of the Seaboard Coast Line. Predecessor Tropical Florida Railroad built their line from Ocala through Belleview in 1882. Currently the line is a vital component of today's CSX Railroad. The depot fell into disrepair after railroad use ceased. It was moved, renovated, and used as the chamber of commerce office. (Courtesy of Florida State Archives.)

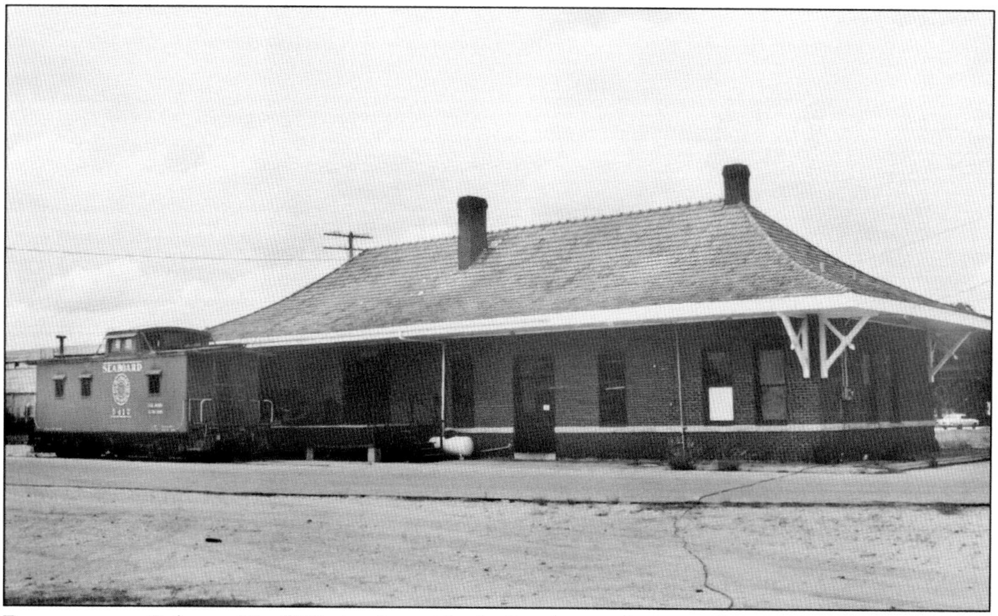

BRADENTON. Caboose No. 5412 sits alongside the Bradenton depot in the summer of 1968. Built in 1914, the depot would lose passenger service that year as the July 1, 1967, merger rationalized company assets. The building would survive until the 1980s. (Courtesy of R. Randolph Stevens.)

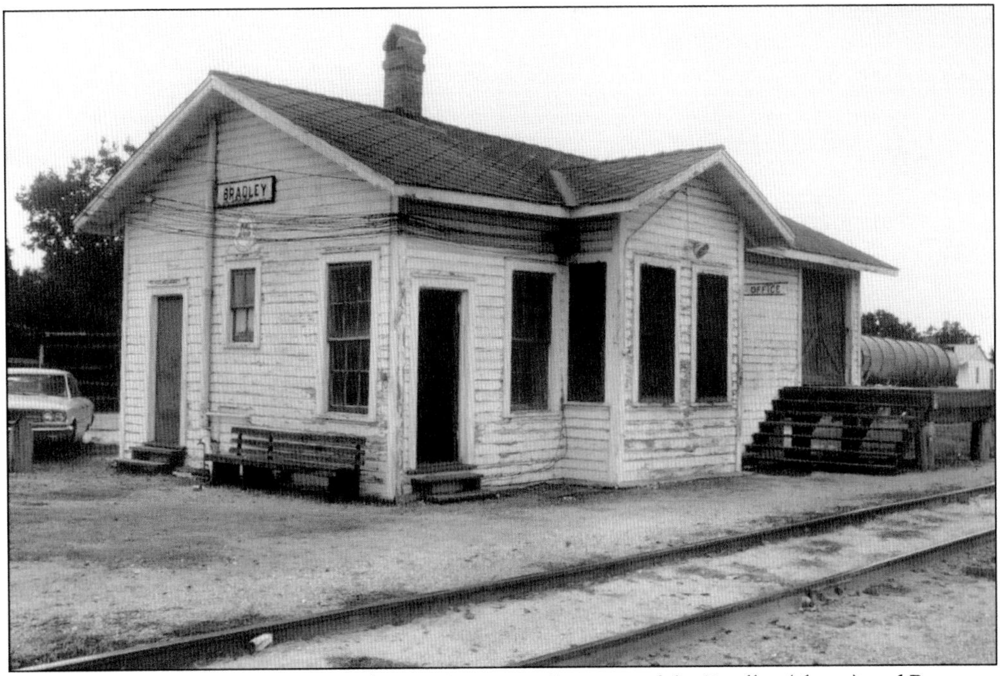

BRADLEY AND BREWSTER. Seaboard Coast Line is making use of the Bradley (above) and Brewster (below) depots on a summer day in 1968. Seaboard rails met the Charlotte Harbor and Northern (CH&N) at Bradley in 1910. Bradley was a community of 154 people in 1929. The station provided postal telegraph and American Railway Express services. Brewster, located just over three miles south of Bradley on the CH&N line, numbered just 75 citizens at that time, but it offered Western Union Telegraph services as well as the others. Both stations had passenger train activity until the late 1950s. Both buildings no longer exist. (Both courtesy of R. Randolph Stevens.)

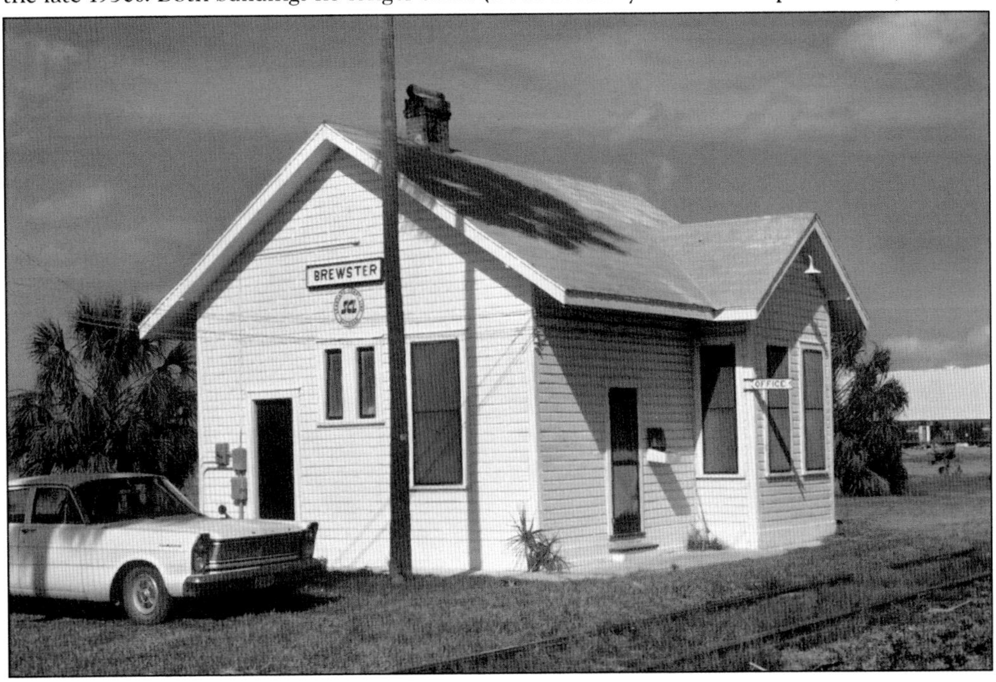

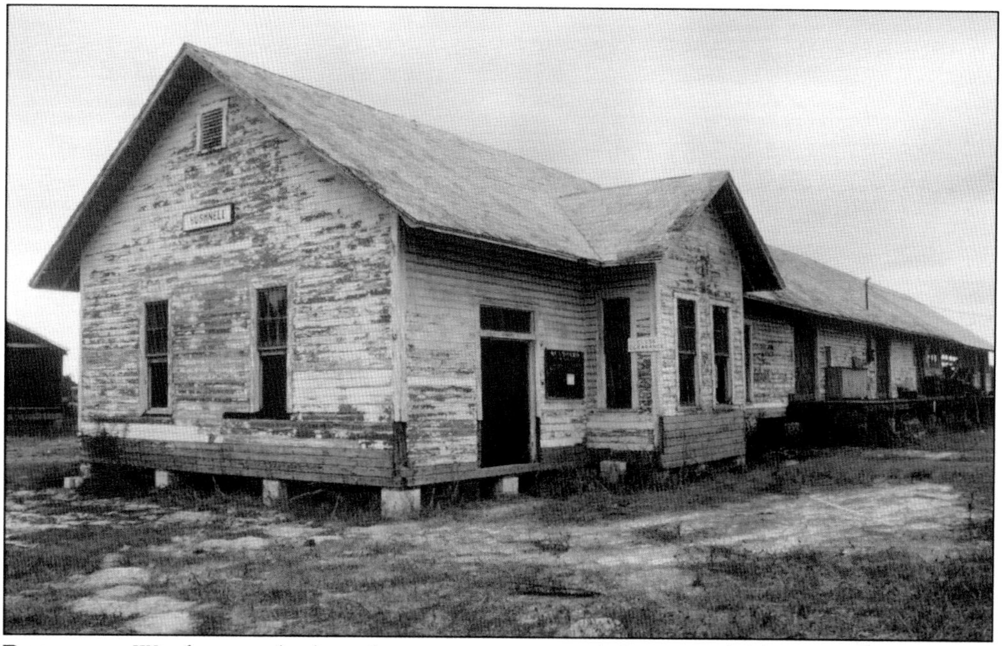

BUSHNELL. Windows are broken, doors are missing, and the general dilapidated condition of Bushnell's depot suggests it will soon be demolished. However, a close study of this early-1969 image points to a recent move to this site. Railroad tracks are not present, steps are missing, and new concrete blocks are providing support to the building. In any event, the structure no longer exists, as it was taken down later that year. (Courtesy of R. Randolph Stevens.)

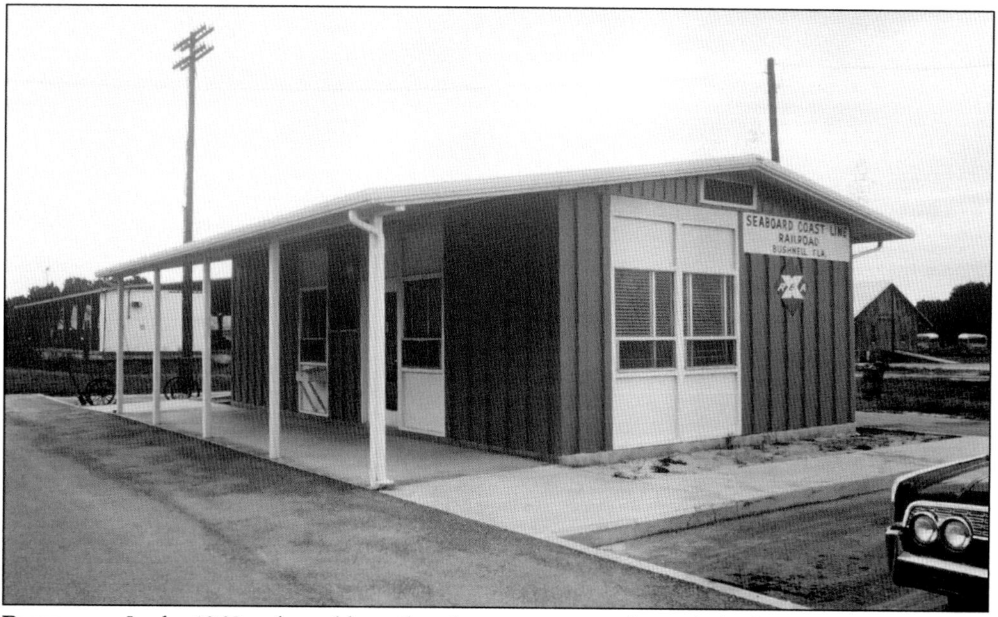

BUSHNELL. In the 1960s, when older railroad structures were deemed obsolete, they were typically replaced by these utilitarian metal boxes. Perhaps this one replaced the one in the previous image. The "Train Bulletin" board is in place, and it is a Railway Express Agency location. This image is from early 1969. Bushnell was listed in a Seaboard Coast Line timetable effective December 15, 1968, with two trains scheduled per day. (Courtesy of R. Randolph Stevens.)

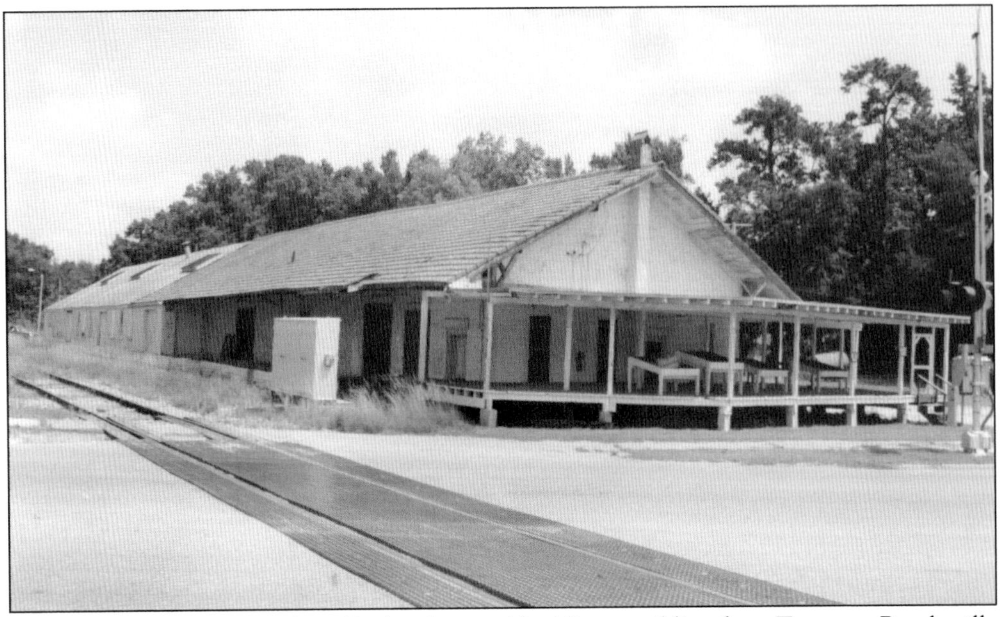

BROOKSVILLE. Tampa Northern Railroad started building a rail line from Tampa to Brooksville in June 1906. Forty-nine miles and 18 months later, it reached Brooksville. In 1910, a depot was built to service the town. On July 25, 1992, the former station was being used for non-railroad-related business. The track is still in place, but the building was torn down later in the 1990s. (Courtesy of Mike Mulligan.)

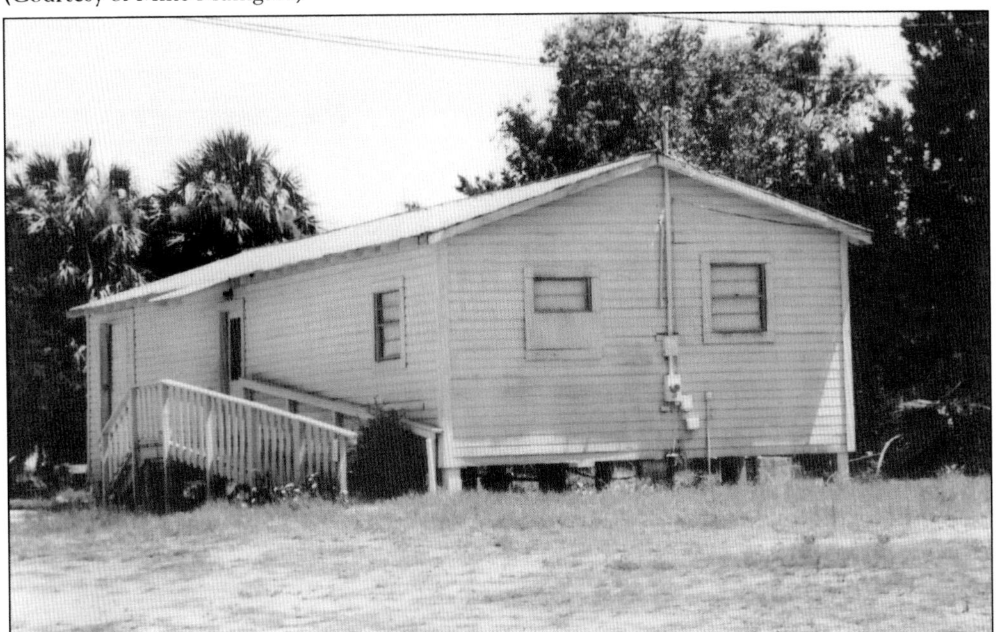

CEDAR KEY. Florida Railroad's line from Fernandina to Cedar Key was completed in 1861. The outbreak of the Civil War would result in the destruction of much of the railroad over the next four years. It was rebuilt after the war, and rail service allowed the town to grow. Railroad service lasted until 1932. The depot, seen in 2001, is one of a few tangible reminders of the town's railroad past. (Courtesy of Jeanne Hickam.)

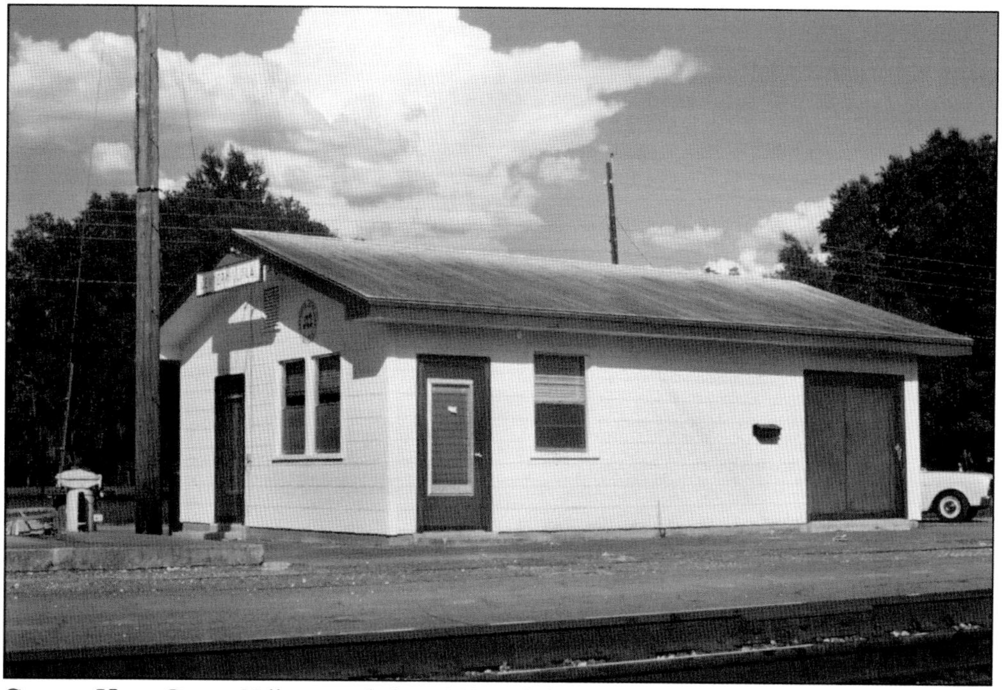

CENTER HILL. Center Hill was settled in 1883, and the area became a large producer of produce, particularly green beans. By 1929, the population was over 700 and the town was served by two railroads. Seaboard Air Line came on the scene in 1925. It built a depot with a long freight-loading dock to handle the numerous carloads of produce shipped from here. Passenger service would last until 1968. These views are from early 1969. (Both courtesy of R. Randolph Stevens.)

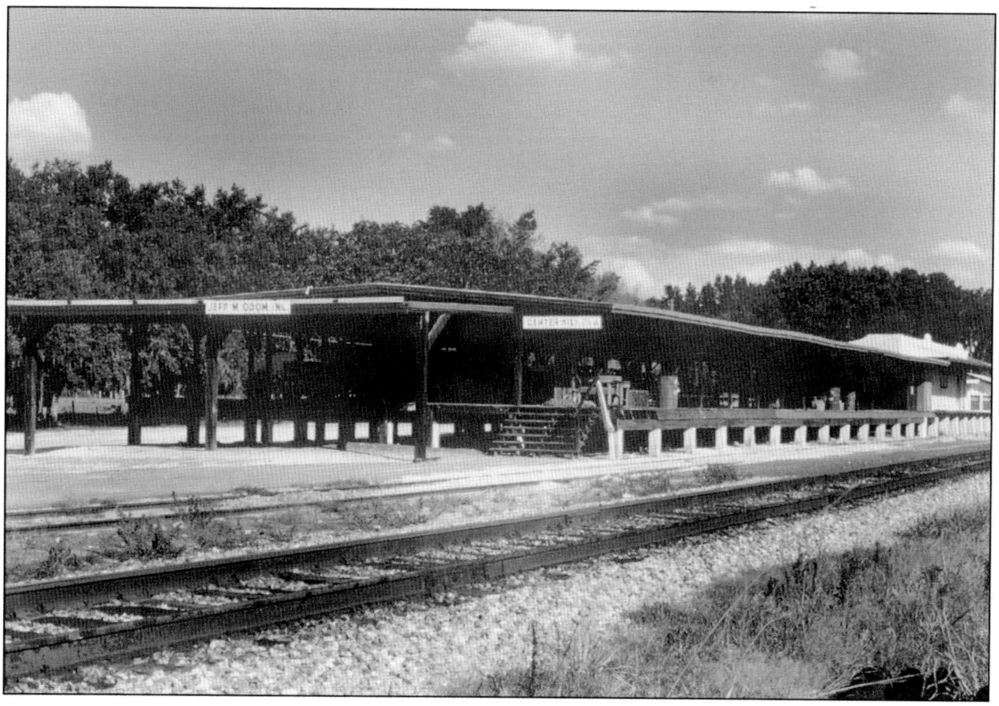

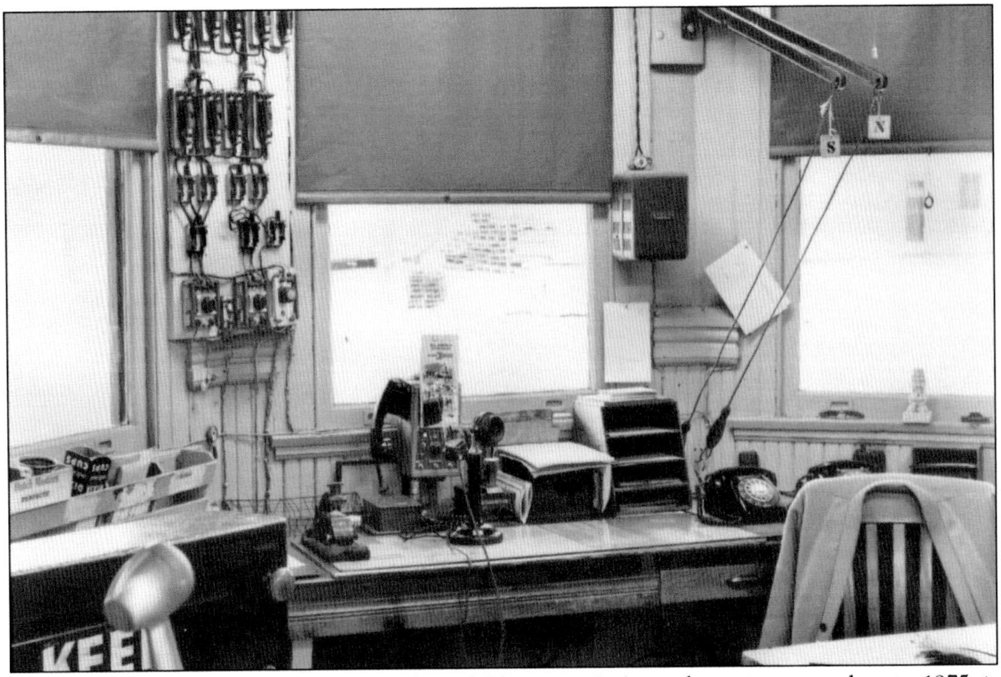

CLEARWATER. Although this interior shot of Clearwater's Amtrak station was taken in 1975, it is a good representation of a station agent's work area over the previous decades. The building was formerly the Seaboard passenger station, built in 1922. It was used by Amtrak into the 1990s. This work area was manned by agents for over 60 years. (Courtesy of Fred Clark Jr.)

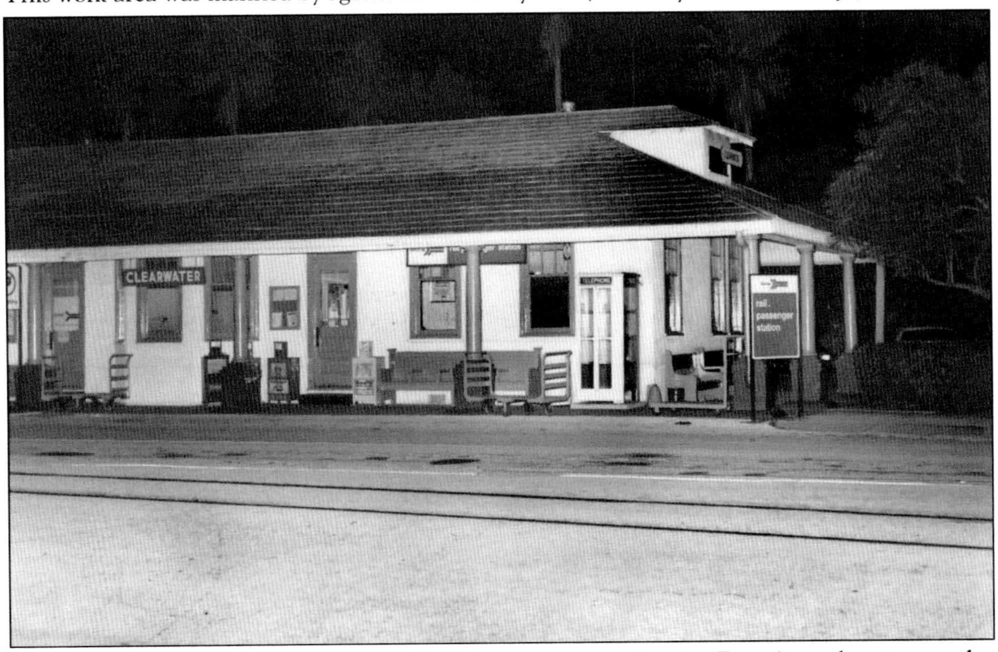

CLEARWATER. Photographed in 1977, the Clearwater station is quiet. Four Amtrak trains per day were on the schedule at this time. After the last train pulled out in 1984, the station was used as a ticketing and motor-coach transfer location. The building was razed around 2004. (Courtesy of Fred Clark Jr.)

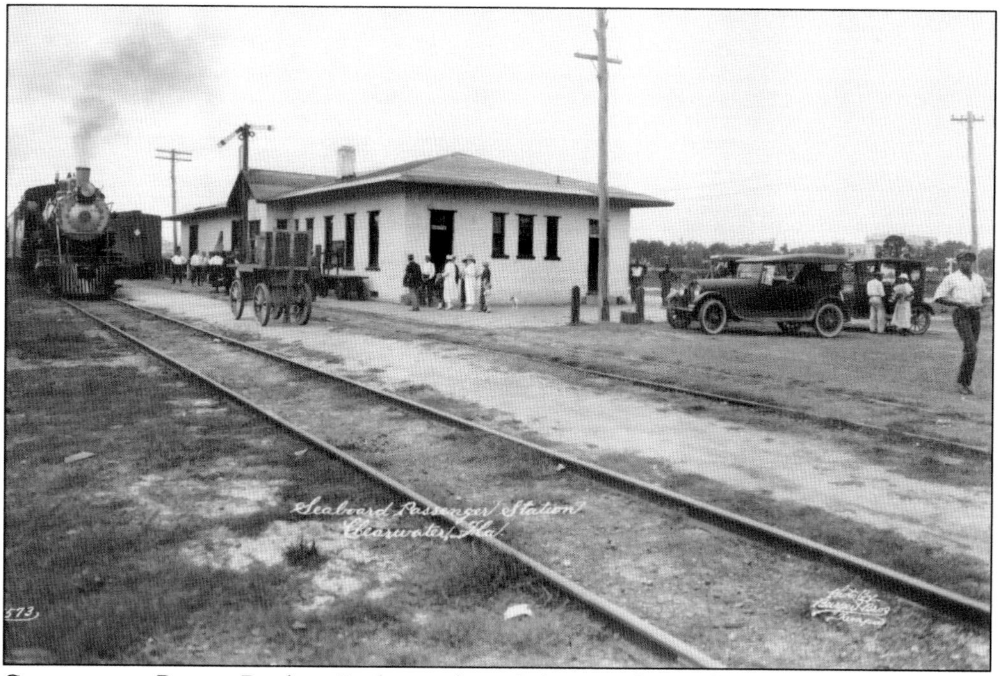

CLEARWATER. Burgert Brothers Studios performed photographic work in the Tampa Bay area for many years. Thankfully many high-quality images were saved after the studio passed into history. Clearwater's Seaboard station that preceded the one featured in the previous caption was the subject of the studio in this 1926 scene. Segregated waiting rooms are evident with "White" and "Colored" posted above the doors. (Courtesy of Tampa-Hillsborough Public Library.)

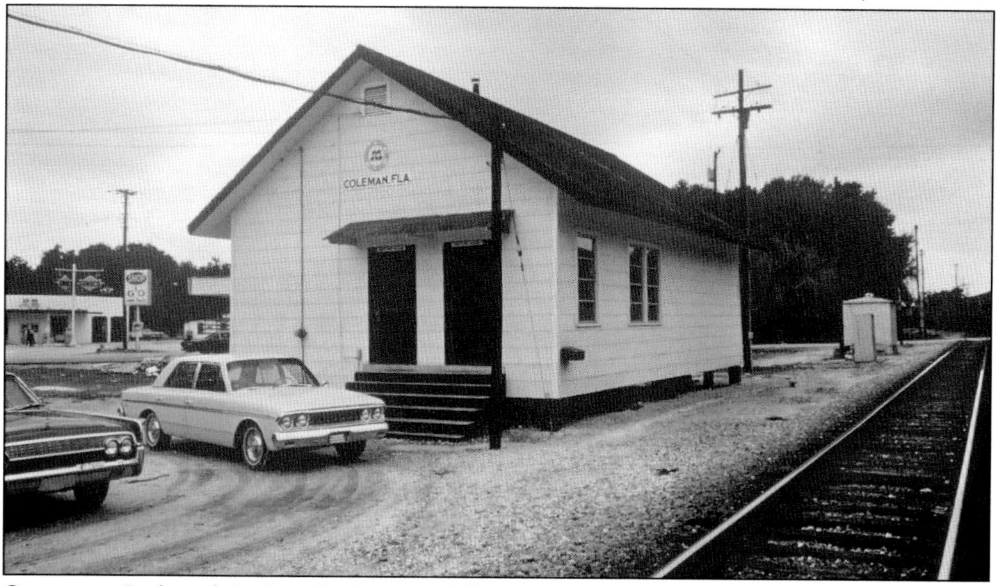

COLEMAN. Seaboard Air Line Railway would build a 204-mile extension to West Palm Beach in 1925. A point just south of the Coleman depot was selected to be the junction. People could still board a train at Coleman up to 1968, which is about the time period of this image. The depot has been moved a few times since and is now a part of a retail antiques complex. (Courtesy of R. Randolph Stevens.)

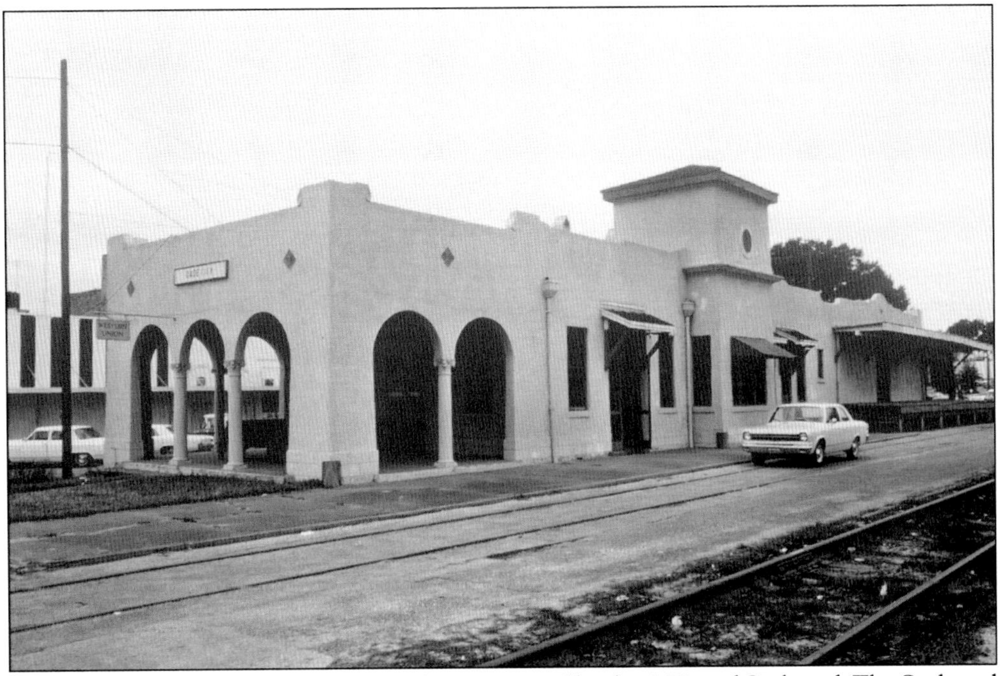

DADE CITY. Dade City is another town that was served by the ACL and Seaboard. The Seaboard depot was located in the business district, while the other was located on the eastern edge of town. The depot pictured here at the end of 1968 opened in 1927. It was torn down in 1971. (Courtesy of R. Randolph Stevens.)

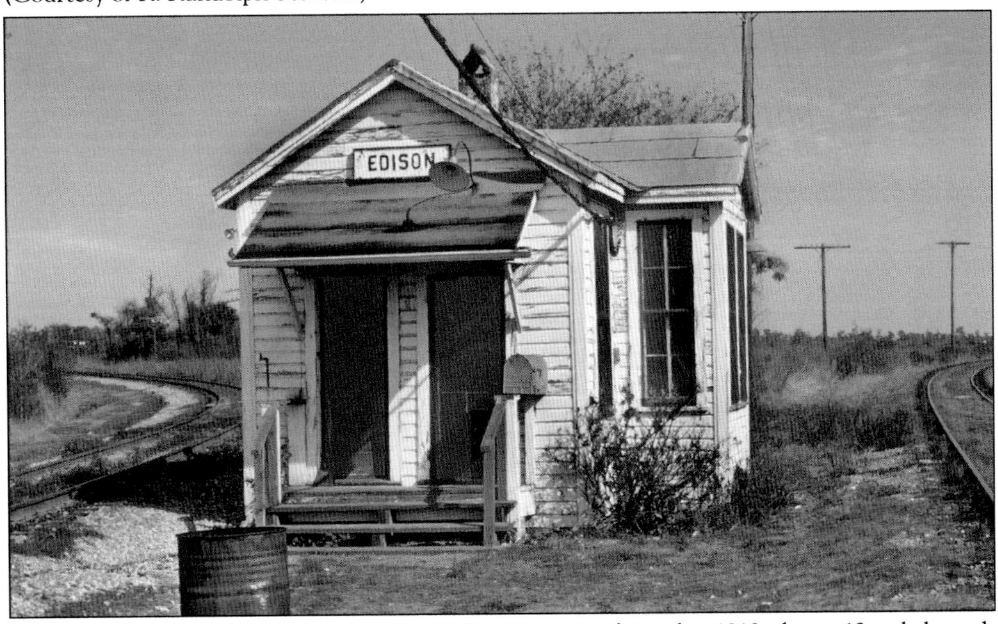

EDISON. The bucolic Edison depot was located at a junction formed in 1910 when a 12-mile branch to Agricola joined a line running between Plant City and Walinwa. Edison is still an important railroad junction in the phosphate-mining area of Florida. The simple wooden depot is seen in early 1969. It was a station stop until the late 1950s. The building was taken down many years ago. (Courtesy of R. Randolph Stevens.)

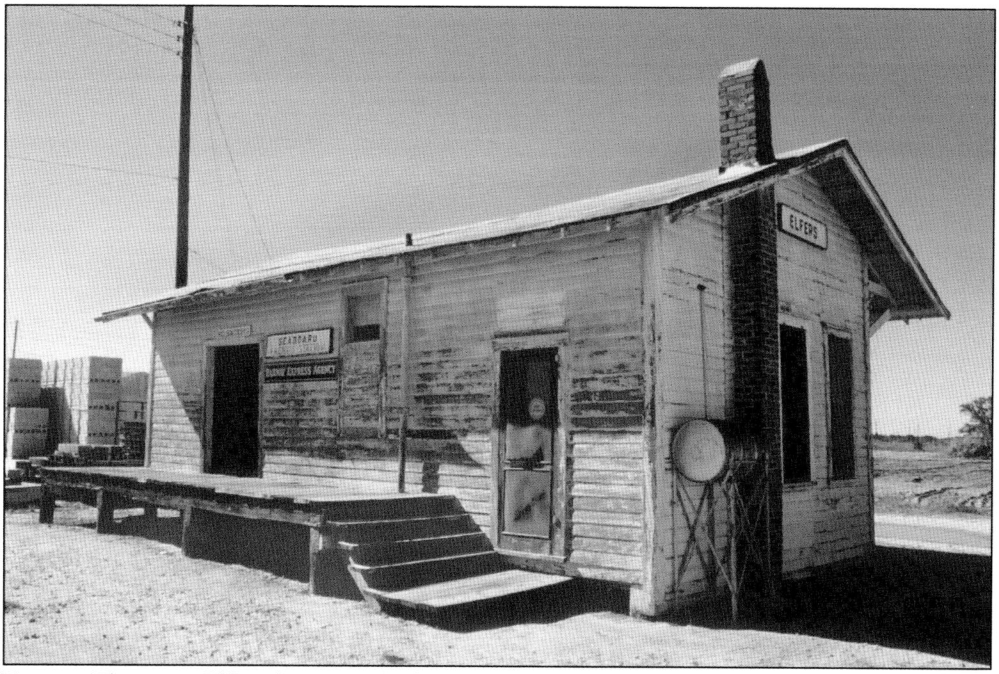

ELFERS. The rustic Elfers depot was built in 1912, railroad service would cease in 1972, and the building would come down in 1985. It was a freight-only facility and is shown at the beginning of 1969. One source indicated that salvaged lumber from the building was used to construct a home nearby. (Courtesy of R. Randolph Stevens.)

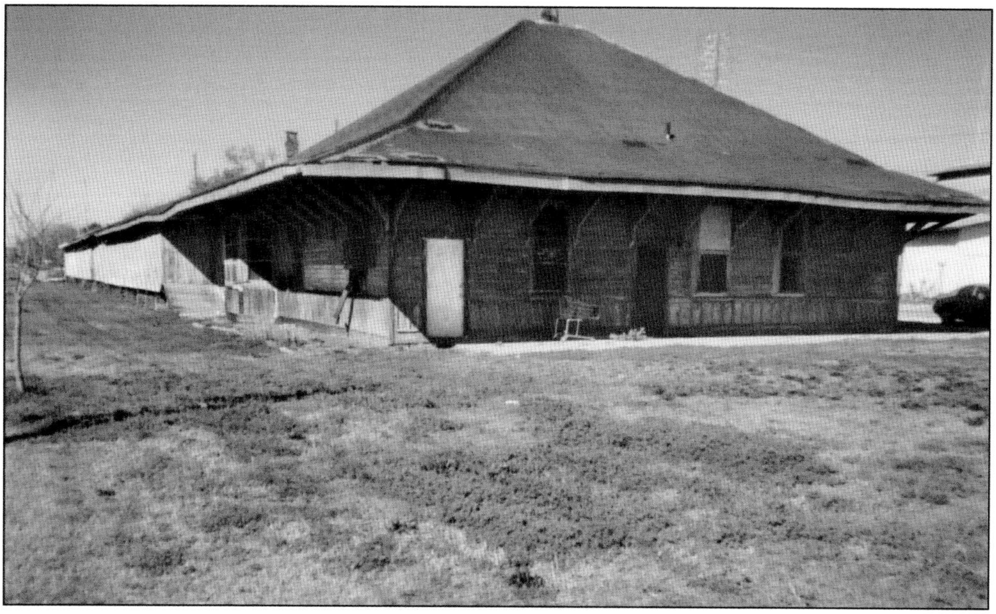

GAINESVILLE. Now referred to as "Old Gainesville Depot," the former Seaboard station is part of a large-scale area remediation project known as Depot Park. This project includes the renovation of the 1907 building and reclamation work on the adjacent former industrial lands located south of the depot. The building is shown in February 2000 looking rundown. It was listed on the National Register of Historic Places in 1996. (Courtesy of Mike Mulligan.)

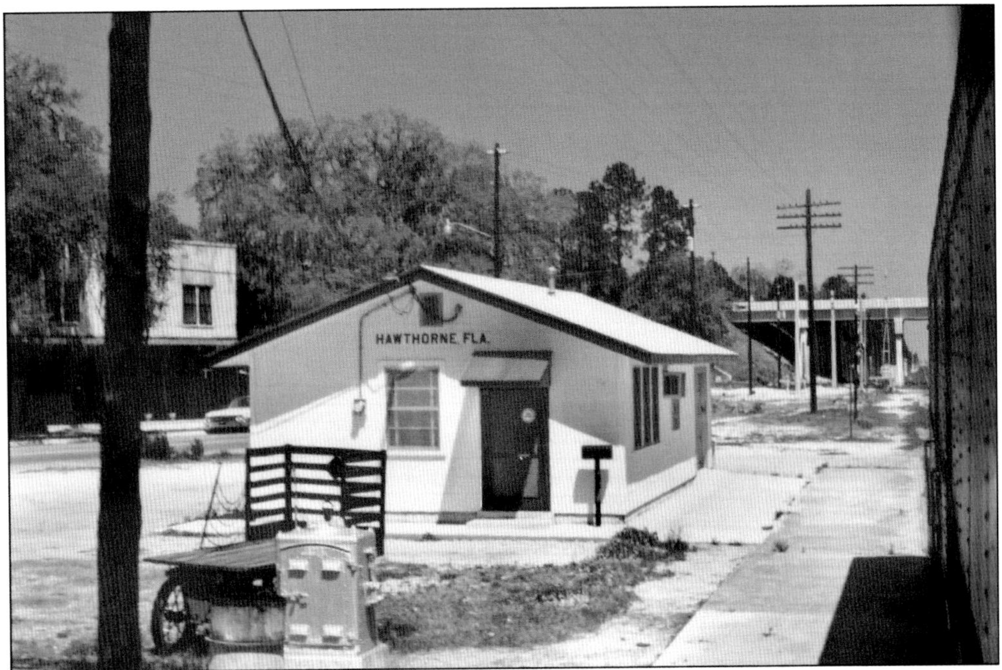

HAWTHORNE. One could still catch the train at Hawthorne in the spring of 1968, when this photograph was taken. Passenger train service would end later that year. The depot is no longer with us, but the railroad through town is still a busy freight corridor for CSX. (Courtesy of Paul Coe.)

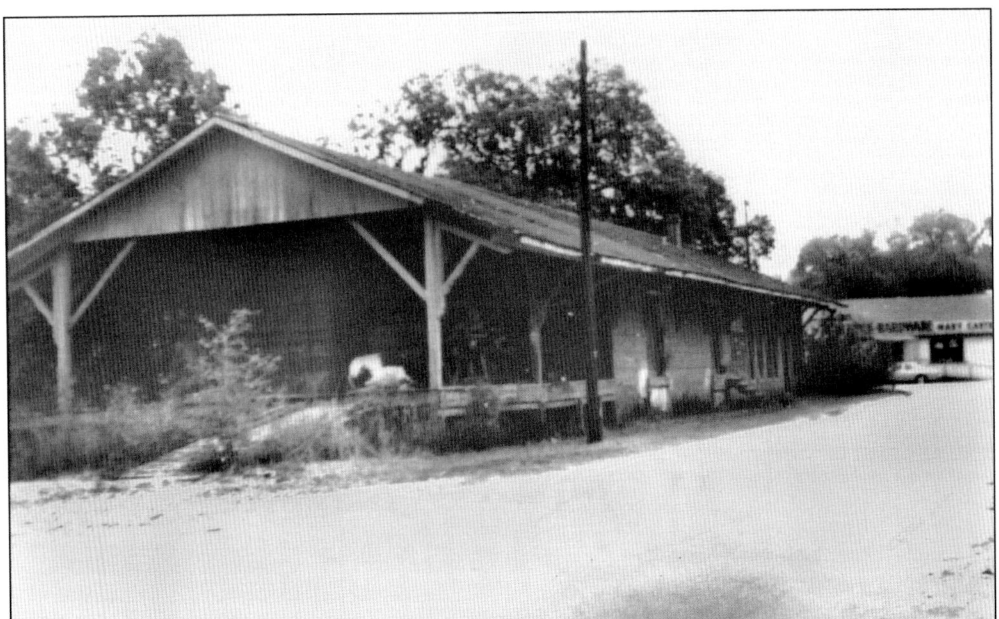

INVERNESS. After sitting unused and rundown for a number of years, the former Inverness Seaboard depot was converted to an office complex in the 1980s. It is still in use as such today. (Courtesy of Old Courthouse Heritage Museum.)

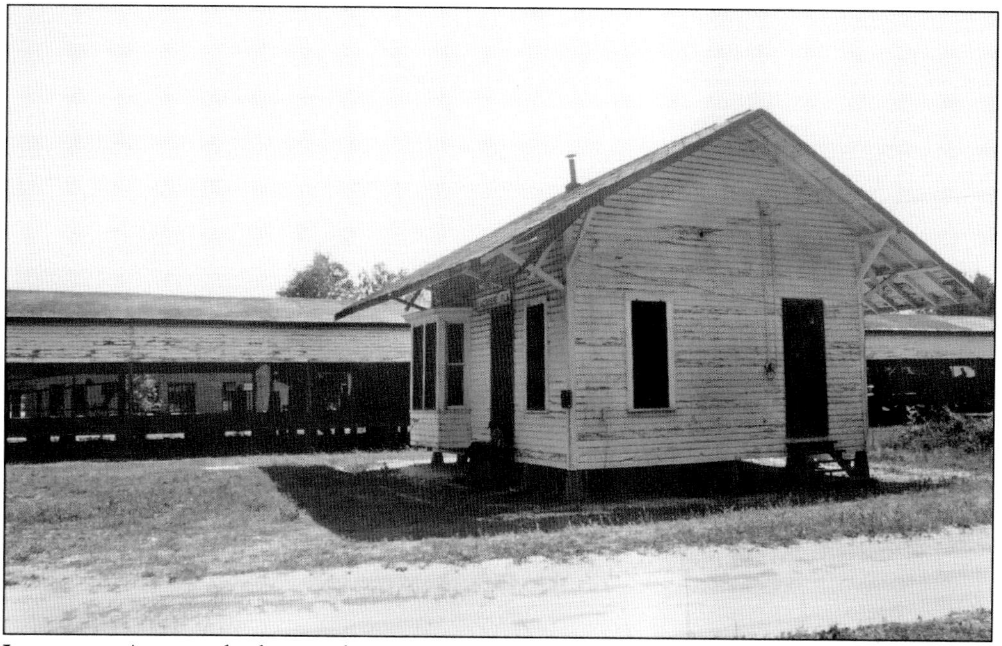

LACROSSE. Apparently the wooden Lacrosse depot has been moved from the railroad right-of-way, as seen in this view from early 1971. CSX Transportation still uses the former Seaboard tracks through town. One source indicates the depot still exists, but the author has been unable to substantiate this information. (Courtesy of R. Randolph Stevens.)

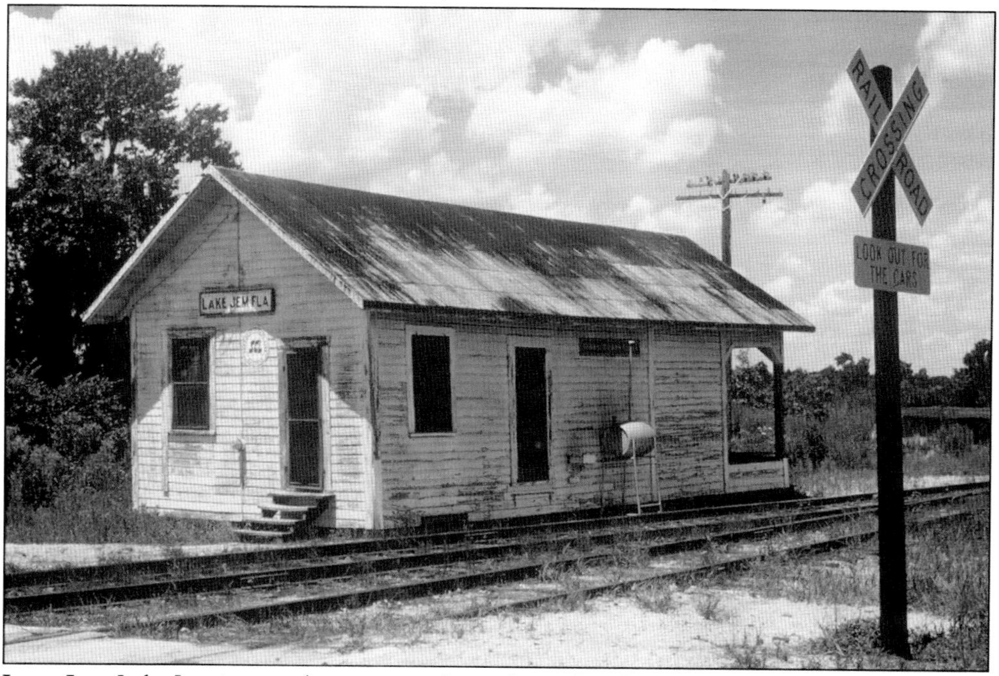

LAKE JEM. Lake Jem is a rural community located on a line between Tavares and Apopka. This simple wood depot provided freight service only after passenger service ended in the 1940s. In the summer of 1969, it was in the service of Seaboard Coast Line Railroad. Trains still run through Lake Jem, but the rustic depot is only a memory. (Courtesy of R. Randolph Stevens.)

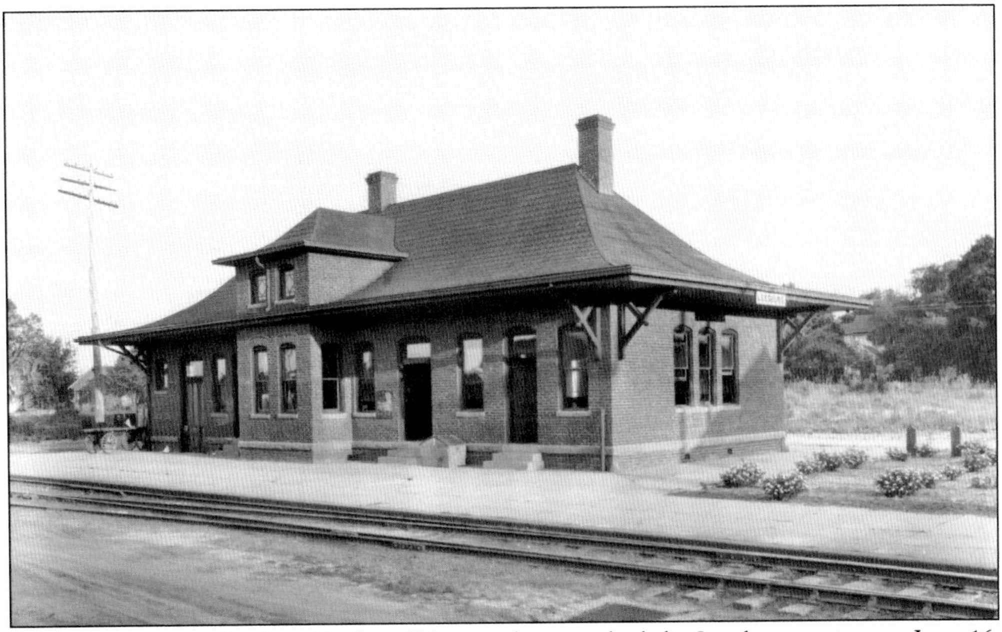

LEESBURG. Burgert Brothers Studio of Tampa photographed the Leesburg station on June 16, 1926, fourteen years after it opened. Rail passengers could go to either Wildwood or Orlando or towns in between. This classic depot stands today and may be used by a local model railroad club in the future. (Courtesy of Tampa-Hillsborough Public Library.)

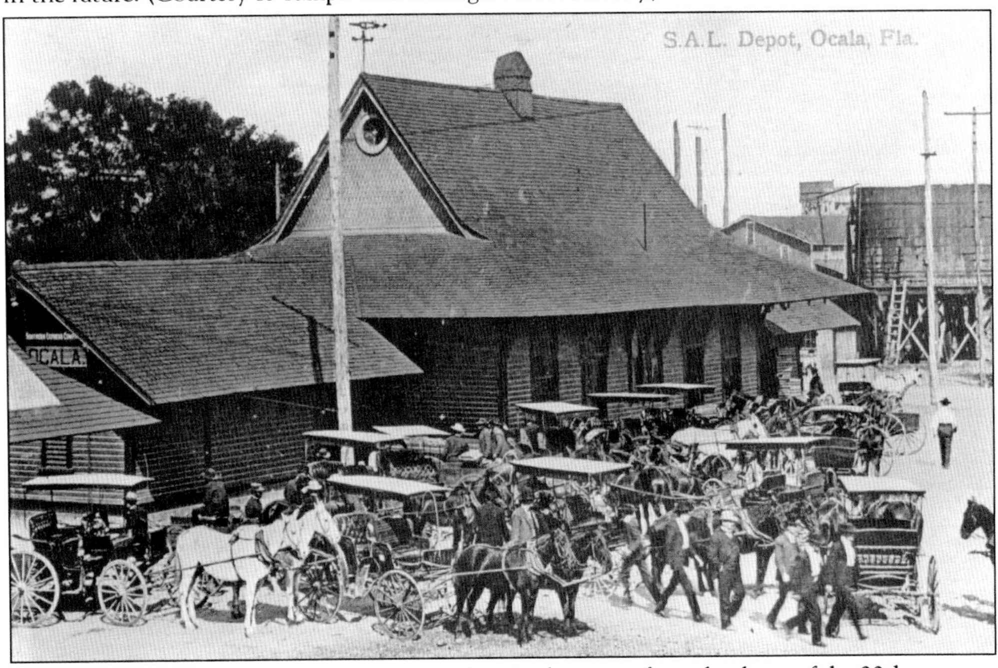

OCALA ACL. Transportation options are evident in this scene from the dawn of the 20th century. There are at least 12 horse teams in this image of the Ocala Seaboard station. A modern Union Station would be built near this site in 1917. The Southern Express Company occupies the left end of the depot. A large water tank is located to the far right to slake the thirst of steam locomotives. (Courtesy of Florida State Archives.)

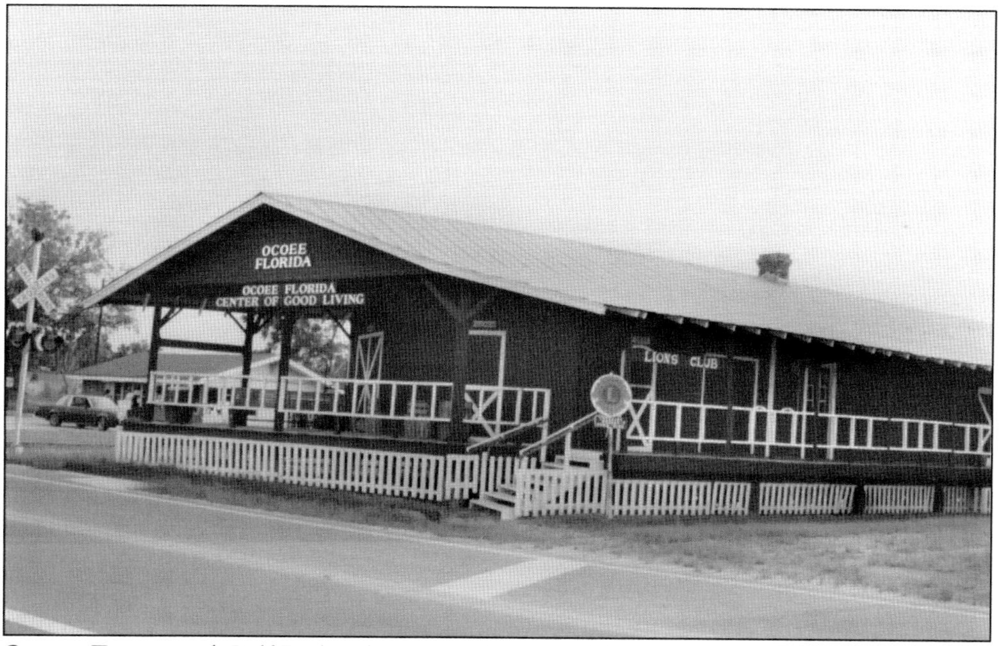

OCOEE. Tavares and Gulf Railroad came to Ocoee in 1914 when an 11-mile branch was built from Waits Junction. A depot was built and opened the same year. It was used by the railroad until 1969. Ocoee Lions Club moved in in 1979 and has occupied it ever since. This image dates from 1991. (Courtesy of Mike Mulligan.)

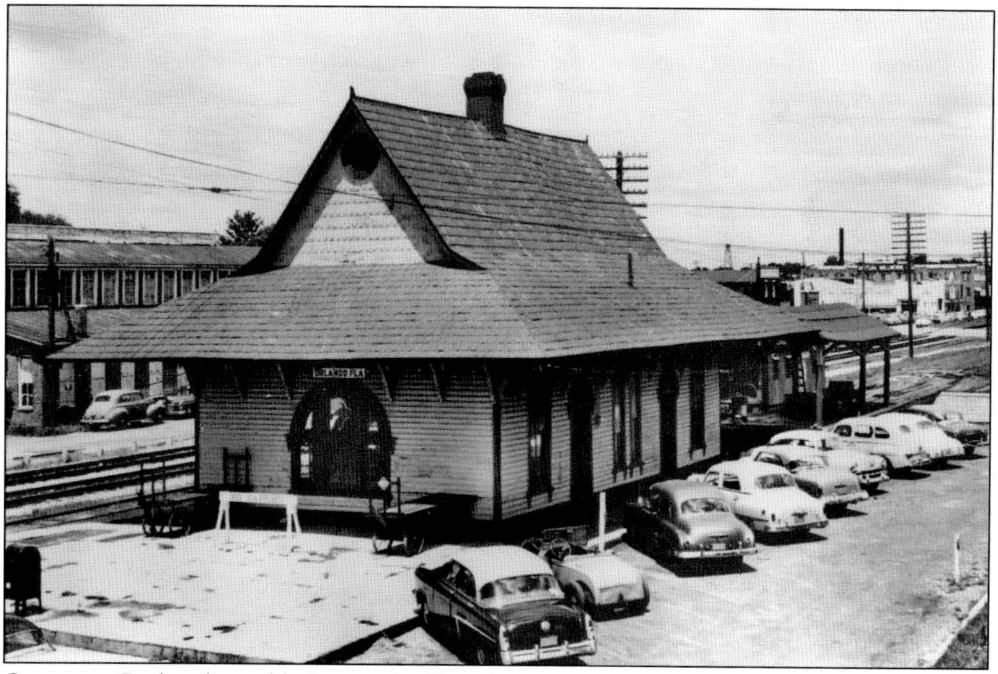

ORLANDO. Railroads would often use building designs over again with minor changes. Orlando's Florida, Central, and Peninsular Railroad depot of 1896 is nearly identical to Ocala's, seen on the preceding page. Vintage cars date this view to around 1950. It, along with an adjacent freight station dating from 1924, was razed in 1955. (Courtesy of Orange County Regional History Center.)

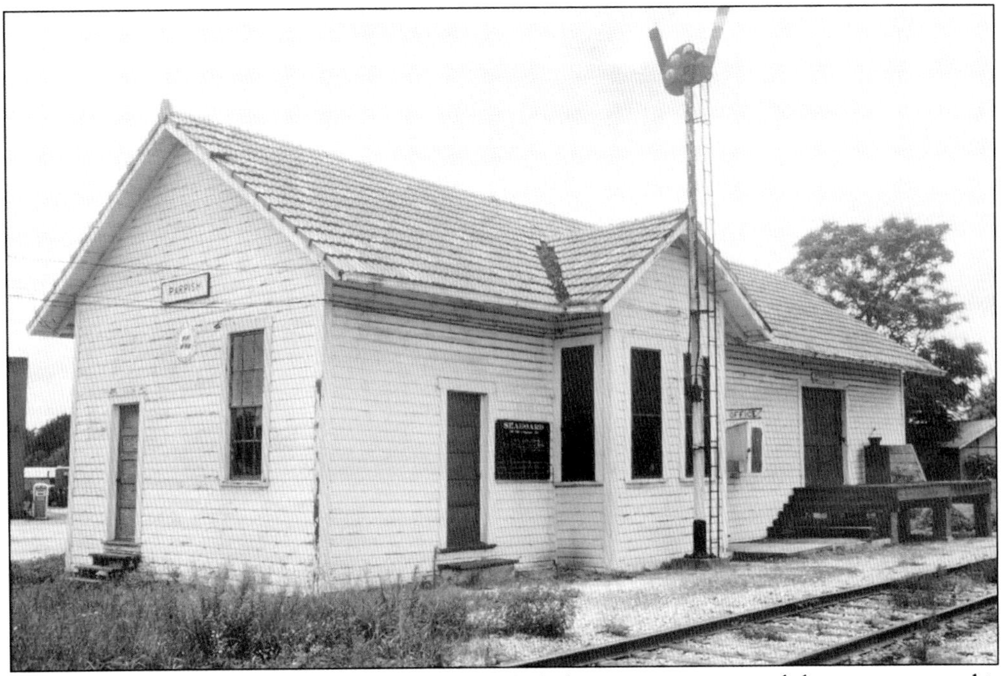

Parrish. Parrish received railroad service in 1902. A depot was constructed the same year and is shown here in the summer of 1968, still a flag stop for two trains per day on the Seaboard Coast Line. Turning the building into a restaurant was attempted in 1988. This venture failed, and the building was consumed by fire by the mid-1990s. (Courtesy of R. Randolph Stevens.)

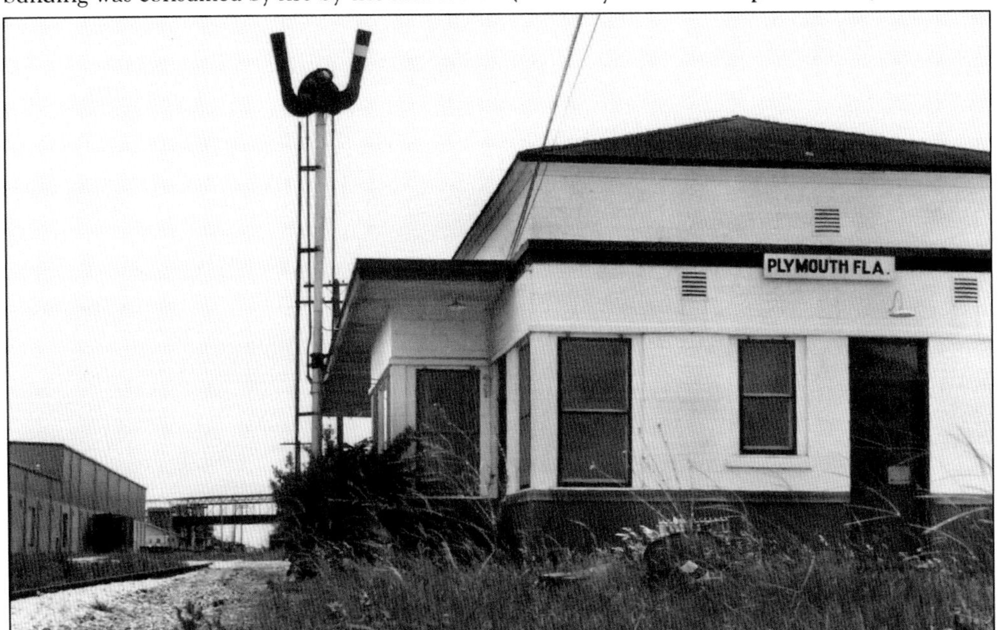

Plymouth. Currently Florida Central Railroad operates out of the former Seaboard station built in 1947 in Plymouth. This freight short line started up in November 1986. In years past, Plymouth Citrus Growers Packing House had an average annual output of 500,000 boxes shipped from the area. There appears to be little activity going on this day in 1975. (Courtesy of Fred Clark Jr.)

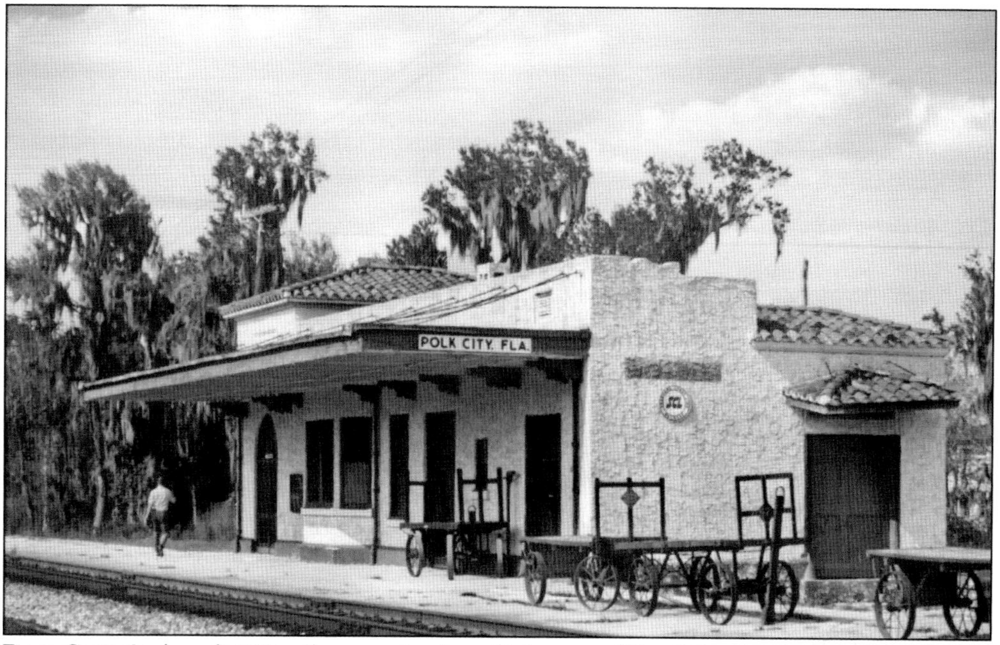

POLK CITY. Seaboard's 204-mile extension from Coleman to West Palm Beach came through Polk City in 1925. The depot was built shortly afterward. In April 1968, it was still a station stop with two trains per day, although the service would end later in the year. (Courtesy of Paul Coe.)

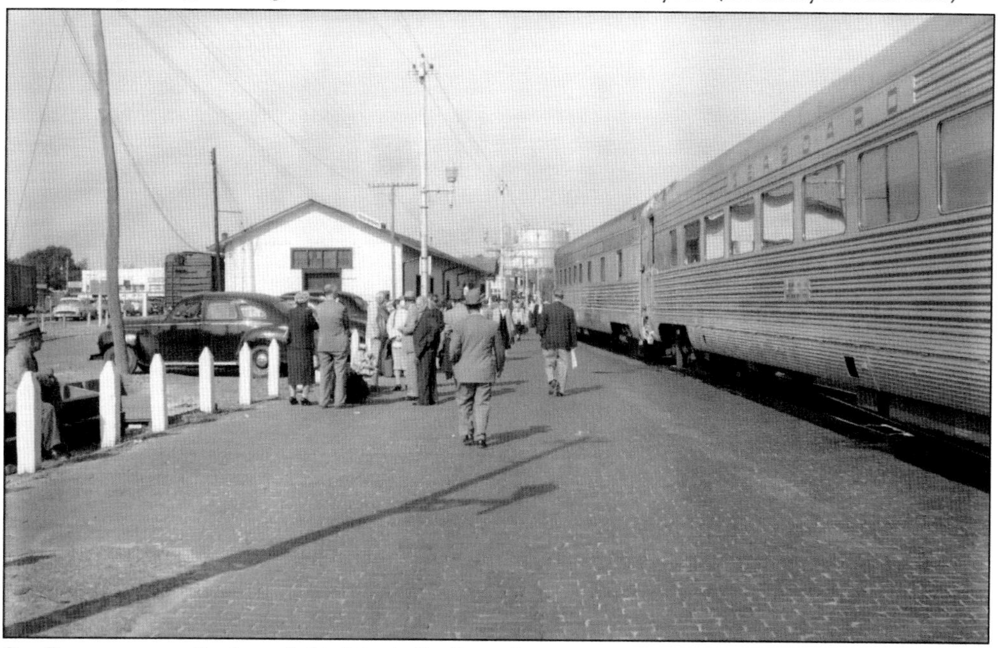

ST. PETERSBURG. Seaboard Air Line's St. Petersburg passenger operations were handled from this modest building opened around 1915. Compare this to the impressive ACL station from the same era featured in the preceding chapter. This building would fulfill the needs of the growing city until 1959. Burgert Brothers Studio captured this scene on March 27, 1956. Its replacement was photographed on March 13, 1959, as seen in the following image. (Courtesy of Tampa-Hillsborough Public Library.)

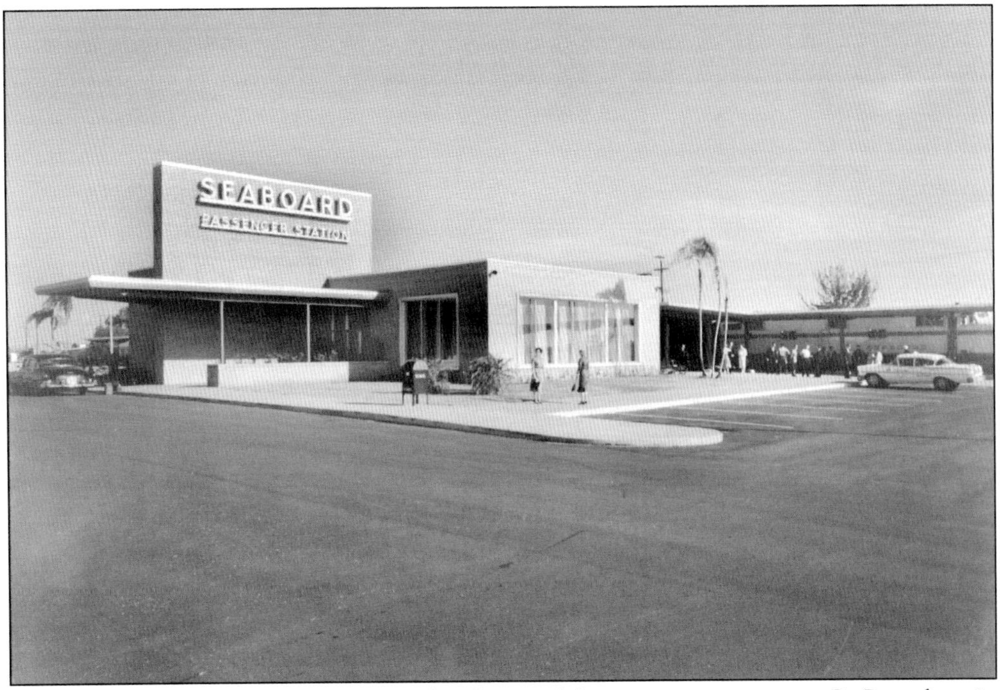

St. Petersburg. Seaboard Air Line Railroad opened this impressive station at St. Petersburg in 1959. Merger talks with the Atlantic Coast Line were in the air then that were consummated on July 1, 1967. Eight months later, a sign was posted to inform customers "effective April 28th. 1968, all passenger trains will arrive and depart from the former A.C.L station." Later it was sold to a lumber company for sales/warehouse use. (Courtesy of Tampa-Hillsborough Public Library.)

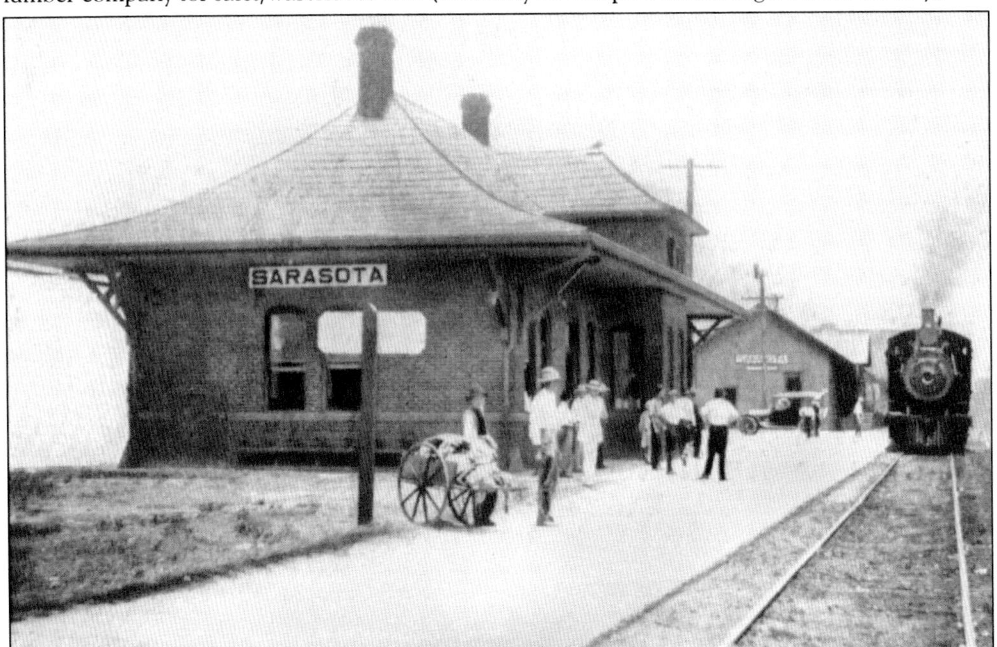

Sarasota. Sarasota's original wooden depot is in the background of this photograph of the new brick depot built in 1912. The building would last until 1937. (Courtesy of Florida State Archives.)

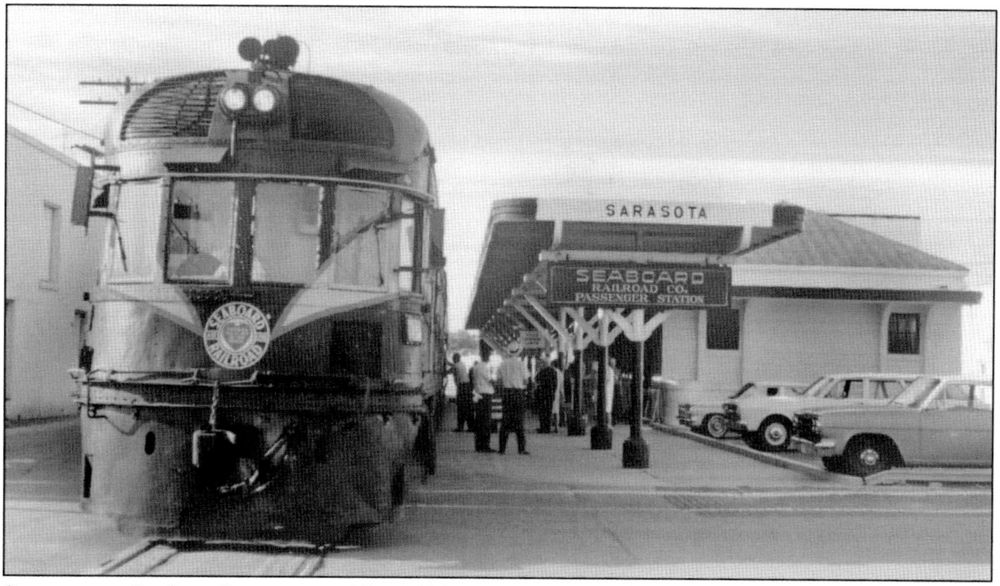

SARASOTA. Seaboard's motorcar No. 2028 is preparing to depart Sarasota a few months after the July 1, 1967, merger with ACL Railroad. Typically, the motorcar would pull two trailing cars. Business appears brisk at the depot, which dates from 1937. Motorcar No. 2028 would operate with the merged company until April 30, 1971. The depot serviced passengers to the same date and was demolished in 1984. (Courtesy of Paul Coe.)

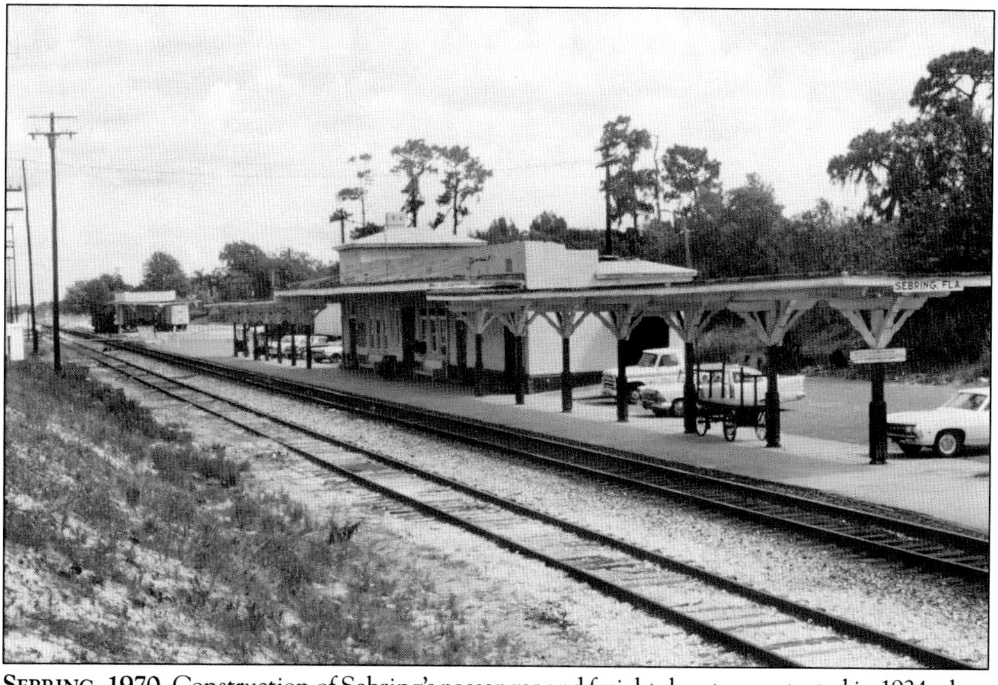

SEBRING, 1970. Construction of Sebring's passenger and freight depots was started in 1924 when the Seaboard's rail line extension from Coleman to West Palm Beach came through town. The freight house is seen in the distance on a spring day in 1970 while automobiles at the passenger station suggest a train arrival is imminent. Six trains per day stopped here then. Currently four Amtrak trains per day serve Sebring. (Courtesy of R. Randolph Stevens.)

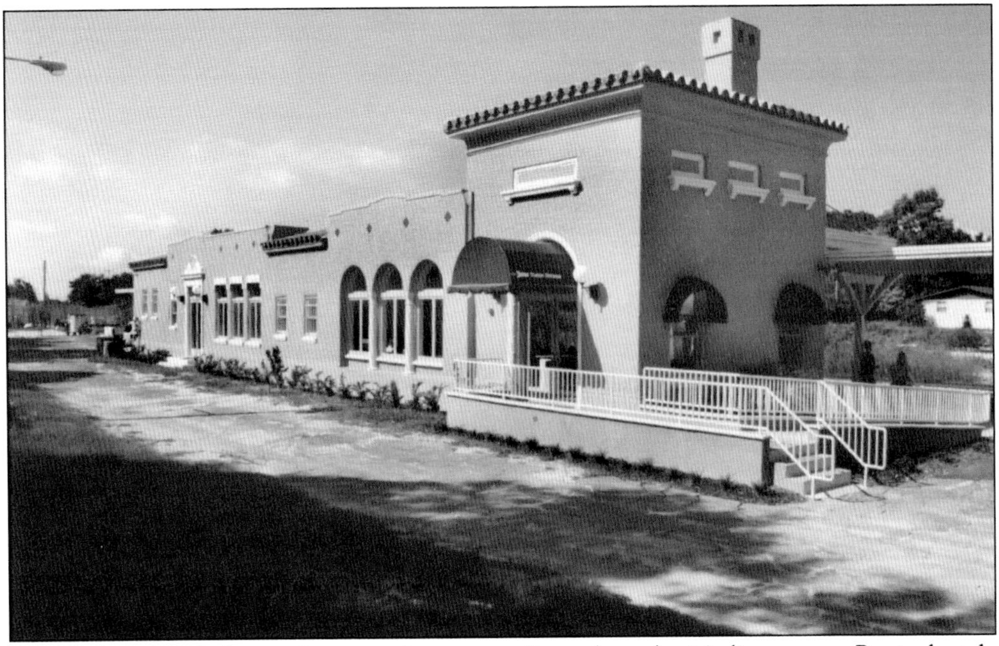

SEBRING, 1998. A thorough renovation was performed on the Mediterranean Revival–style Sebring depot in 1997–1998. It was captured on film in August 1998, shortly after completion of the project. The building was placed on the National Register of Historic Places in 1990. Amtrak's *Silver Meteor* and *Silver Star* make a total of four stops daily. (Courtesy of Mike Mulligan.)

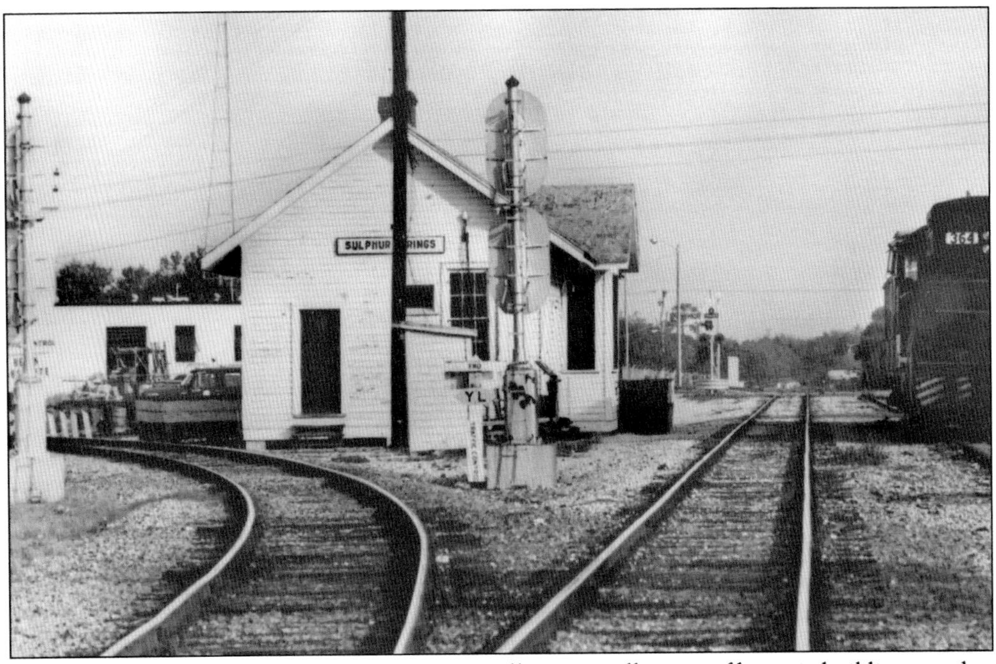

SULPHUR SPRINGS. Opened in 1977, Heritage Village is a collection of historic buildings used to interpret life in years past. A featured exhibit is Sulphur Springs's depot, built in 1924. It is used to tell the story of railroading and the impact it made in the community. In 1977, the depot was still trackside in adjacent Hillsborough County just north of Tampa. (Courtesy of Fred Clark Jr.)

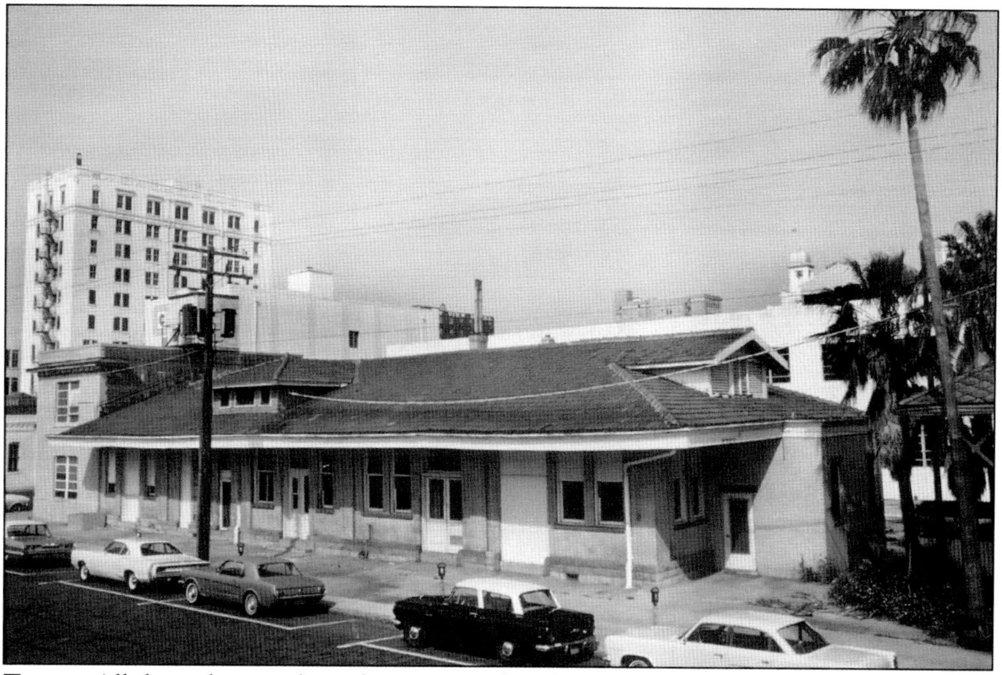

TAMPA. All that is known about this image is that the time frame is early 1969, the location is Tampa, and the railroad origin of the building is listed as Seaboard. It is believed to have been a freight station. Anyone who can shed further light on its history can contact the author at mulliganm@juno.com. (Courtesy R. Randolph Stevens.)

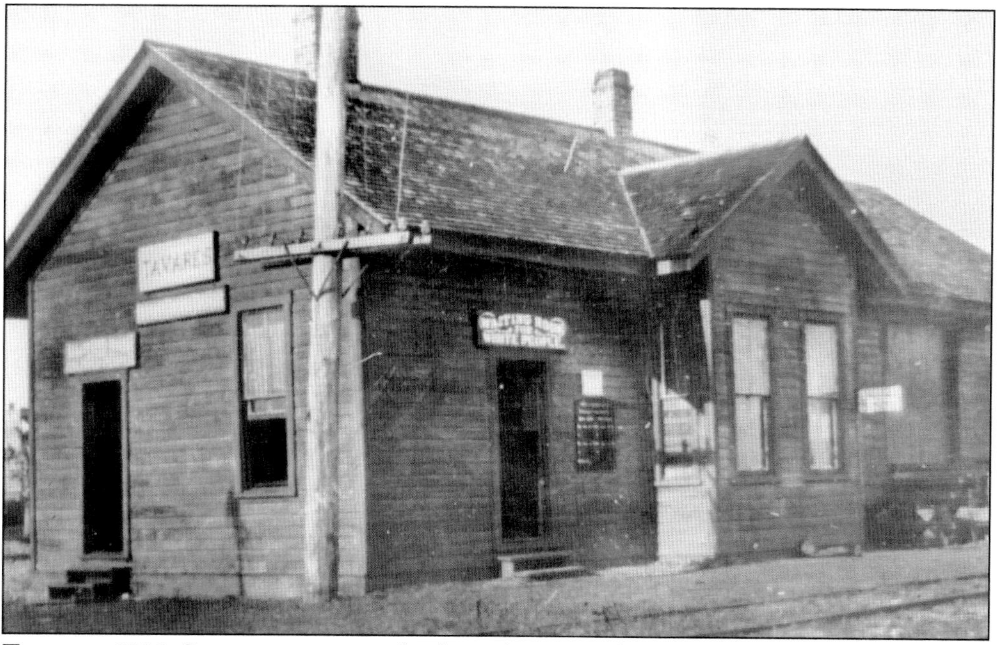

TAVARES, 1910. Segregation is seen clearly in this image from Tavares around 1910. Separate waiting rooms and toilets at the depot were standard. On trains, there would be segregation by car, or people would be separated in some fashion whenever a coach was shared. This continued up to the Equal Rights Act of 1964. (Courtesy of Florida State Archives.)

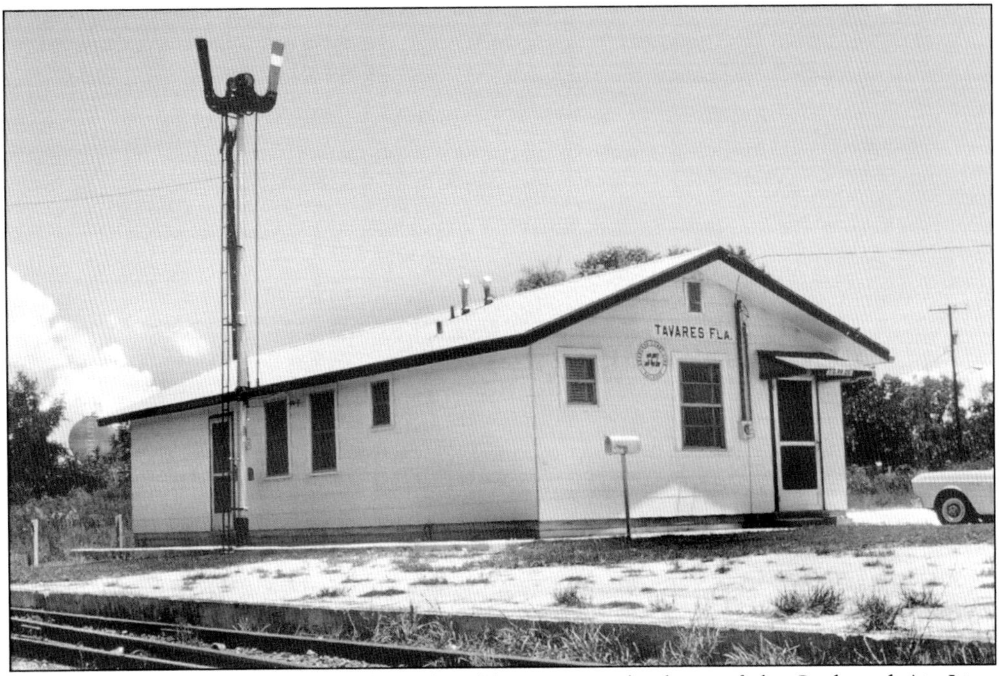

TAVARES, 1969. Tavares and Gulf Railroad became a subsidiary of the Seaboard Air Line Railway in 1926 when Seaboard purchased controlling shares of stock. The Tug and Grunt, as it was affectionately called, would operate as an independent company until the merger creating Seaboard Coast Line on July 1, 1967. Taken two years later, this image shows the station built earlier in the decade still labeled (on the awning) for the T&G Railroad. (Courtesy of R. Randolph Stevens.)

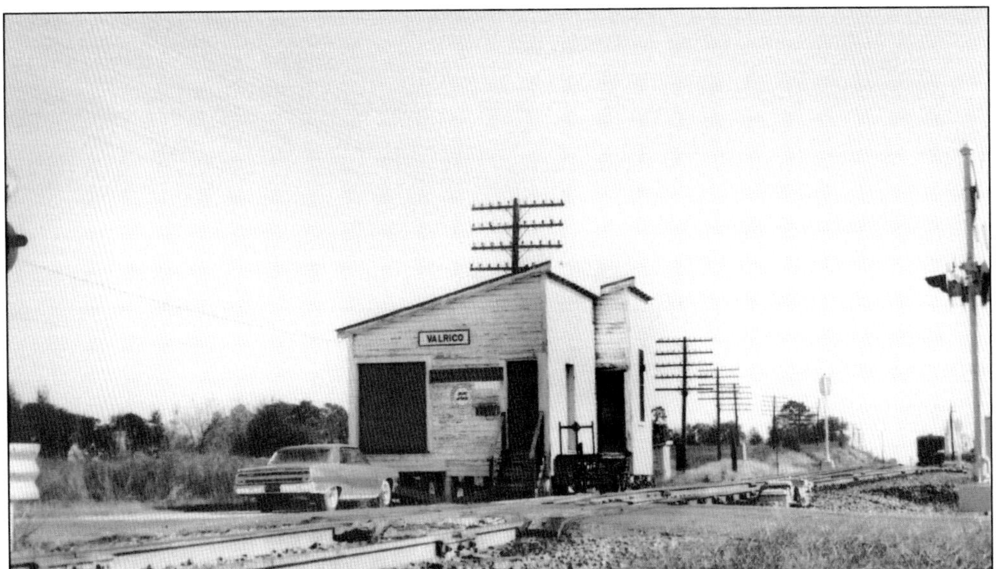

VALRICO. The unique wooden Valrico depot was just a discharge stop by 1968 and would leave the timetable altogether before the end of the year. Tracks are still in place through Valrico, but the station is no longer with us. (Courtesy of Paul Coe.)

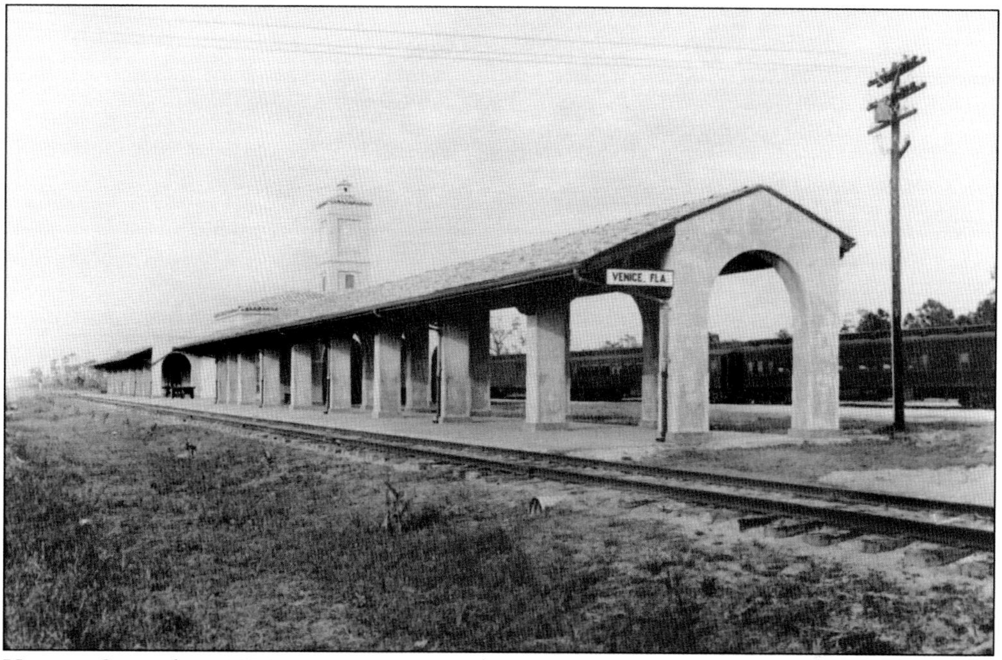

VENICE. Opened in 1927, Venice's station cost $47,500 to construct. It featured a 400-foot covered platform and tower. Later the tower was removed. The building would see the last passenger train leave on April 30, 1971. It would fall into disrepair over the next few decades. Purchased by Sarasota County in 1998, it was restored to its original appearance in 2003 at a cost of $2.3 million. Depicted in 1927 (above) shortly after opening with passenger cars in the background, it is then seen 41 years later (below) without the tower. (Above courtesy of Venice Archives and Area Historical Collection; below courtesy of R. Randolph Stevens.)

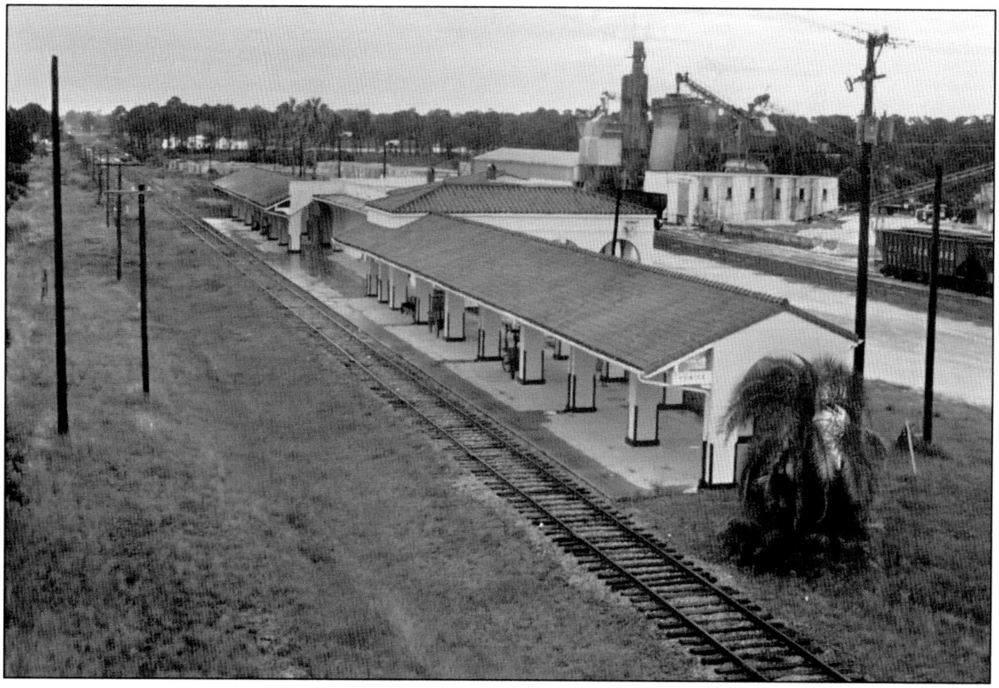

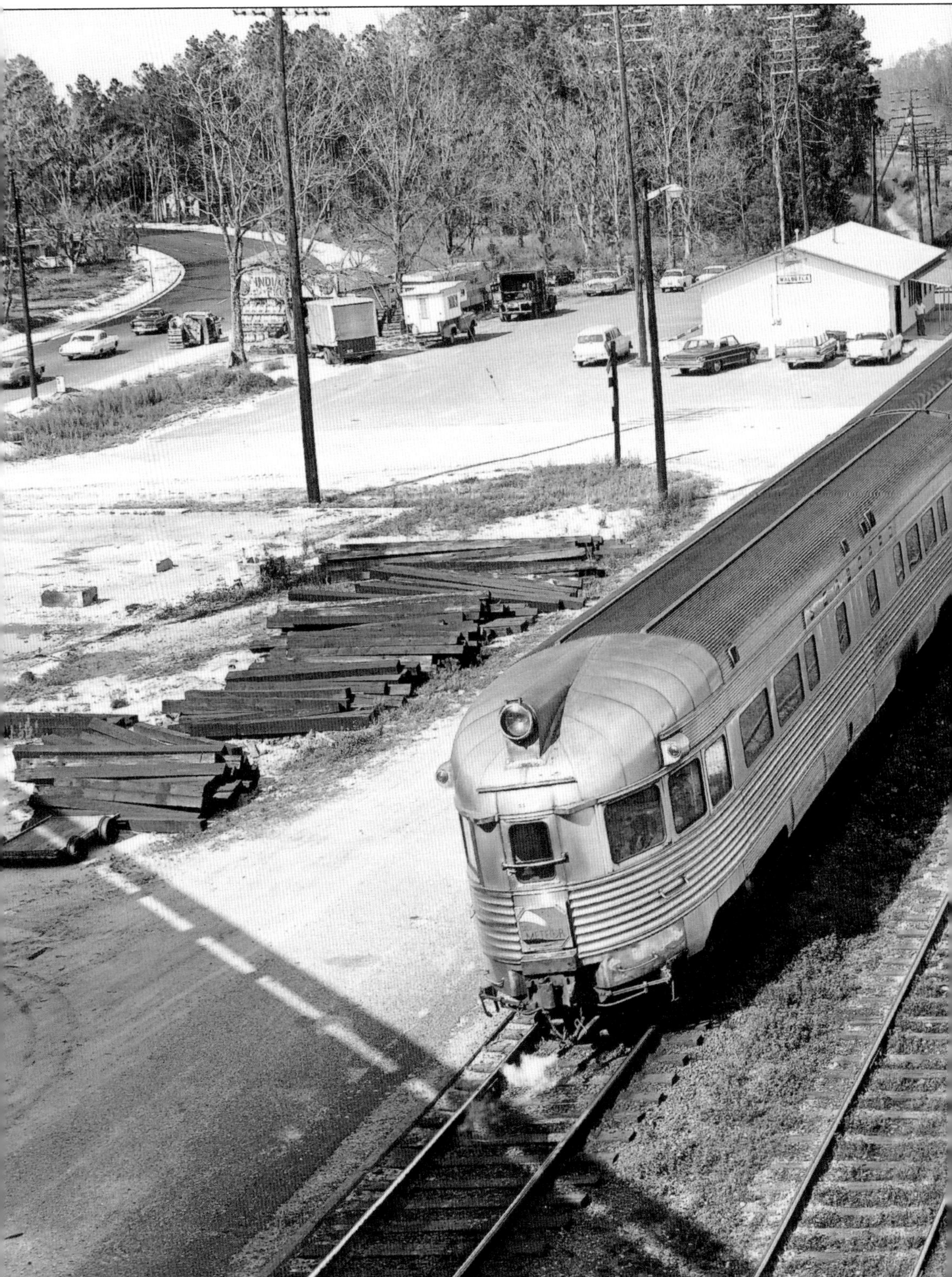
WALDO FLA

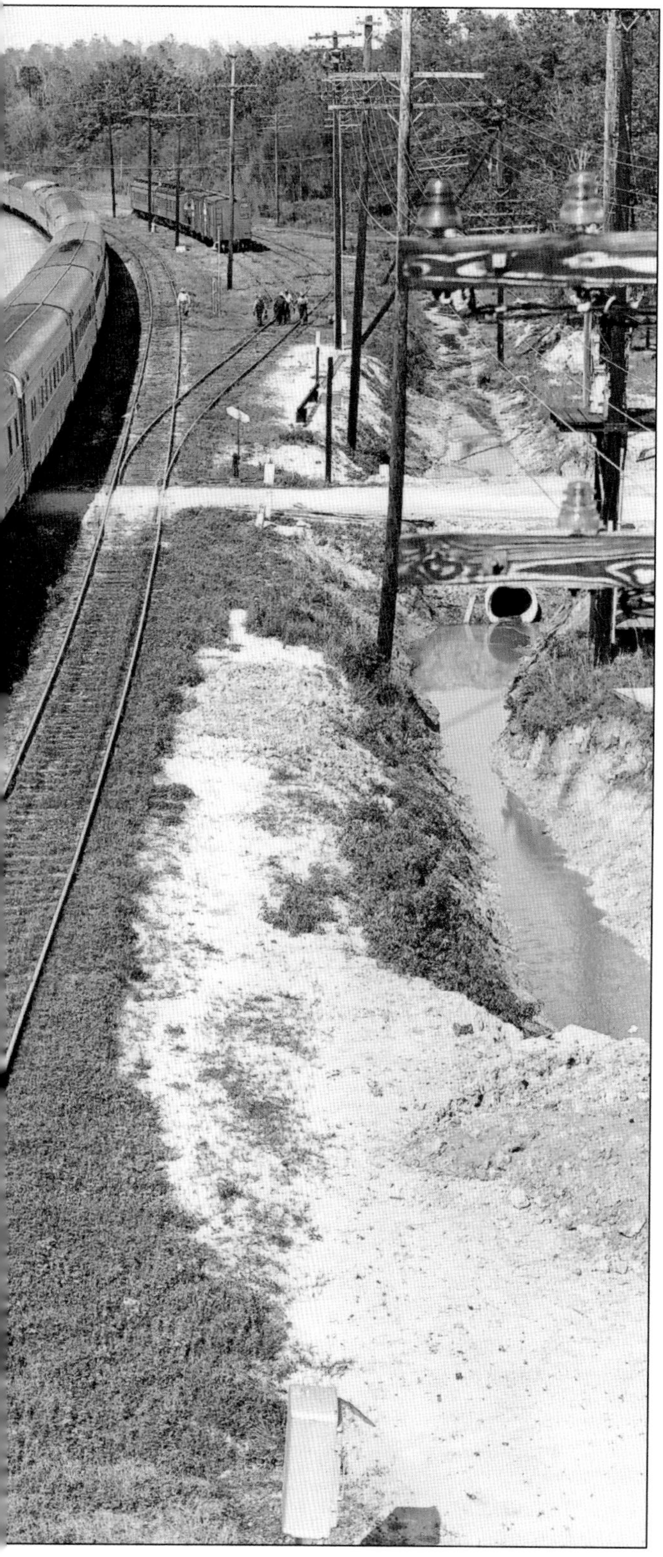

WALDO. Train No. 58, the northbound *Silver Meteor*, is shown departing Waldo 30 minutes late on March 26, 1965. Waldo is the closest stop on the Seaboard's main line to serve the University of Florida and Gainesville. Tavern-observation car No. 6602 brings up the rear. (Courtesy of David W. Salter.)

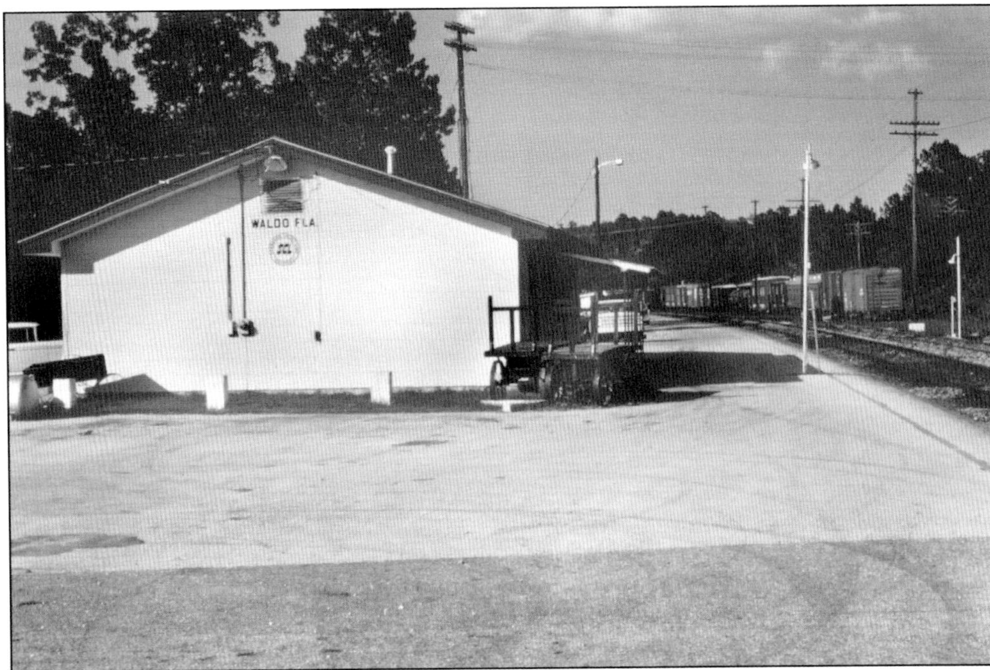

WALDO, 1969. At one time, Waldo had a two-story depot with a large freight room and was a divisional headquarters for the Seaboard. By 1930, the depot was reduced in size by removal of the top floor and a portion of the freight room. In 1963, a smaller depot was built to take its place. The replacement depot is seen on a summer day in 1969. Amtrak trains stopped here until 2004. (Courtesy of R. Randolph Stevens.)

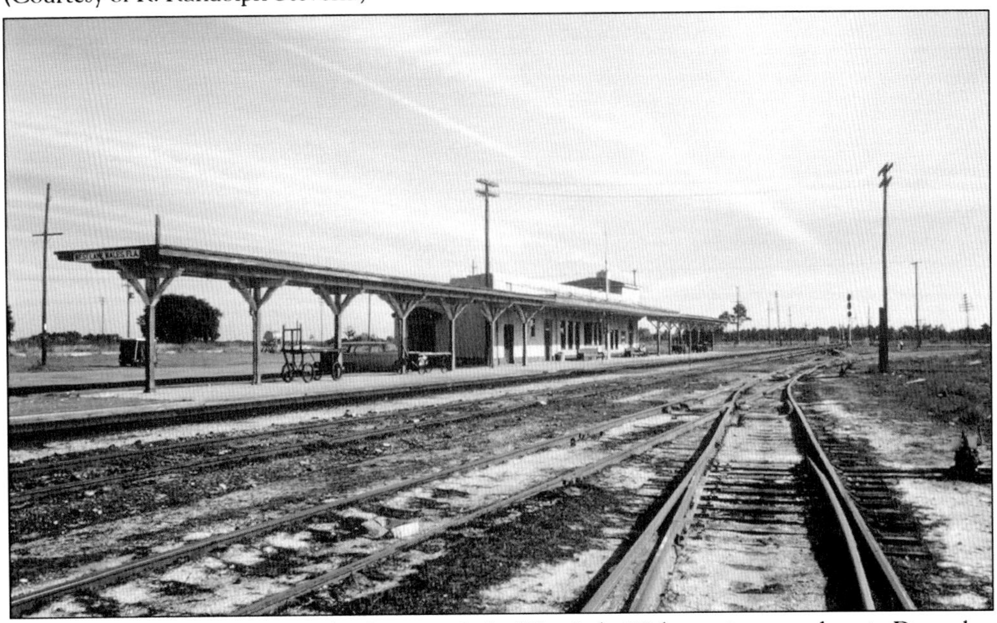

WEST LAKE WALES. Wide-open land surrounds the West Lake Wales station, seen here in December 1968. The building was located on the Seaboard's main line three miles from Lake Wales and was constructed in 1924. It was listed in the timetable as a flag stop as late as 1971. After sitting unused for a number of years, it was razed around 1993. (Courtesy of R. Randolph Stevens.)

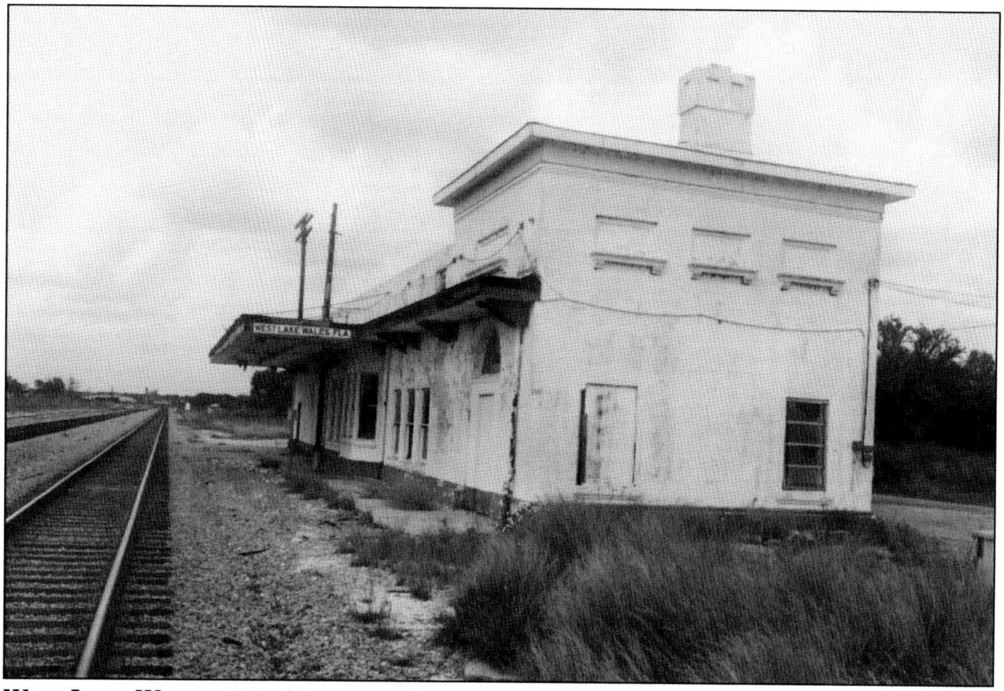

WEST LAKE WALES, 1991. Here is another view of the West Lake Wales depot a few years before demolition. (Courtesy of Mike Mulligan.)

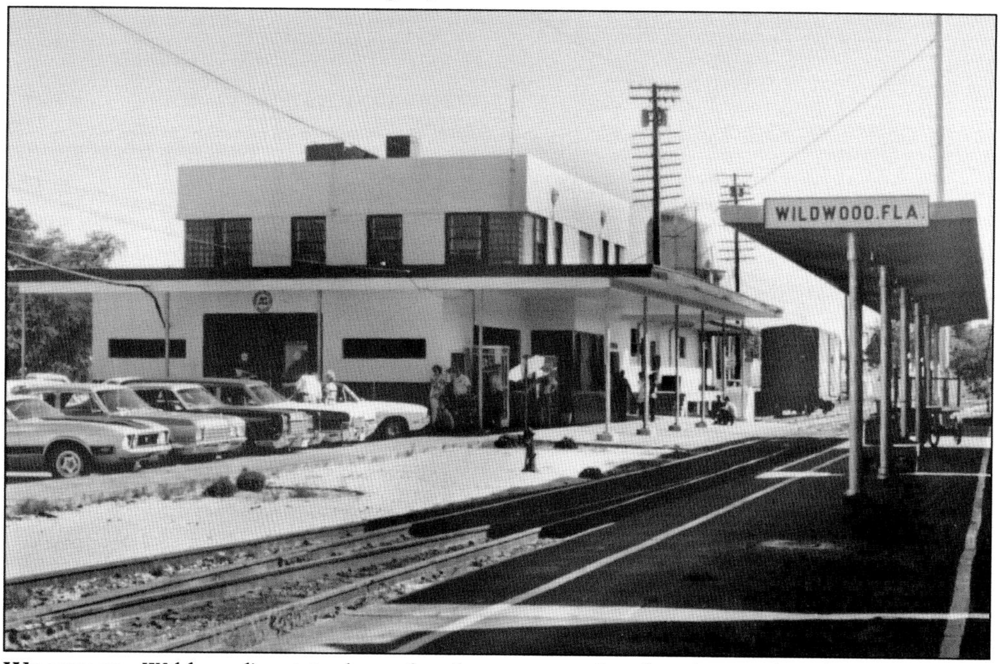

WILDWOOD. Wildwood's original wooden depot was replaced with a modern building around 1948. It is shown on a 1973 spring day. At 158 feet long by a varying width of 34 to 43 feet, the two-story building was quite large for a town of 2,300 people. This can be attributed to several large resort towns located in the vicinity. Amtrak stopped here until 2004, and CSX Railroad continues use today. (Courtesy of Paul Coe.)

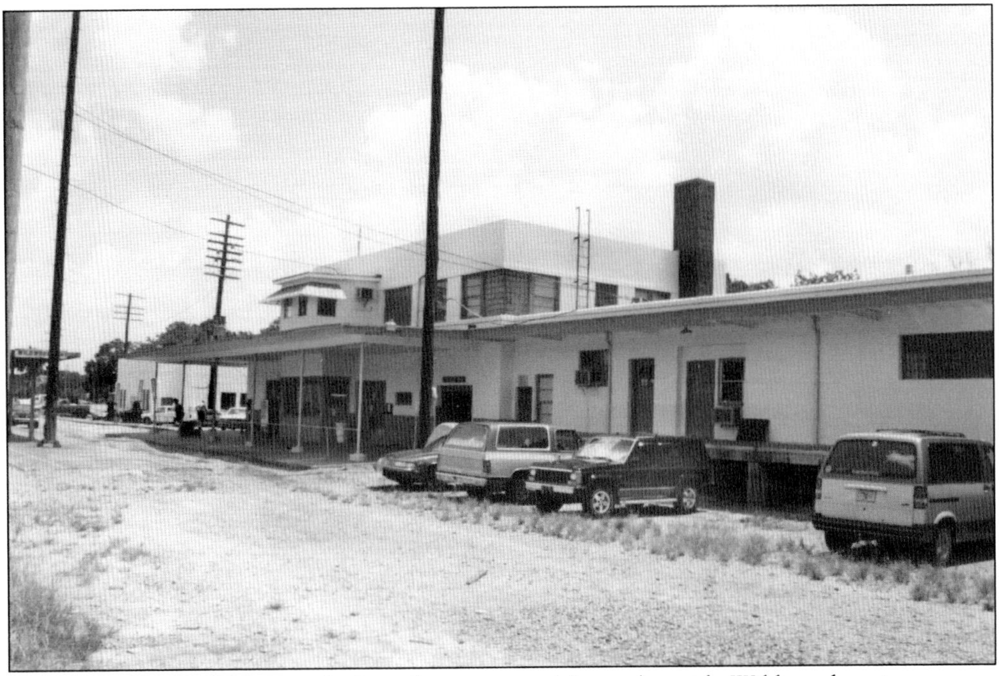

WILDWOOD, 1992. House tracks have been removed from alongside Wildwood station as seen in this 1992 photograph. This vantage point shows the freight end of the building. (Courtesy of Mike Mulligan.)

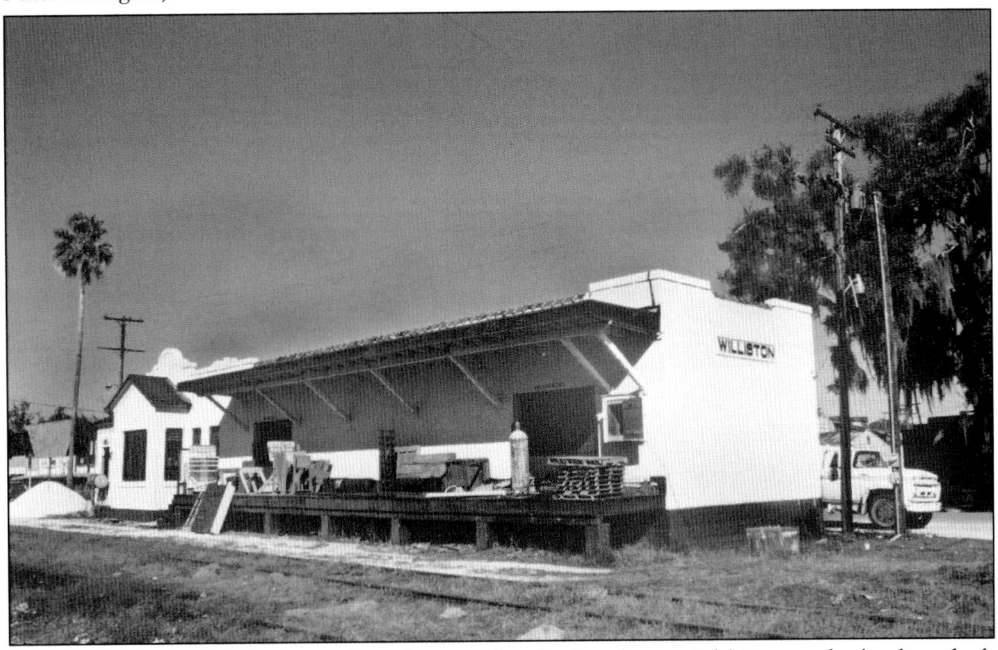

WILLISTON. Overgrown rusty rails and non-railroad-related material lying on the loading dock indicate Williston's depot is no longer used by the railroad. Florida Central and Peninsular Railway came to town in 1891. This depot was built around 1920 and has been used for a landscape supply store and real estate office in recent years. Tracks by the building have been gone for many years, but the old depot lives on. (Courtesy of R. Randolph Stevens.)

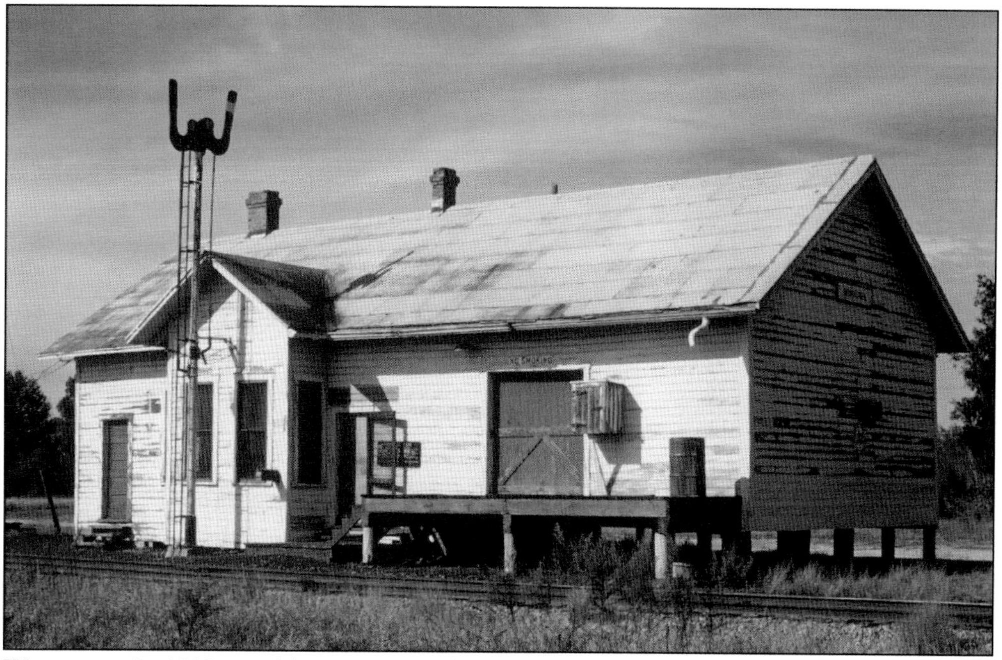

WIMAUMA. In 1903, a rail line was extended from Durant, located a few miles south of Plant City, to Palmetto. The community of Wimauma was established at that time, and a depot constructed. It would serve as a passenger stop until 1968, the same year this photograph was taken. Tracks were taken out in 1984, and the depot was removed years before that. (Courtesy of R. Randolph Stevens.)

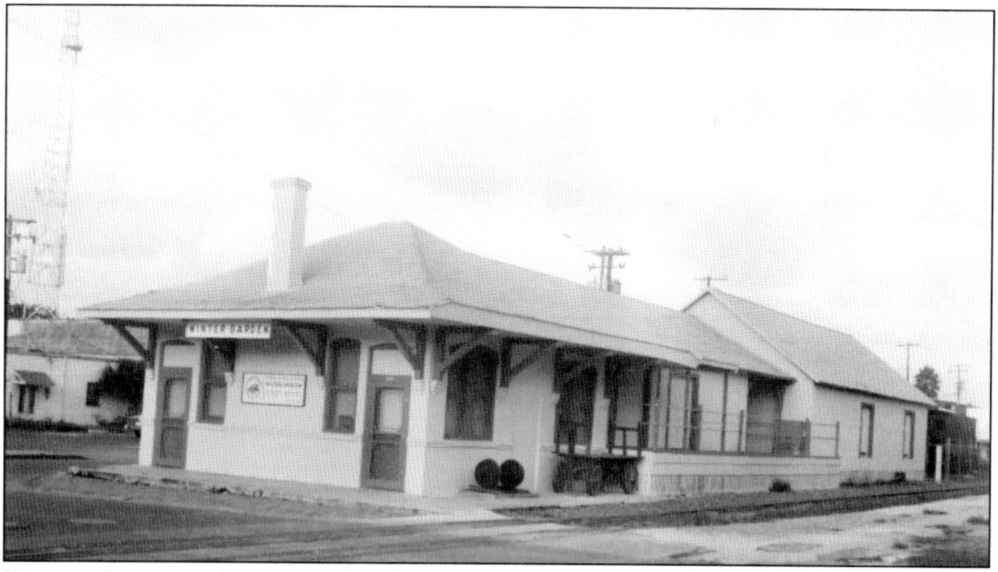

WINTER GARDEN. The Central Florida Chapter, National Railway Historical Society, purchased the former Tavares and Gulf Railroad depot in 1979. Constructed in 1913, the depot would pass to Seaboard Air Line control in 1926 and to successor Seaboard Coast Line in 1967. It remained a freight office until 1978. Upon acquisition, the chapter implemented a restoration project and converted the building into a railroad museum, completed by 1983. (Courtesy of Mike Mulligan.)

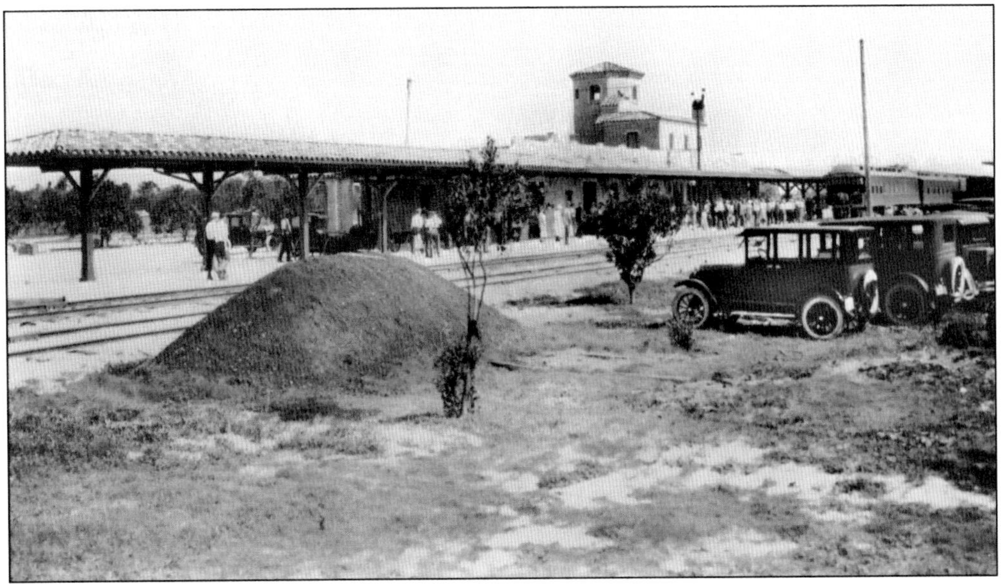

WINTER HAVEN. Seaboard Air Line's 204-mile-long extension from Coleman to West Palm Beach brought the railroad to Winter Haven in 1924. An impressive Mediterranean Revival–style building was opened shortly after. A large crowd is at the station in this scene (above) around 1925. A heavyweight platform observation car is on the rear of the train. These suggest some VIP has come to visit. This station would last in railroad service just over 20 years, as a replacement (below) was opened in 1947. The replacement station is seen in 1990 in the service of Amtrak. It was built on the other side of the tracks from the original depot. The original Seaboard station was demolished about 2007. The replacement is still in Amtrak service with four trains per day making stops. (Above courtesy of Polk County Historical Museum; below courtesy of Mike Mulligan.)

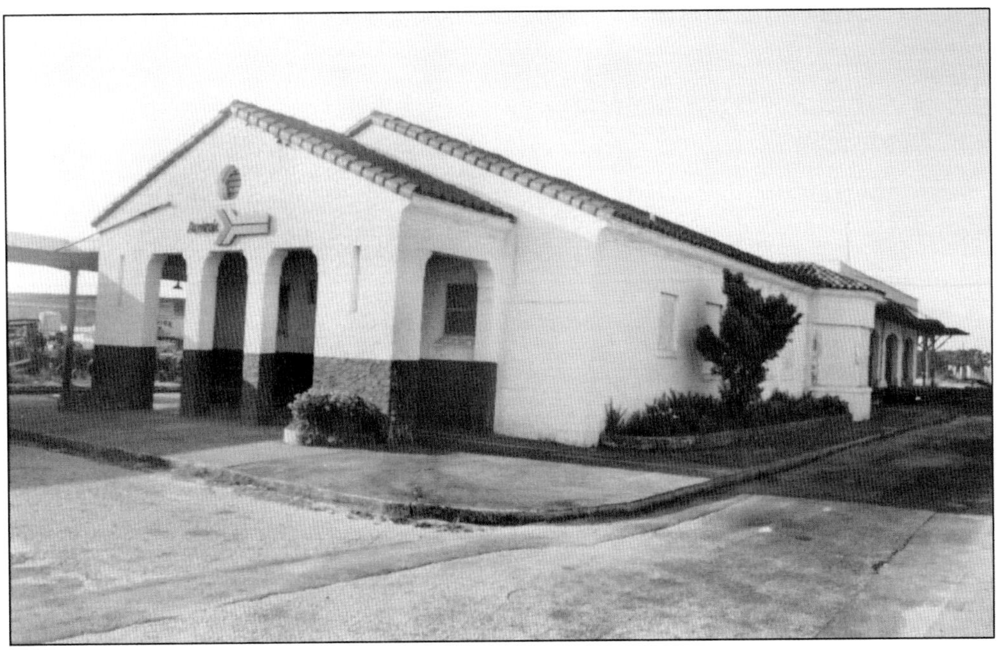

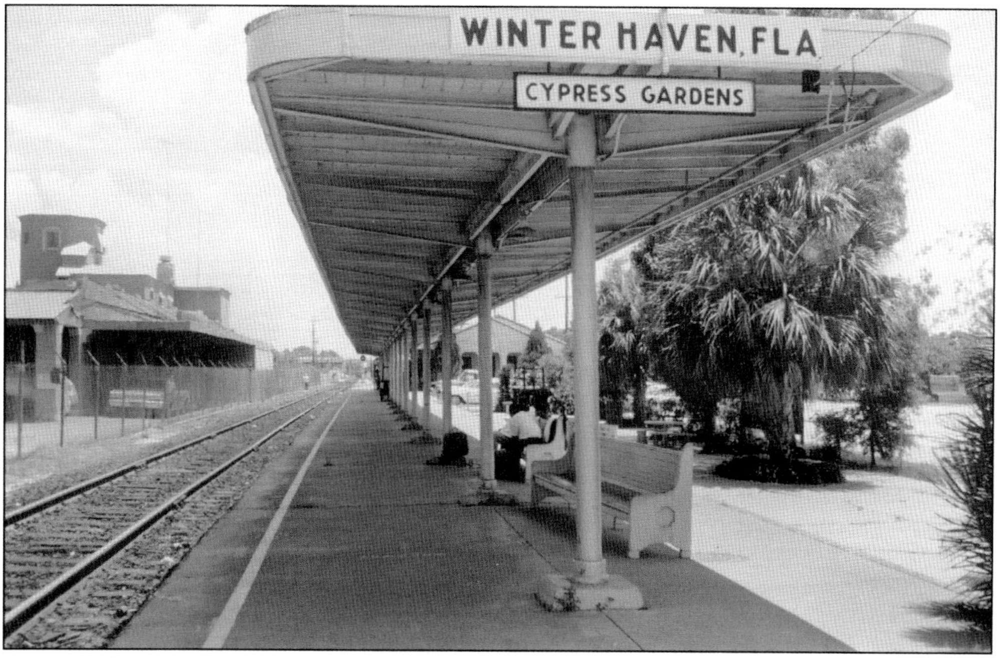

WINTER HAVEN, 1968. A summer 1968 photograph shows the original Winter Haven Seaboard station to the left and the replacement to the right. Cypress Gardens, Florida's first theme park, receives acknowledgment for being a major attraction for the city. The park is located about two miles from the station. (Courtesy of R. Randolph Stevens.)

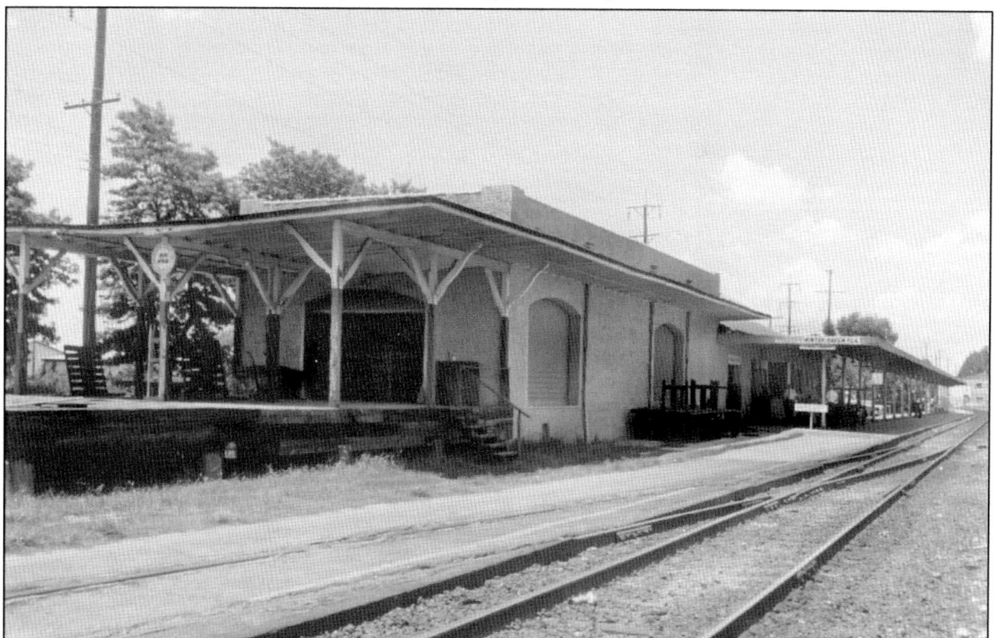

WINTER HAVEN, 1968. Seaboard Coast Line's logo is in place on Winter Haven's freight room to identify the new company to the public. This scene is just one year after the 1967 merger. SCL would last until 1982, when it merged with the Louisville and Nashville Railroad, creating Seaboard System Railroad. (Courtesy of R. Randolph Stevens.)

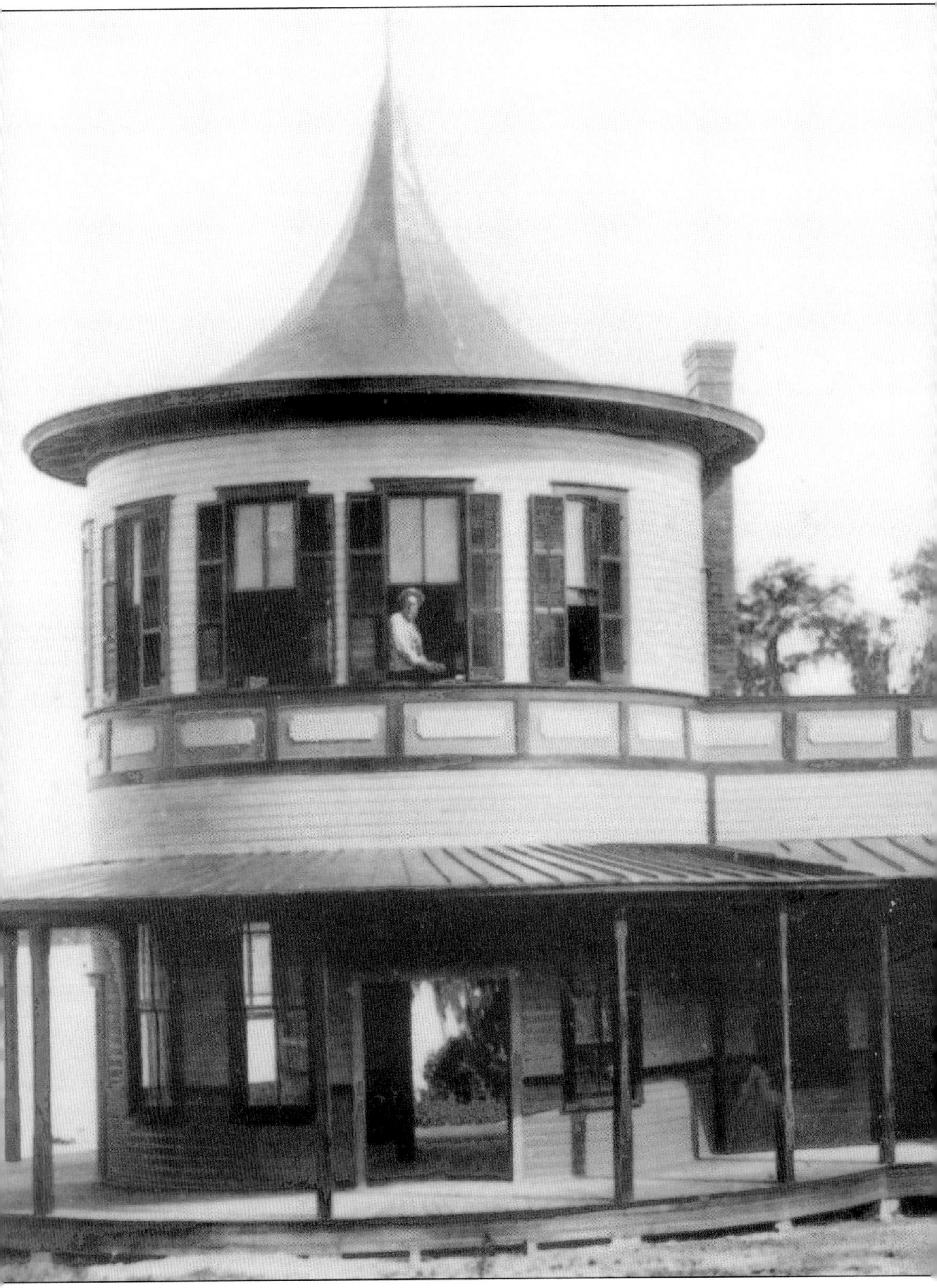

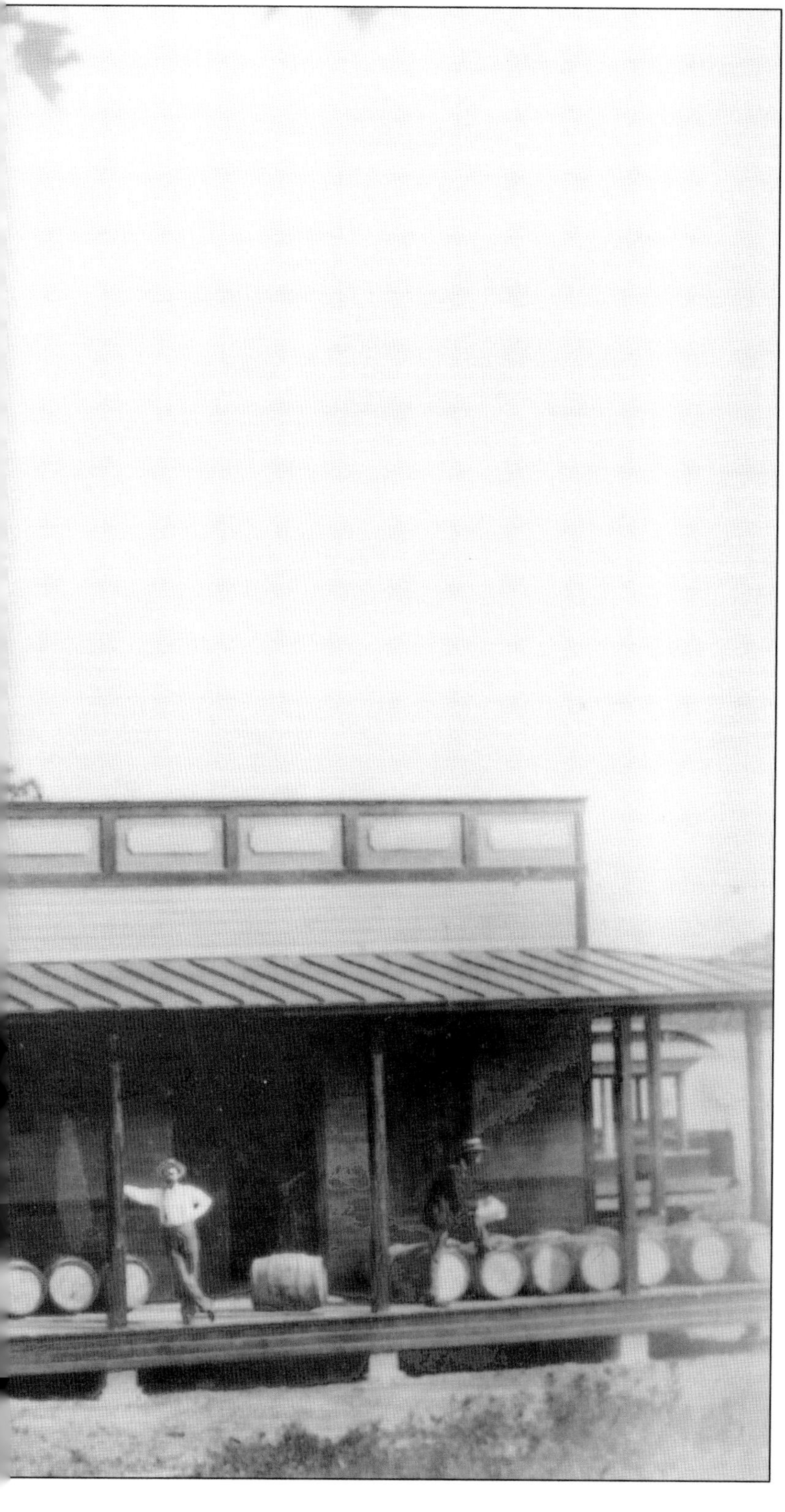

DINKY LINE. Orlando and Winter Park Railway built a 6-mile line between its namesake points that was completed by 1889. The railway's primary riders were Rollins College students. The students nicknamed the railway "Dinky Line" because of the narrow-gauge line's smallness. A depot was built to the east of the college campus on the shore of Lake Virginia, and tracks were widened to standard gauge in 1890. In 1903, it became a part of the Seaboard Air Line system. After Seaboard's merger with the Atlantic Coast Line in 1967, the former Orlando and Winter Park Railway became redundant to the needs of the new company, and parts were abandoned beginning in 1969. Little physical evidence remains of the Orlando and Winter Park Railway. The location of the Winter Park depot is now a park called Dinky Dock Park. (Courtesy of Rollins College.)

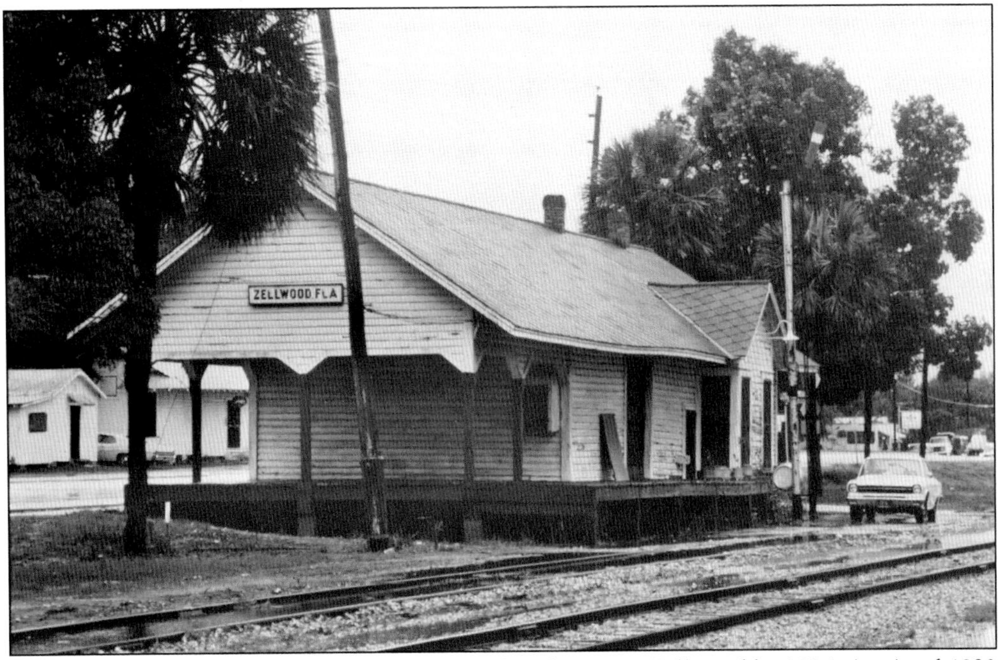

ZELLWOOD. Tavares, Orlando, and Atlantic Railroad came to Zellwood by 1884. An April 1930 timetable shows two passengers trains per day stopping with service to Wildwood and Orlando. By the 1950s, bus service was substituted for the trains. This arrangement appeared on the timetable until the merger. In this early-1971 image, the depot appears to be no longer in service. Later it was used as a feed store before being removed. (Courtesy of R. Randolph Stevens.)

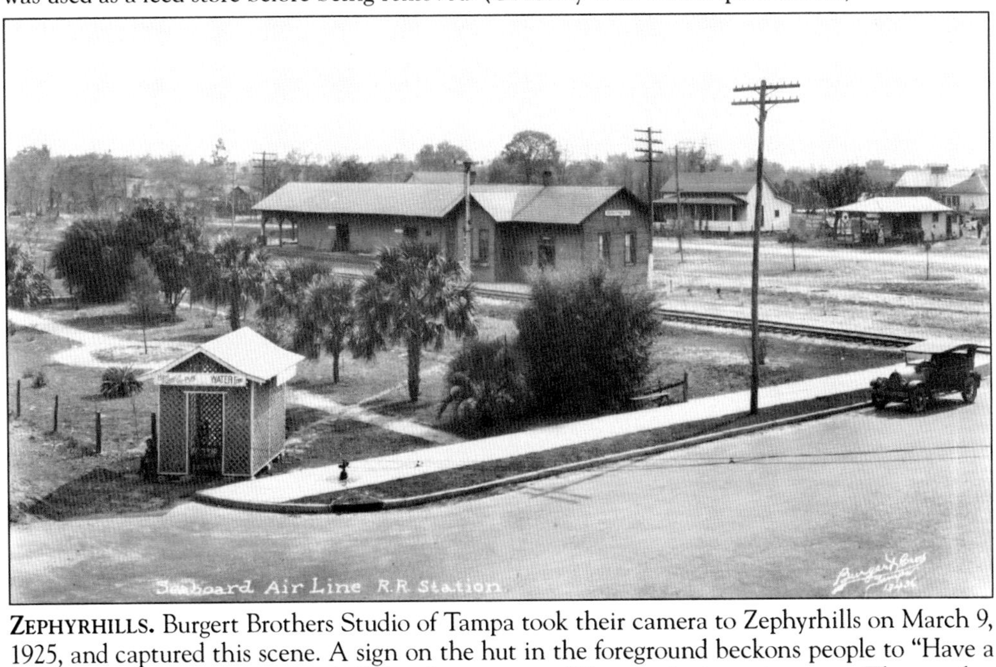

ZEPHYRHILLS. Burgert Brothers Studio of Tampa took their camera to Zephyrhills on March 9, 1925, and captured this scene. A sign on the hut in the foreground beckons people to "Have a drink of our pure water . . . free." Today the town is well known for its springwater. The wooden depot was built in 1911, and passenger trains would stop here until 1968. (Courtesy of Tampa-Hillsborough Public Library.)

Three

Florida East Coast Railway and Predecessors

Florida East Coast Railway Company came into existence on September 7, 1895. One predecessor company was the Florida Coast and Gulf Railway, incorporated on May 28, 1892, with the goal of building a railroad to link Jacksonville with the Gulf Coast at Tampa. On October 31, 1892, the Florida Coast and Gulf Railway name was changed to the Jacksonville, St. Augustine, and Indian River Railway Company. The efforts of these two companies and predecessors would build a railway that would stretch from Jacksonville to West Palm Beach by March 1894.

Various railways or railroads were to become a part of the Florida East Coast Railway (FEC), including the Southeastern Railway Company, formed to take over assets of the Atlantic Coast, St. Johns, and Indian River Railway Company on May 10, 1899. The latter company had a 36-mile-long railway between Enterprise and Titusville. Twenty-one miles of this line between Titusville and Lake Henry was originally constructed by the St. Johns and Indian River Railroad. The first 8-mile segment was built in 1876.

Ormond Bridge Company incorporated in 1887 to build a railroad bridge and rail connection between Ormond Beach and Ormond station—a distance of 1.76 miles.

Atlantic and Western Railroad Company formed in 1888 to acquire the assets of the Blue Springs, Orange City, and Atlantic Railroad Company. The latter had completed just over 25 miles of railroad between a point on the St. Johns River to New Smyrna by 1886.

St. Johns and Halifax River Railway took over operations of the St. Johns and Halifax Railroad and Palatka Bridge Company in 1888. It completed construction of a line from Rollestown to Palatka, which included a bridge over the St. Johns River connecting East Palatka with Palatka.

In 1889, St. Augustine and Halifax Railroad was incorporated to take over 22 miles of railroad formerly known as St. Augustine and Palatka Railway Company. The St. Augustine and Palatka had been incorporated in 1885.

Primarily, Volusia and Brevard Counties were served by the Florida East Coast in the geographic region covered in this book.

Florida East Coast Railway (FEC) ceased passenger train service in 1968, but the railroad is still an independent, successful freight railroad. Many depots were removed soon after passenger service was terminated. A few FEC depots survive today.

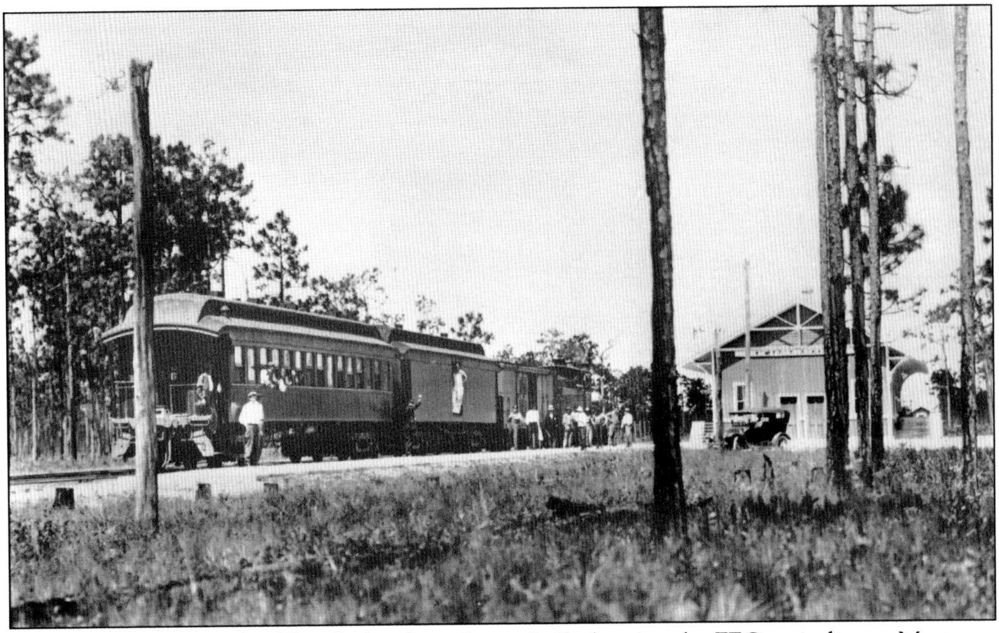

CHULUOTA. In 1913, the Okeechobee branch was built, leaving the FEC main line at Maytown and extending 122 miles south to Okeechobee by January 1915. Chuluota was the third station stop heading south on the branch that later extend along the eastern shore of Lake Okeechobee to Lake Harbor. Northbound train No. 132 is at the depot in 1922. The station was off the timetable by early 1942. Line abandonment occurred in 1947. (Courtesy Jonathan Nelson Collection.)

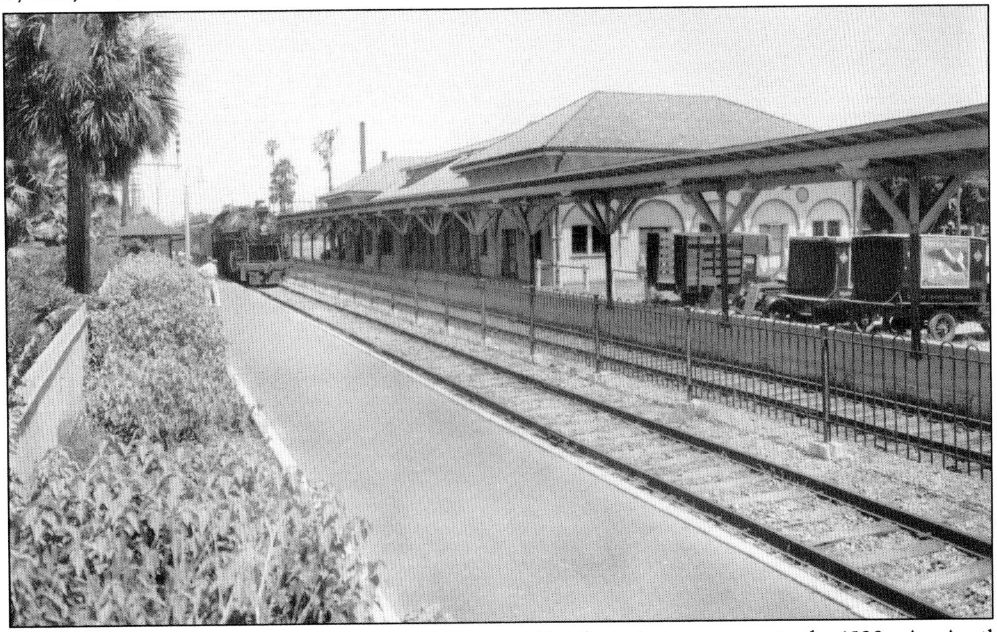

DAYTONA BEACH. A train is pulling into the Daytona Beach station sometime in the 1920s. An April 1930 timetable lists seven daily trains stopping at the station. FEC would terminate all passenger service in 1968. The station was considered architecturally significant by many in the community and was listed on the local history walking tour, but it was torn down without announcement in March 1984. (Courtesy Jonathan Nelson Collection; photograph by Harry Wolfe.)

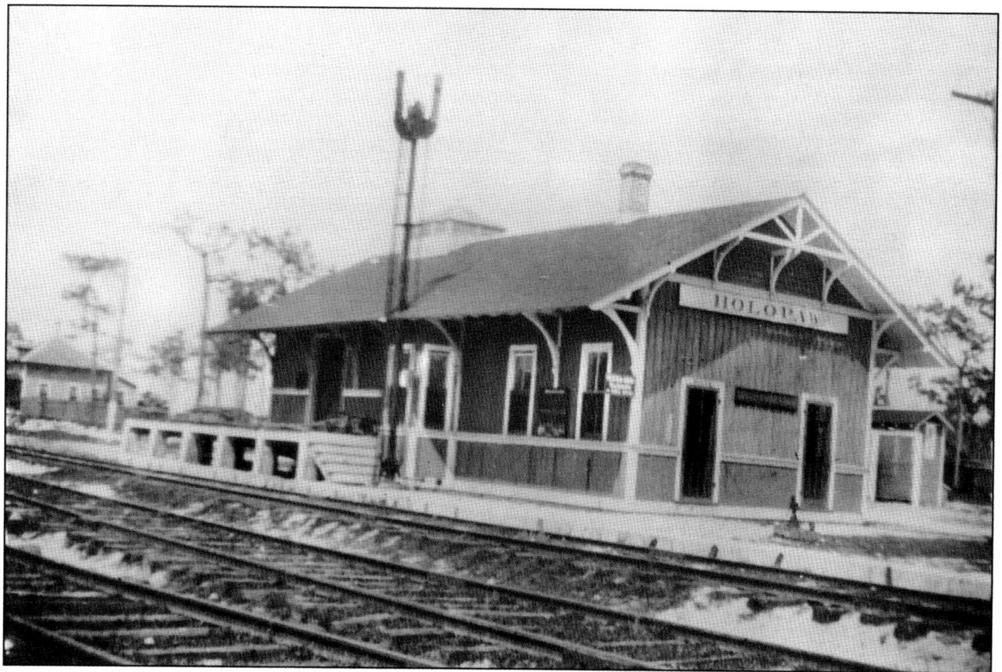

HOLOPAW. The railroad came to Holopaw in 1914. Rail transportation provided the means to exploit the large stands of cypress and pine trees in the area. A lumber mill operated to process the timber. About 2,000 people worked and lived here at one time. When all the timber was removed, everyone moved away as well. Abandonment of the railroad occurred in 1947. Nowadays Holopaw is a ghost town. (Courtesy of Florida State Archives.)

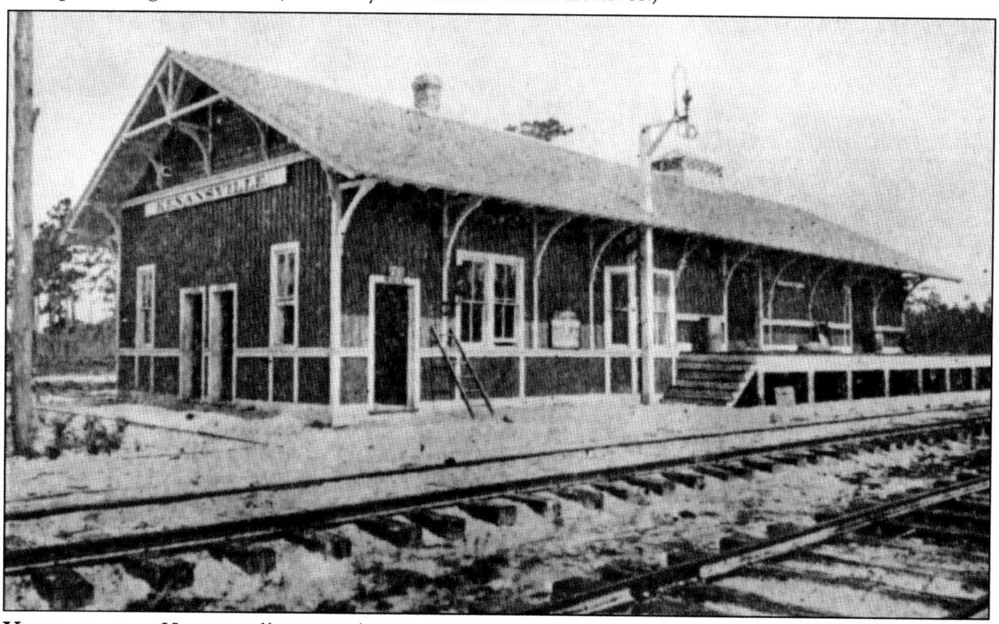

KENANSVILLE. Kenansville is another stop located on the Okeechobee branch, also referred to as the Kissimmee Valley Line. It was 49 miles north of Okeechobee and 73 miles south of Maytown. The community lost its mixed train service by 1942, and the line was abandoned in 1947. Today it is a semi-ghost town with only a few people living here. (Courtesy of Florida State Archives.)

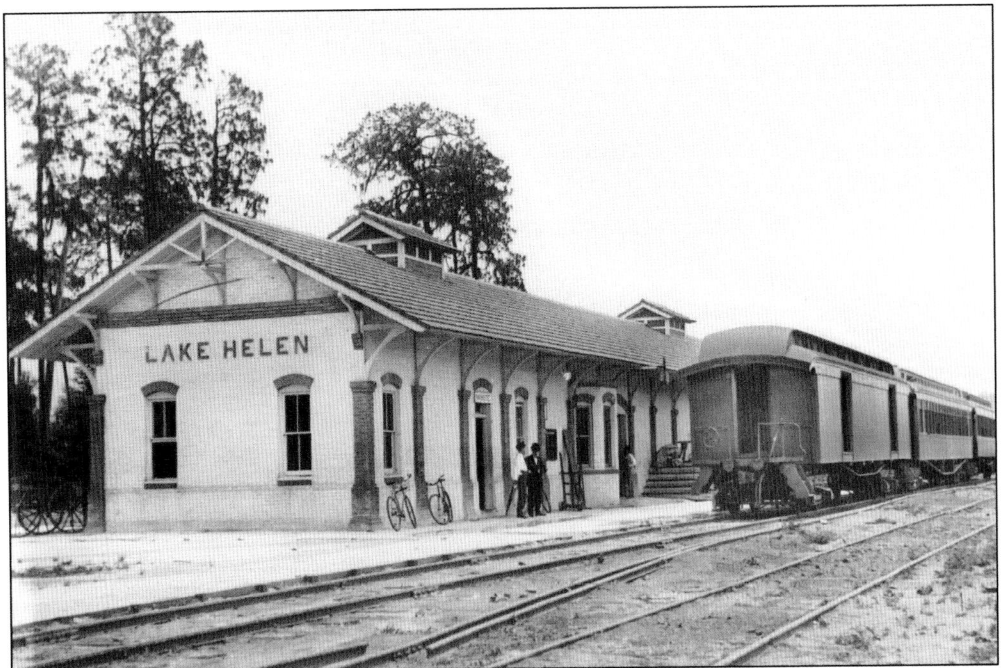

LAKE HELEN. Blue Springs, Orange City, and Atlantic Railroad came to Lake Helen in 1886. This unique double-cupola depot was built around 1910. Lake Helen was located on the 28-mile-long Orange City branch that ran between New Smyrna and Orange City Junction. Passenger trains stopped here until the early 1930s. Connections with ACL trains were made at Orange City Junction. The track and station have been removed. (Courtesy of Florida State Archives.)

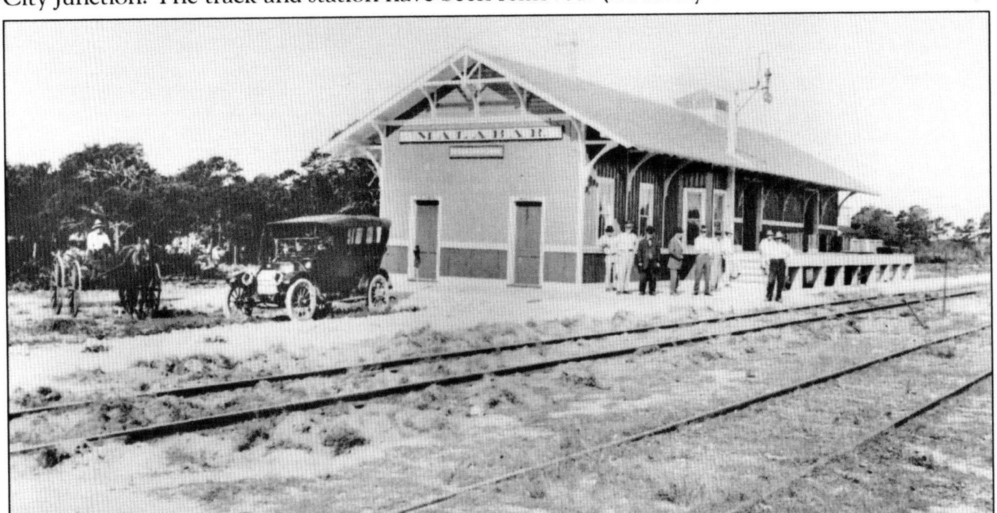

MALABAR. Located in southern Brevard County, Malabar had a population of 138 in 1939, and the main employer was a sawmill. Today the town has around 3,000 people. In 1939, two passenger trains per day stopped. Nowadays only freight trains rumble through on the FEC main line between Miami and Jacksonville. Either a train is soon to arrive or these men just wanted to be photographed around 1920. (Courtesy of Brevard County Historical Commission.)

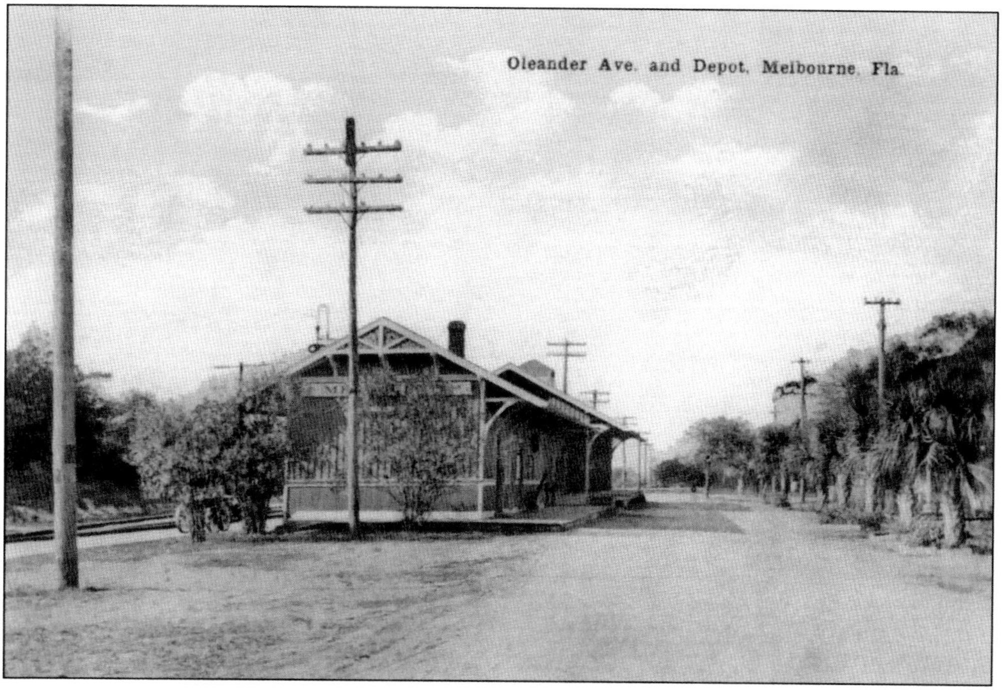

MELBOURNE. Two views of Melbourne's depot from different years in the 1920s are seen here. In the top image, a change in roofline defines the beginning of the freight house. In the lower scene, the freight house has been removed or was perhaps the victim of fire. The passenger depot would survive to the 1960s. (Both courtesy of Brevard County Historical Commission.)

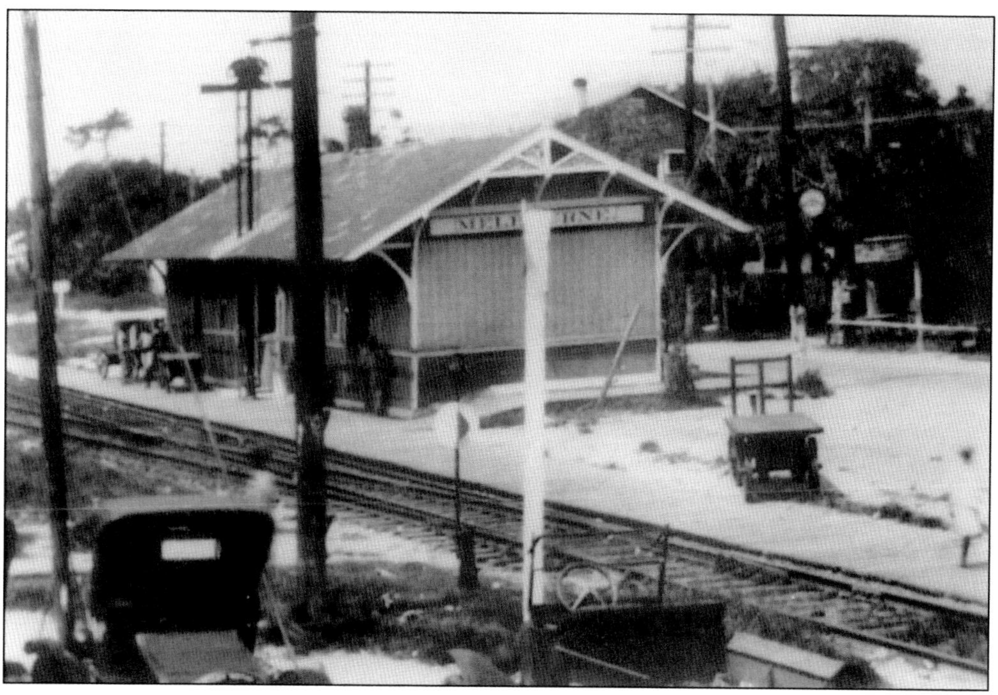

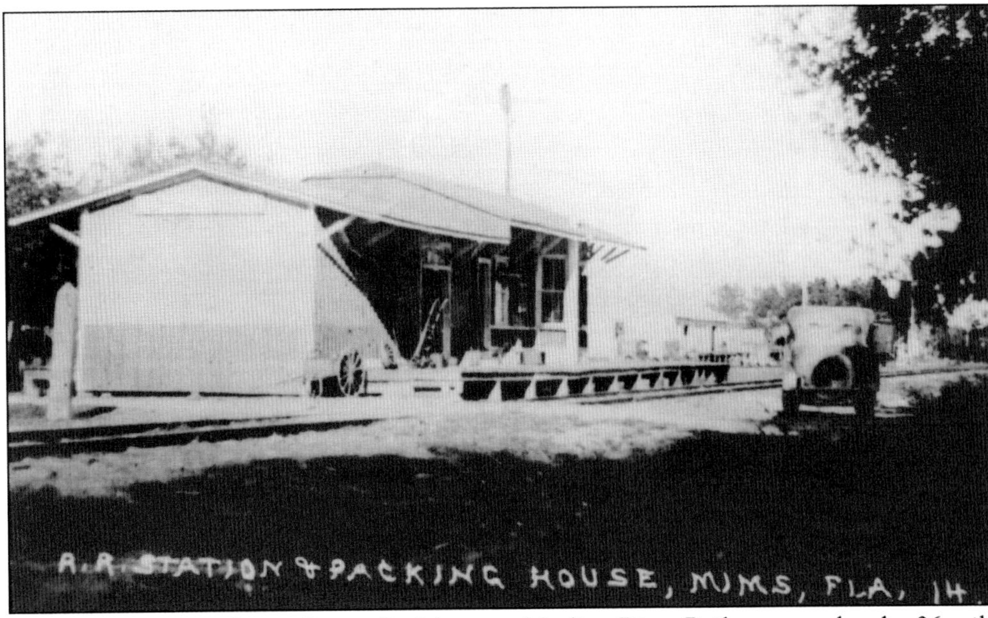

MIMS. Originally Atlantic Coast, St. Johns, and Indian River Railway completed a 36-mile rail line from Sanford to Titusville in 1885. This line passed through Mims, which is located four miles from Titusville. Later the line would become part of the Jacksonville, Tampa, and Key West Railway; in 1903, it became a part of the FEC Railway. (Courtesy of Brevard County Historical Commission.)

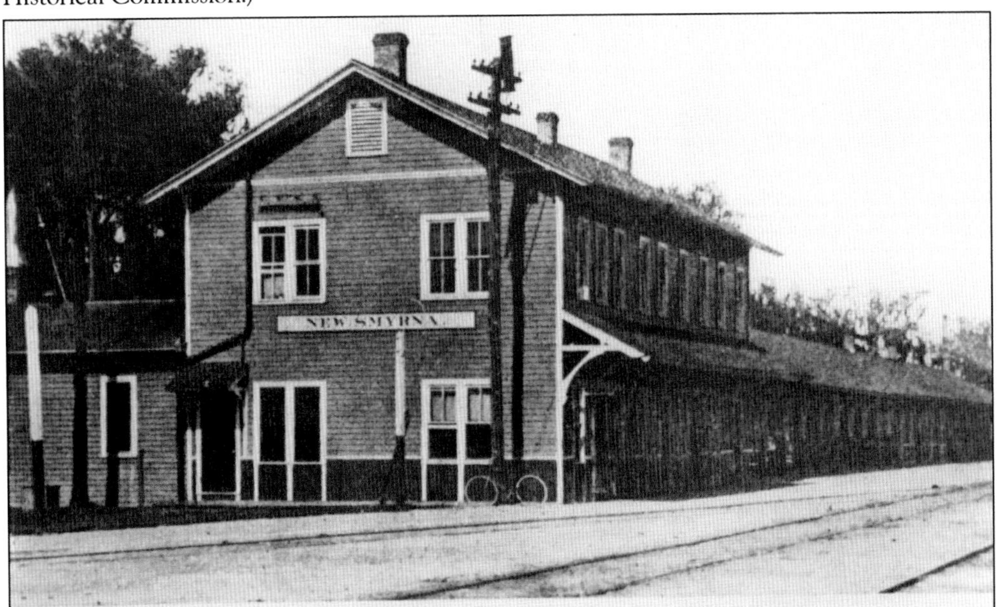

NEW SMYRNA. Jacksonville, St. Augustine, and Indian River Railway extended the railway south through New Smyrna to Fort Pierce by 1894. A single-story wooden depot was built that would be replaced by 1914 with a two-story building. The new building housed a restaurant that provided meal breaks for train passengers. It would serve into the 1960s. (Courtesy of Florida State Archives.)

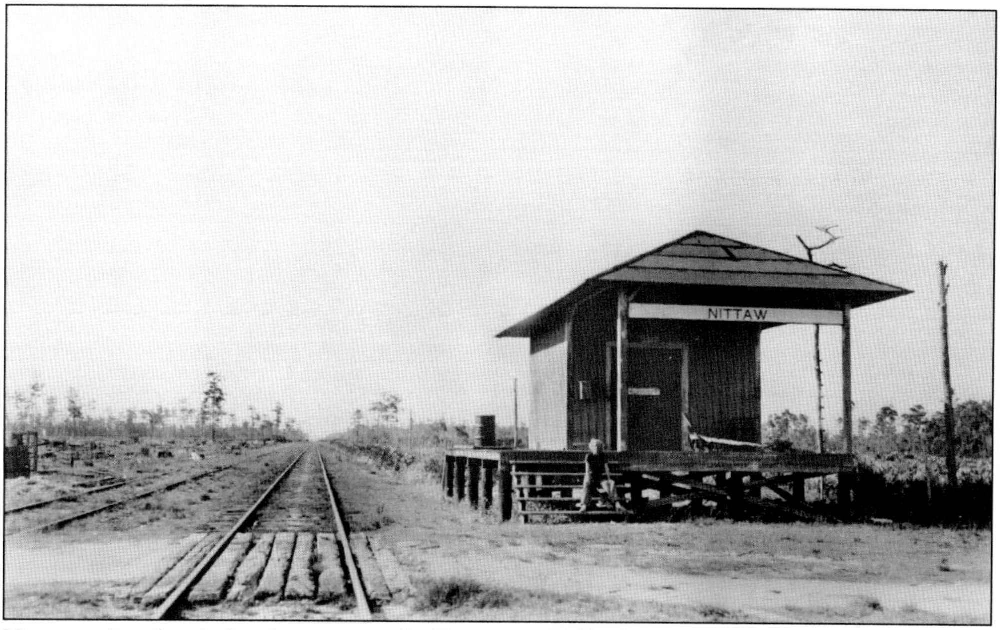

Nittaw. Another isolated station on the Kissimmee Valley Line was Nittaw. At one time, it was a sawmill town in a remote area of Osceola County. There was a post office and a depot, seen in this image from 1940. Nittaw is a ghost town today with little evidence a community ever existed. (Courtesy of Jonathan Nelson Collection; photograph by William Monypeny.)

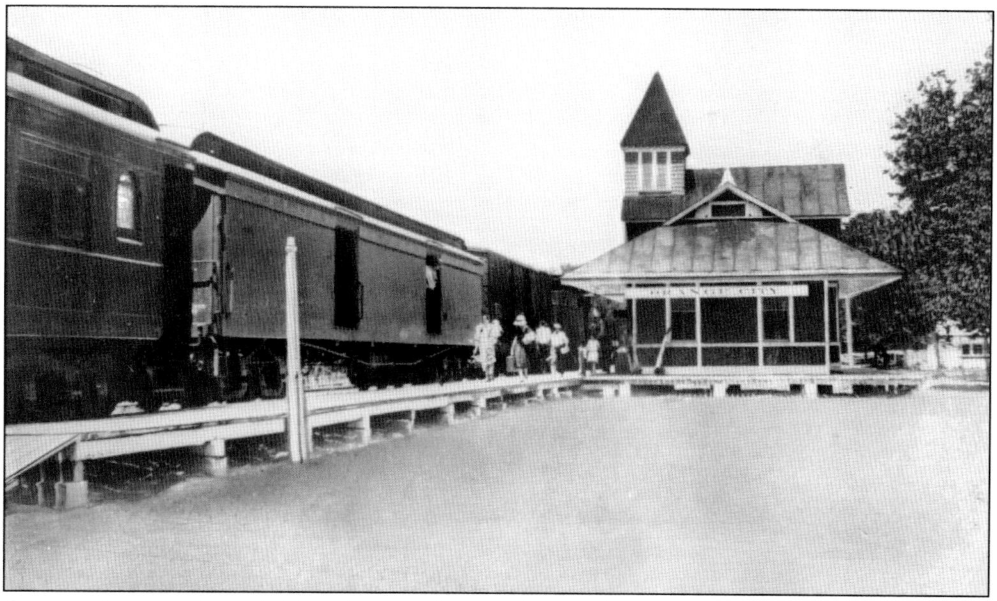

Orange City. Originally Blue Springs, Orange City, and Atlantic Railroad operated the line from Orange City to New Smyrna. Later it became Atlantic and Western Railroad (A&W) and finally the A&W branch of the Florida East Coast. This depot was built in 1891. Passenger service stopped in 1930. The line was abandoned by 1934, and the rails and depot were removed. (Courtesy of Florida State Archives.)

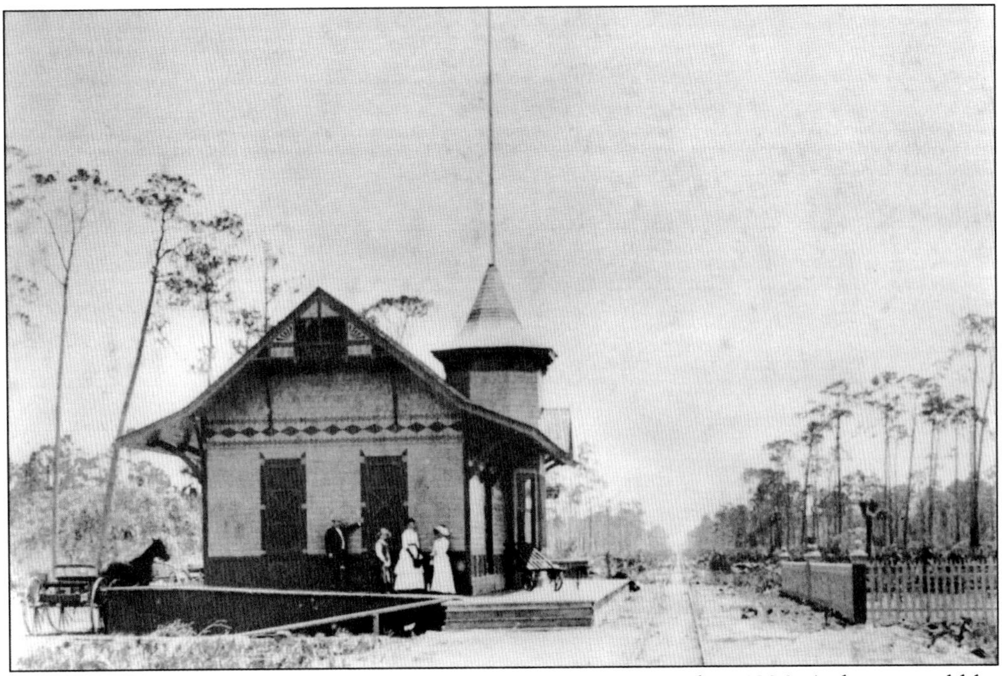

ORMOND. St. Johns and Halifax River Railway came to Ormond in 1886. A depot would be opened in the same year. It would serve until 1900 before it was replaced by a two-story building that included an agent apartment. (Courtesy of Florida State Archives.)

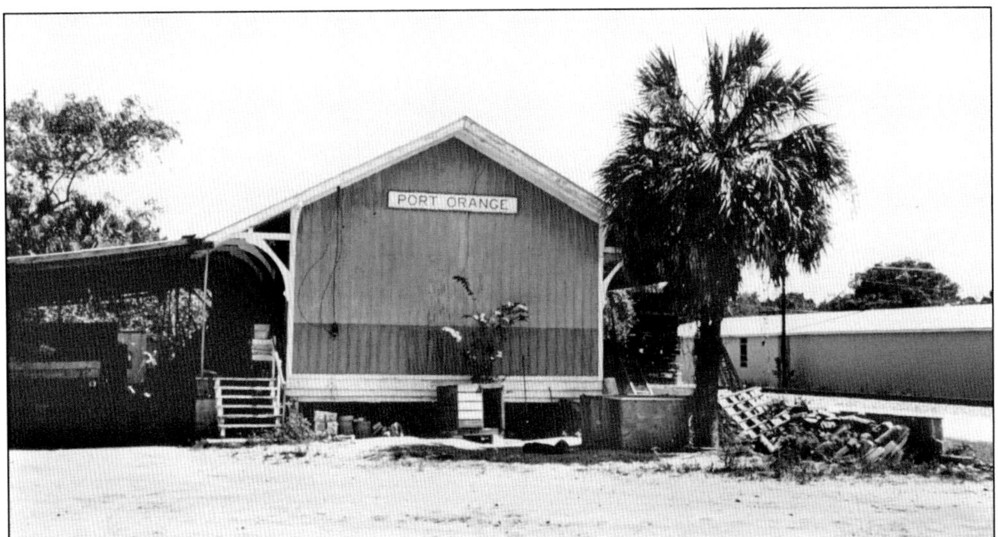

PORT ORANGE. Port Orange's freight depot was built in 1894 and was placed on the National Register of Historic Places in 1998. It was purchased and relocated 500 feet north of its original location in 1966. Port Orange was still listed as a flag stop as late as 1955. Efforts to save the depot are currently under way. (Courtesy of Jonathan Nelson Collection.)

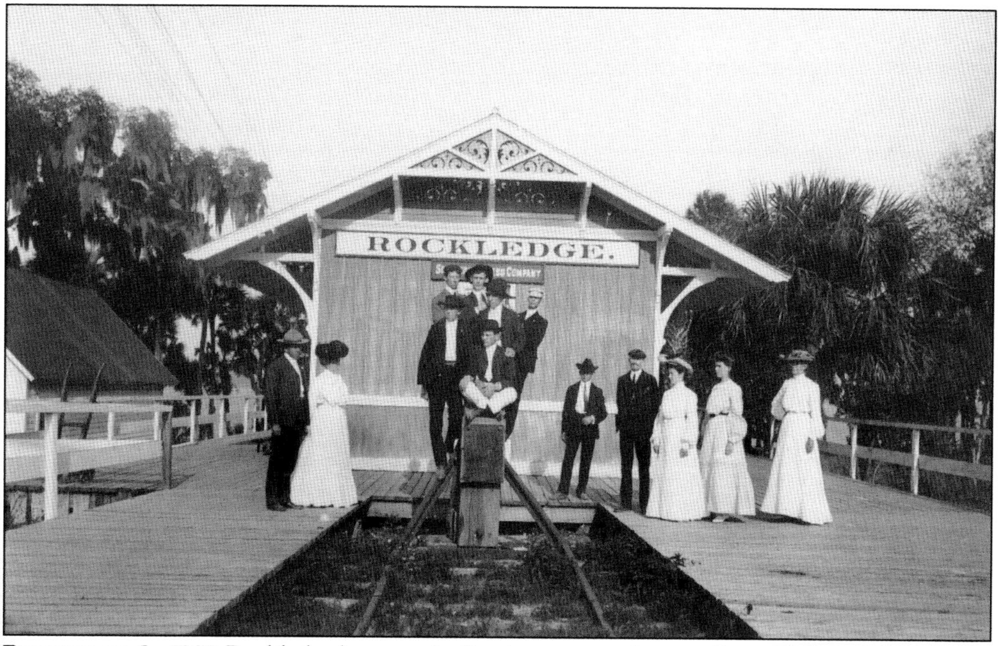

ROCKLEDGE. In 1889, Rockledge became the first incorporated city in Brevard County. Originally the depot was located off the main line on a spur track between the Indian River and Plaza Hotels. FEC Railway owner Henry Flagler wanted to purchase the 300-room Plaza in 1908, but its owners decided not to sell. After a short time, workers overnight removed the spur track and relocated the depot to the main line. (Courtesy of Brevard Historical Commission.)

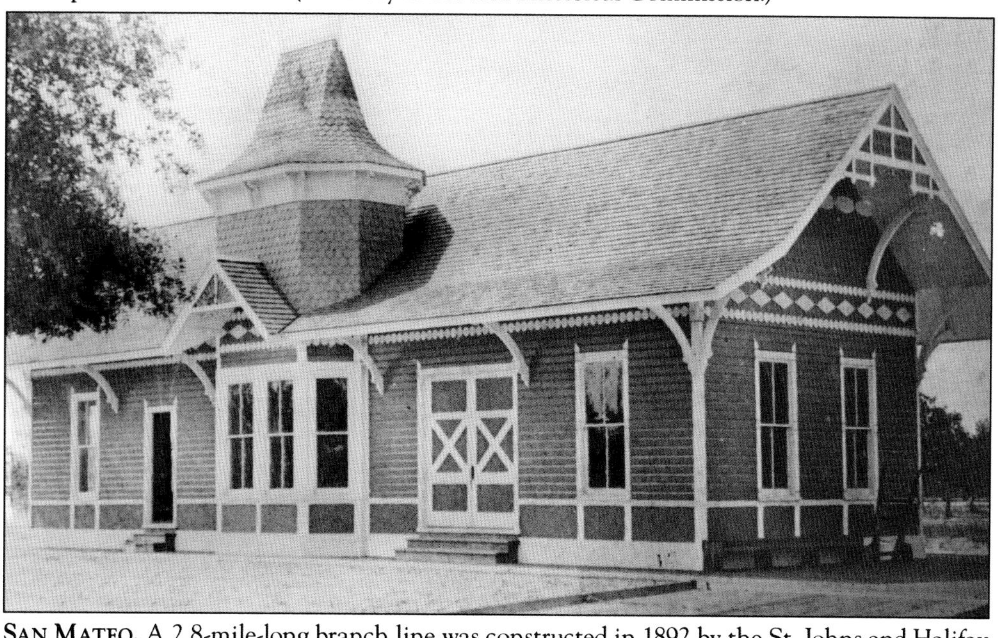

SAN MATEO. A 2.8-mile-long branch line was constructed in 1892 by the St. Johns and Halifax River Railway from East Palatka to San Mateo. The area produced large quantities of fruits and vegetables that needed reliable rail transportation. A beautiful Victorian-styled station served as the terminal. Daily passenger train service would last into the early 1930s, and the line survived until abandoned in late 1942. (Courtesy of Florida State Archives.)

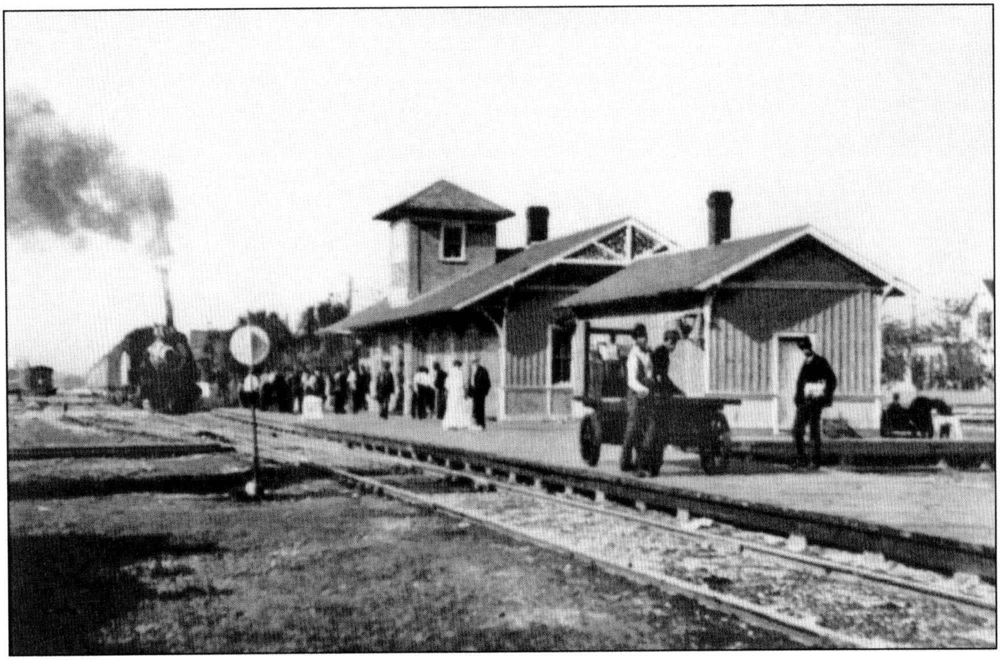

TITUSVILLE. Beginning in 1894, Titusville was served by a wooden, board-and-batten depot (top). At that time, the town numbered around 700 hardy souls. A replacement station made of concrete and stucco (below) came along in 1925. By then, the town had grown to about 2,000 people. They enjoyed daily departures of numerous trains running on the main line of the FEC Railway. The bottom photograph is from June 1975. (Above courtesy of Florida State Archives; below courtesy of Jonathan Nelson Collection.)

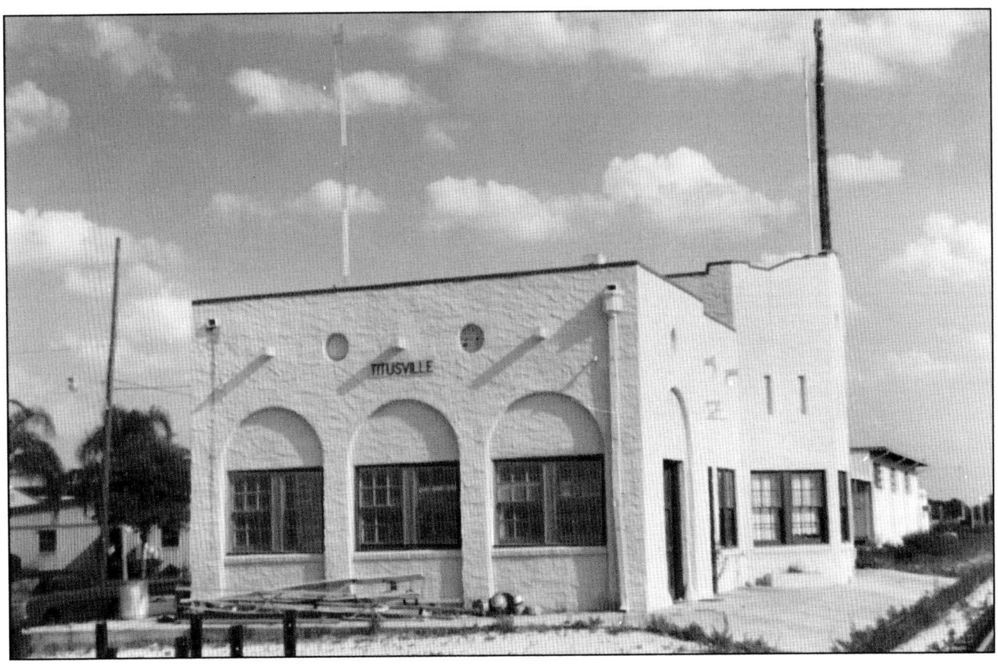

Four

Union Depots with a Bit of Southern and a Dash of Amtrak

When two or more railroad companies agreed to share a railroad depot or station, maintain it, and operate the depot or station, a "Union" facility was created. This brought the trains of the various railroads to the same location in the city or town served. Union depots were encouraged by city or town governments to alleviate traffic congestion and excessive consumption of land and provide better services to the traveling public.

Some Union Stations were jointly owned with a separate company set up by the owning railroads to manage the facility. These were typically larger stations with more than two railroads involved. The station company would oversee construction, operation, and maintenance of the terminal. Tampa Union Station Company was such an entity. Each participating railroad paid user fees based on the amount of business produced at the facility.

Others were a landlord-tenant arrangement with the owning railroad primarily responsible for operations and maintenance. Examples of this arrangement existed at Ocala and Palatka.

There are some Union Stations that were not truly Union, as the various railroads serving the building were either subsidiary, controlled, or owned outright by the parent railroad. Perhaps it was hard to let the memories of predecessor lines go that once rolled into town. Sanford's station of the 1920s is such an example.

Another Union arrangement existed when the railroad met the steamboat landing. Steamboats would remain a transportation option in Florida into the 1920s. Silver Springs stands out as such a place in the geographic area covered here.

Added to this chapter is the Georgia Southern and Florida Railway, which just enters the area covered in the book at Putnam County and Palatka. This railroad would be controlled by the Southern Railroad in 1895 but continued to operate as an independent company. In addition, Amtrak and the City of Lakeland were involved in the only new station construction in the geographic area covered over the past 30 years.

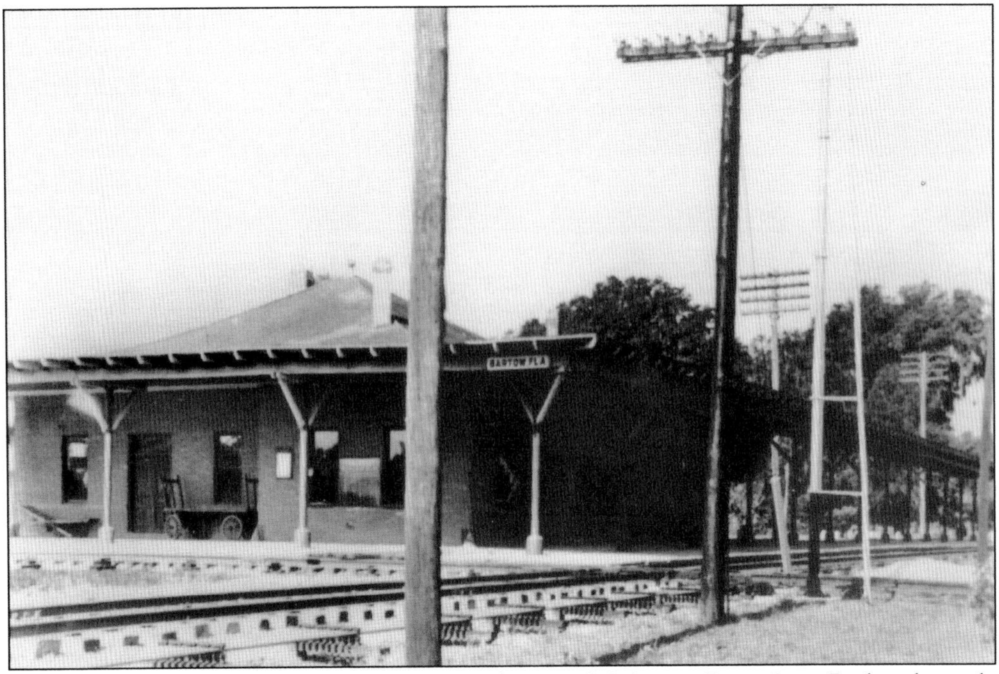

BARTOW. In 1915, the Seaboard Air Line Railway and Atlantic Coast Line Railroad jointly built a Union Station at Bartow, where the respective lines crossed. The red brick station featured two covered platforms. Unfortunately, this Union Station would last just three years, as customers were dissatisfied with the location and disagreement between the railroads. Each railroad returned to existing depots previously used, and the building was razed. (Courtesy of Polk County Historical Museum.)

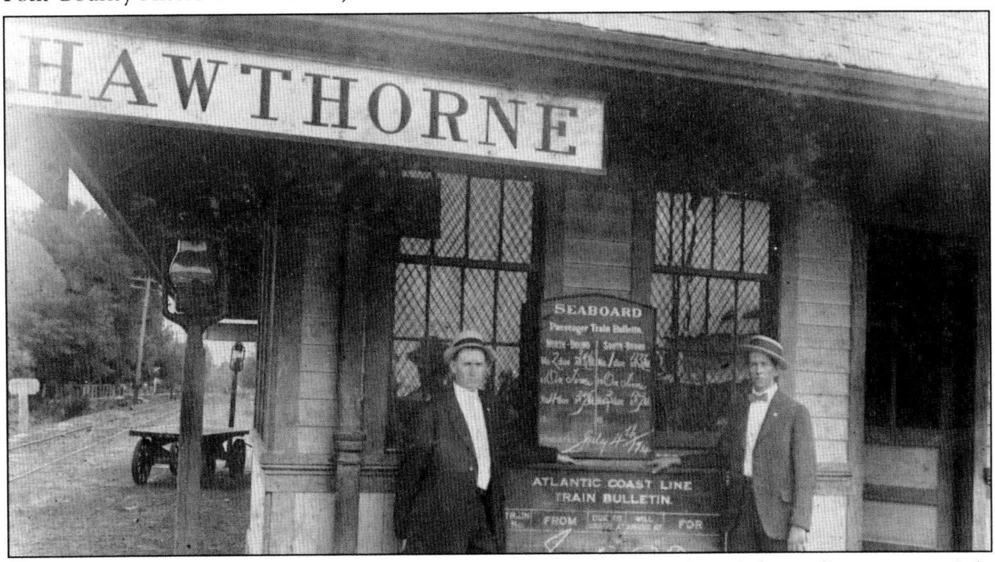

HAWTHORNE. Close examination of the Seaboard train bulletin board dates this image to July 4, 1914. Both Seaboard trains are on time. It is unclear what the Atlantic Coast Line board is indicating. However, the ACL line would carry passengers until 1941. The Seaboard would serve the town until 1968, but this station was long gone before that time. (Courtesy of Florida State Archives.)

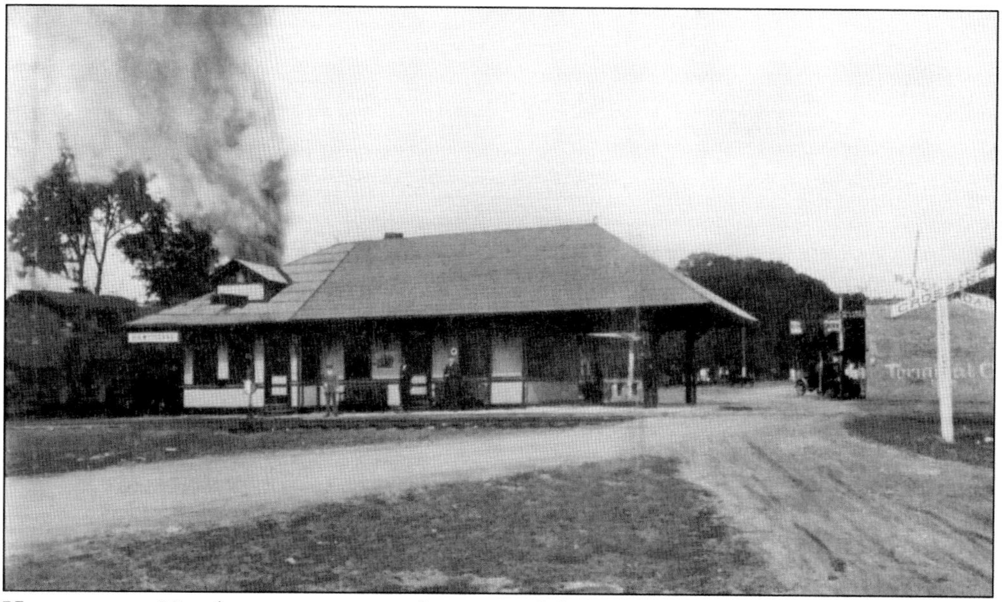

HAWTHORNE. Hawthorne is seen again from around the same time period as the previous image. A large plume rises above the left end of the depot, indicating a train is at the station. The ACL secondary tracks ran east-west between Palatka and High Springs. Seaboard's main line from Jacksonville came through Hawthorne and then extended to Plant City and points south. Hawthorne is 70 miles south from Jacksonville Union Terminal. (Courtesy of Florida State Archives.)

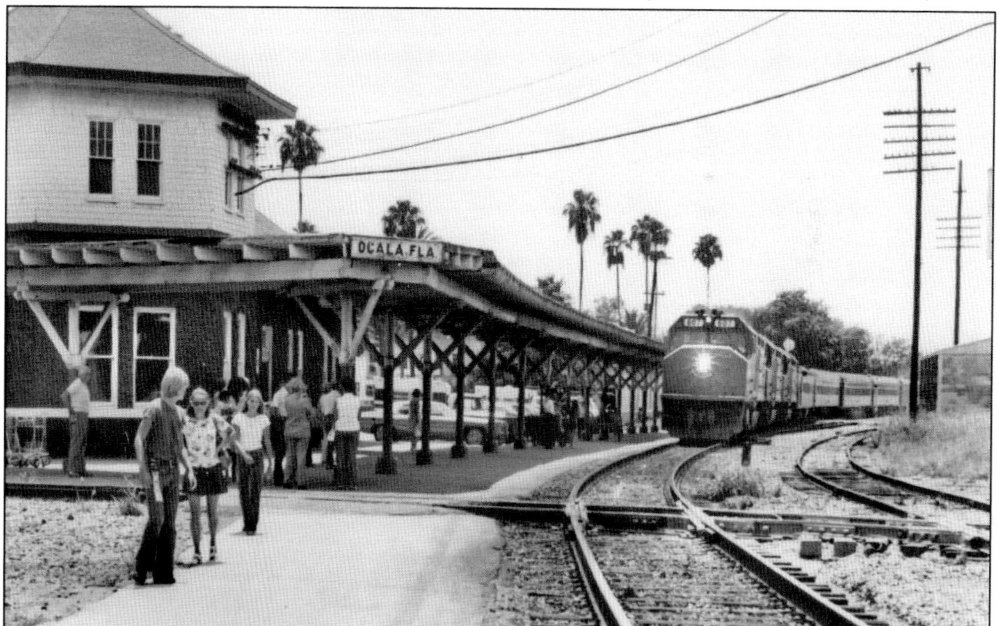

OCALA. The cover image from 1975 appears again in a complete view. Ocala's Union Station was opened in 1917. It would serve passenger trains until 2004. A major renovation of the facility was completed in 1998. Currently it serves Greyhound and local transit buses, and a city police office is located here. It was listed on the National Register of Historic Places in 1997. (Courtesy of Fred Clark Jr.)

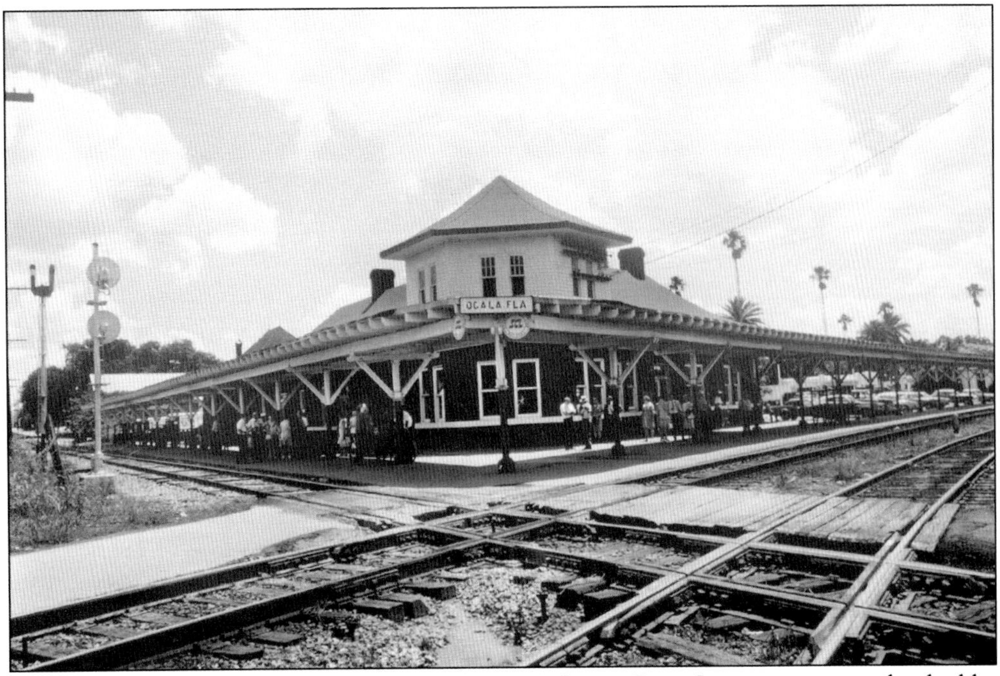

OCALA, 1970 AND 1969. The single-track former Atlantic Coast Line crosses over the double-track Seaboard at Ocala Union Station. This after-merger view (top) is from the spring of 1970, and judging from the number of people on the platform, train arrival is imminent. The timetable effective December 11, 1970, indicates six passenger trains stopping per day in Ocala. Two of these were routed on the former ACL line, arriving at 1:25 p.m. and 1:40 p.m. The photographer is facing east in the scene below from summer of 1969, with the Seaboard's loading platform as the subject. (Both courtesy of R. Randolph Stevens.)

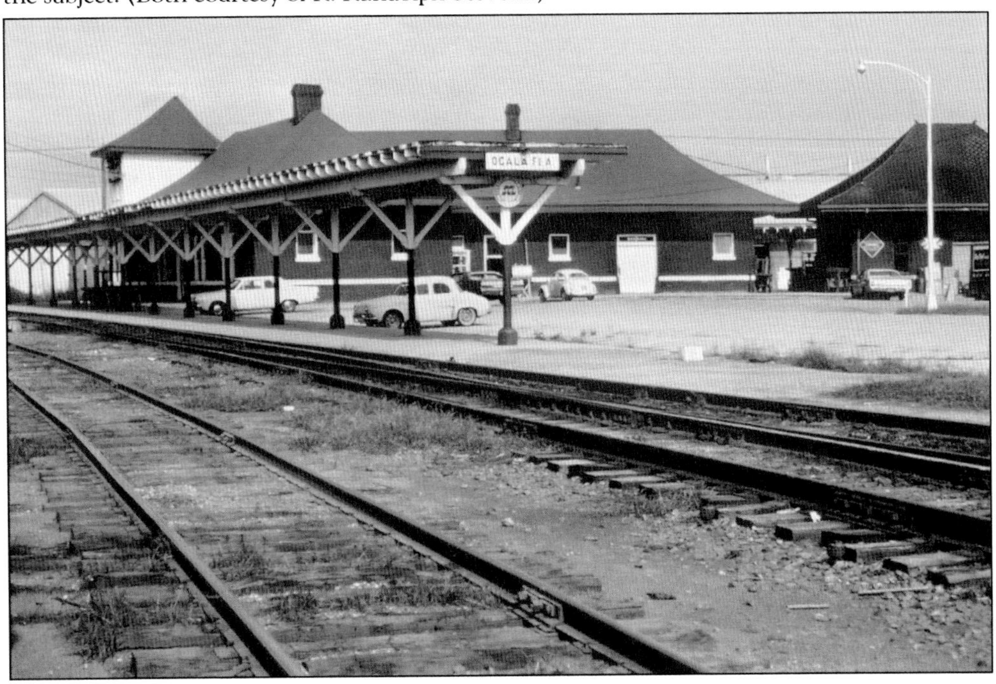

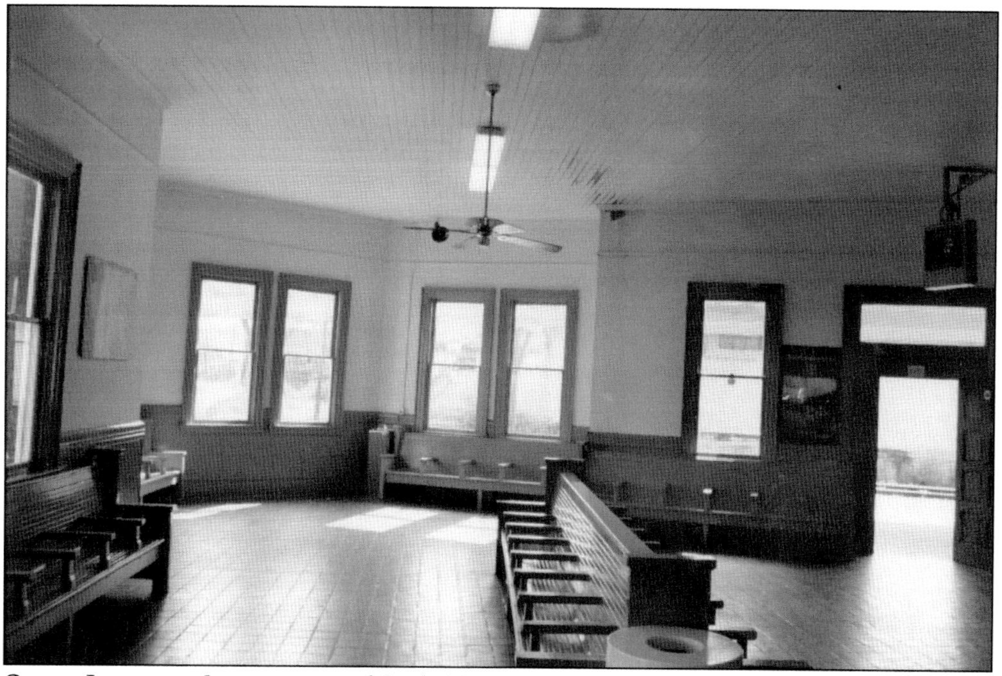

OCALA INTERIOR. Interior views of Ocala Union Station from July 26, 1992, show a very clean, well-kept building. The ceiling in the top view is showing a bit of water damage from a roof leak, but otherwise the building presents a good image for Amtrak. A major renovation of the building was completed by December 1998. Unfortunately, this station would lose service in 2004 when Amtrak rerouted their *Silver Star* trains to the former Atlantic Coast Line route via Palatka and Orlando. (Courtesy of Mike Mulligan.)

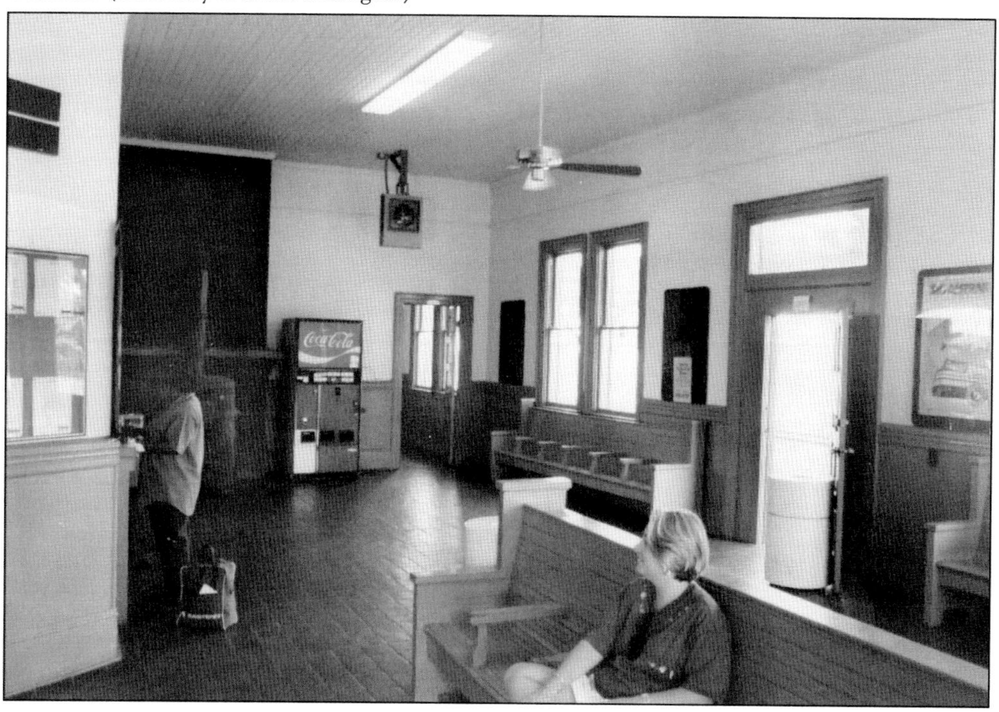

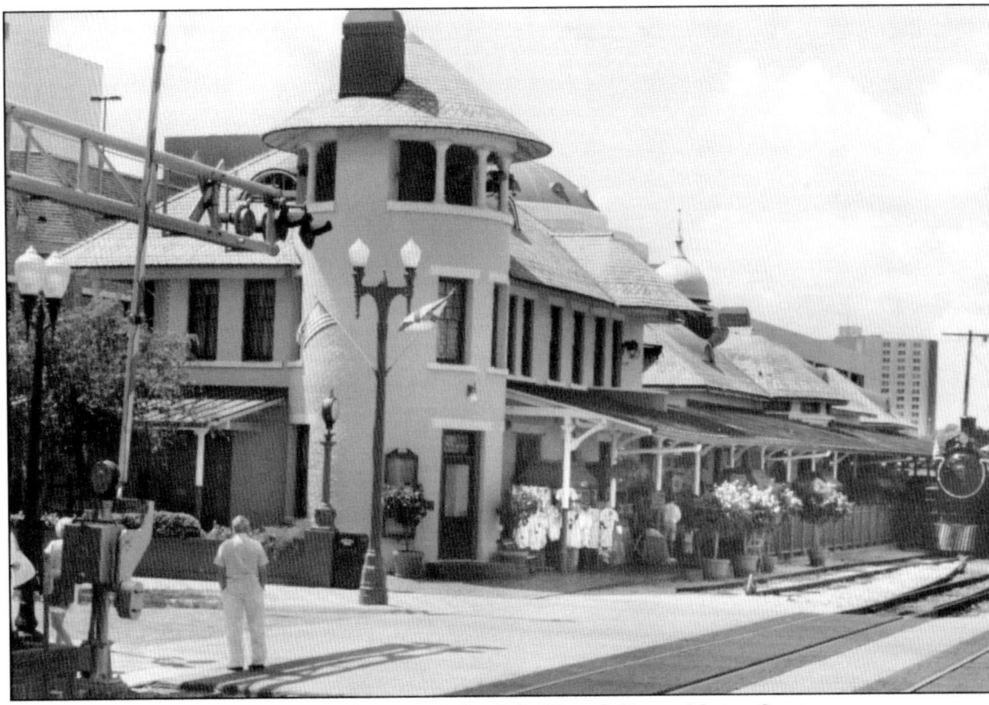

ORLANDO, CHURCH STREET. At the time Orlando's Church Street Union Station was constructed by the South Florida Railroad in 1890, Orlando had service from two other railroads. They were Tavares, Orlando, and Atlantic Railroad and Orlando and Winter Park Railway. Perhaps one or both offered rail service from the Church Street facility for it to be referred to as a "Union Station" on Sanborn Insurance maps of the period. It would serve as the ACL station until 1927. In the 1980s, the building was converted for use in a shopping and entertainment complex. Although successful in the first decade or so, it fell out of favor in the late 1990s. Recently it was in foreclosure, but there is a hope it can regain interest in a very competitive tourist market. The top view is from 1991, and the bottom from 1975. (Above courtesy of Mike Mulligan; below courtesy of Fred Clark Jr.)

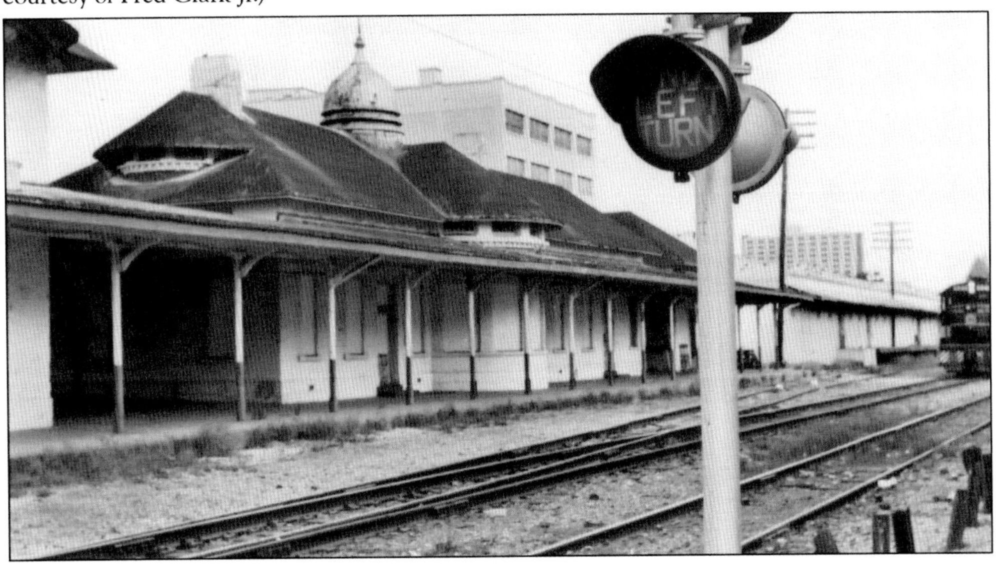

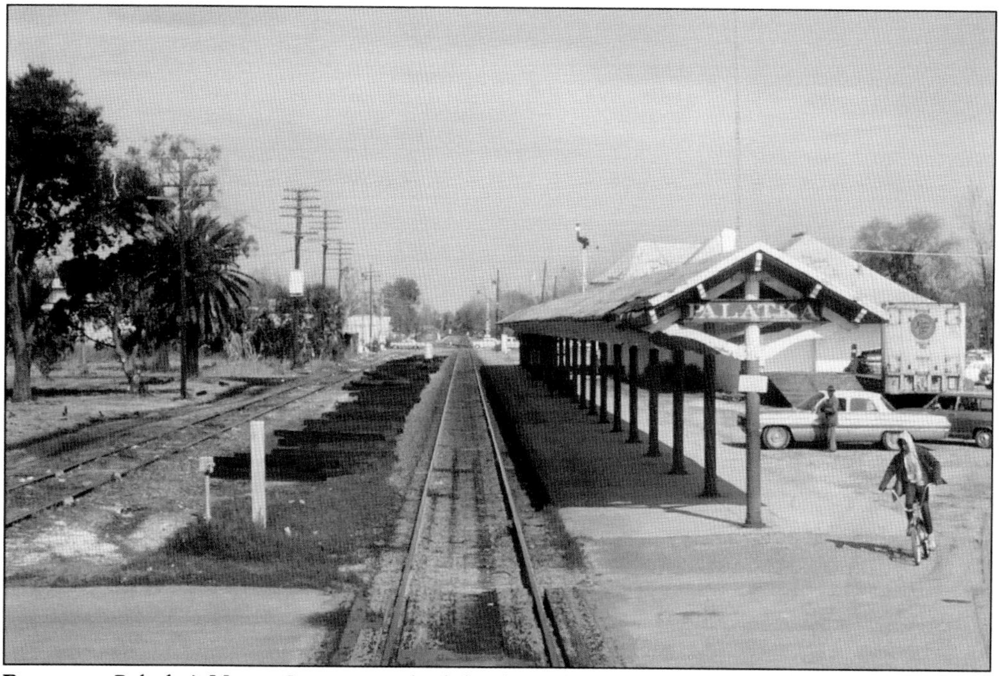

PALATKA. Palatka's Union Station was built by the Atlantic Coast Line Railroad and opened in 1908 at a cost of $25,000. Florida East Coast Railway and Georgia Southern and Florida served the building as well. The image above is from early 1970 and is looking north, showing the long covered platform. The ACL logo adorns the truck trailer on the right. The view below is of the north end of the building and clearly shows the dual agent bay windows. It was taken on October 21, 1973. The north end housed the FEC agent, while on the building side is the ACL agent's office. There was a covered platform that extended along the northern end when the FEC was a tenant. It is currently an Amtrak station and also home to the Palatka Railroad Preservation Society. (Above courtesy of R. Randolph Stevens; below courtesy of Jonathan Nelson Collection, photograph by August Staebler.)

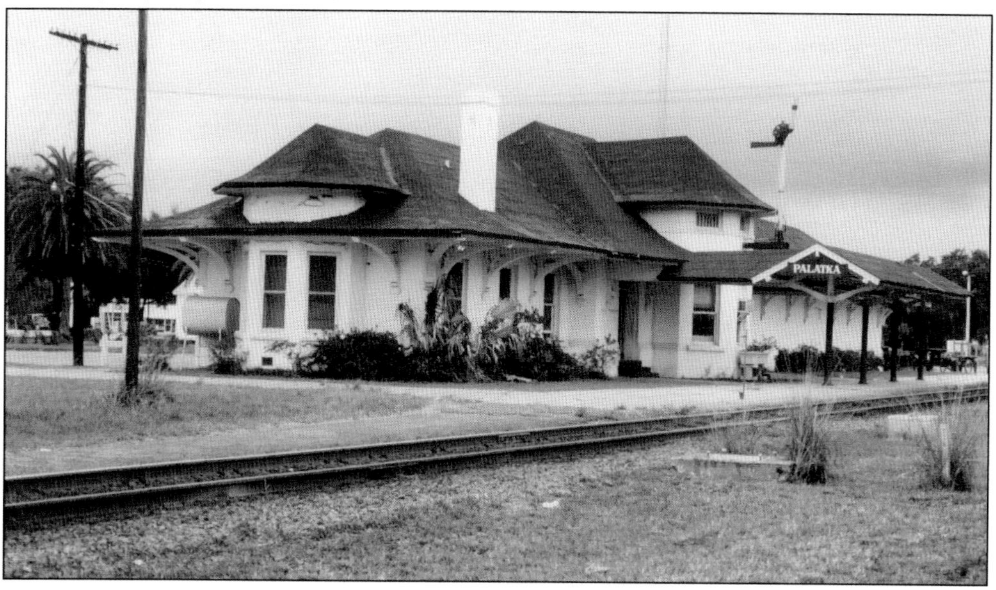

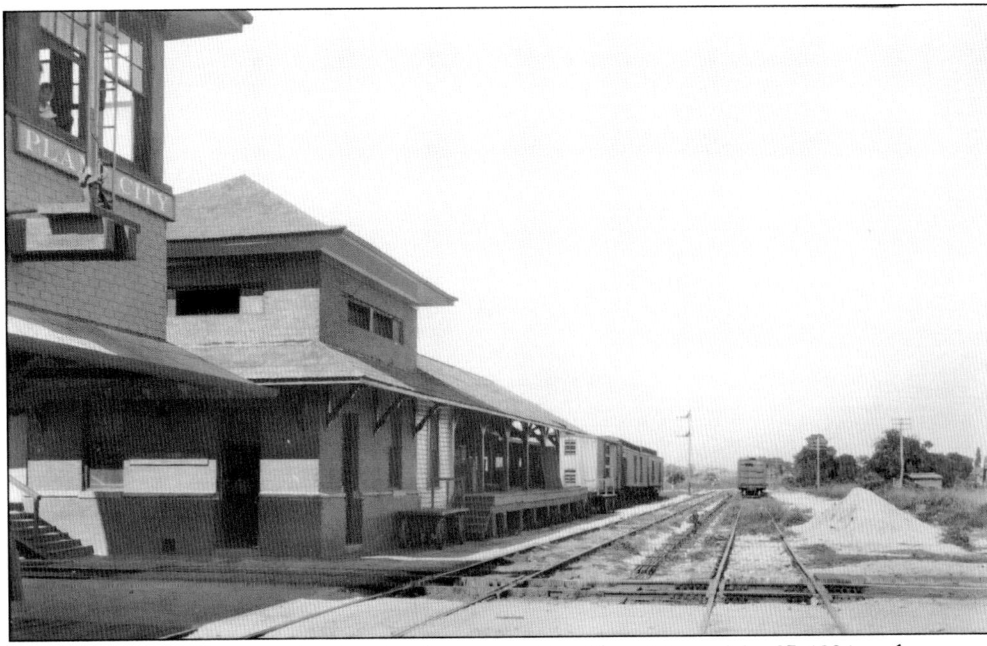

PLANT CITY, 1924. Burgert Brothers Studio was working Plant City on May 27, 1924, and captured this view of the freight house at the station. The second floor of the passenger station just shows on the left. A boy is peering out the tower window. This is looking down the ACL main with the single-track Seaboard crossing over. (Courtesy of Tampa-Hillsborough Public Library.)

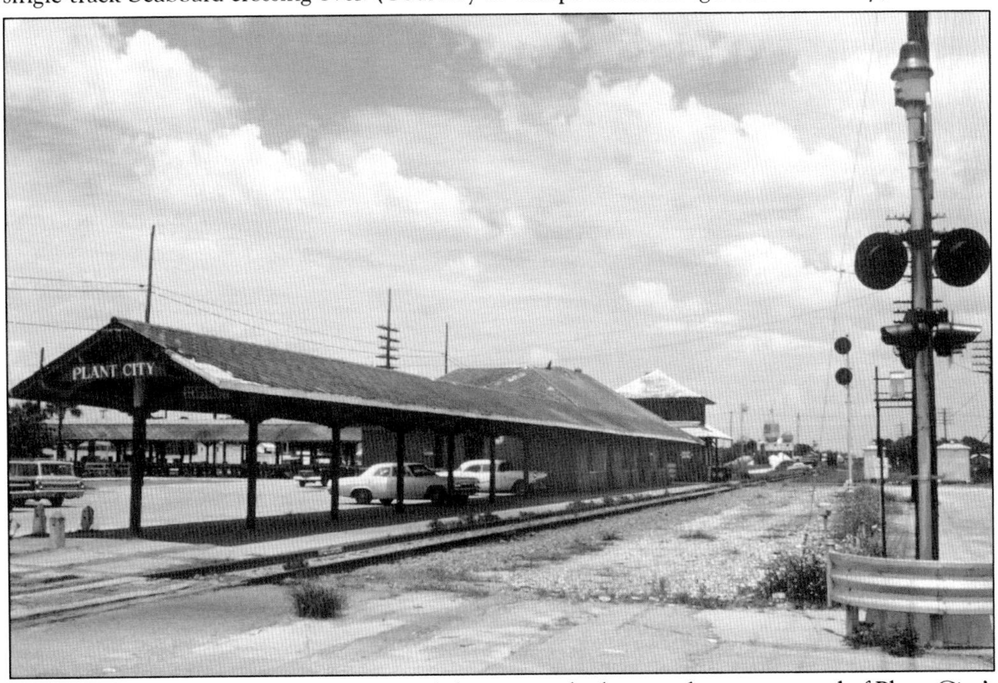

PLANT CITY. It's the summer of 1968, and this view is looking at the western end of Plant City's covered platform. The control tower has long been removed from the passenger station. The timetable effective December 1967 listed six passenger trains per day on the schedule. Trains would continue to stop here into 1971. (Courtesy of R. Randolph Stevens.)

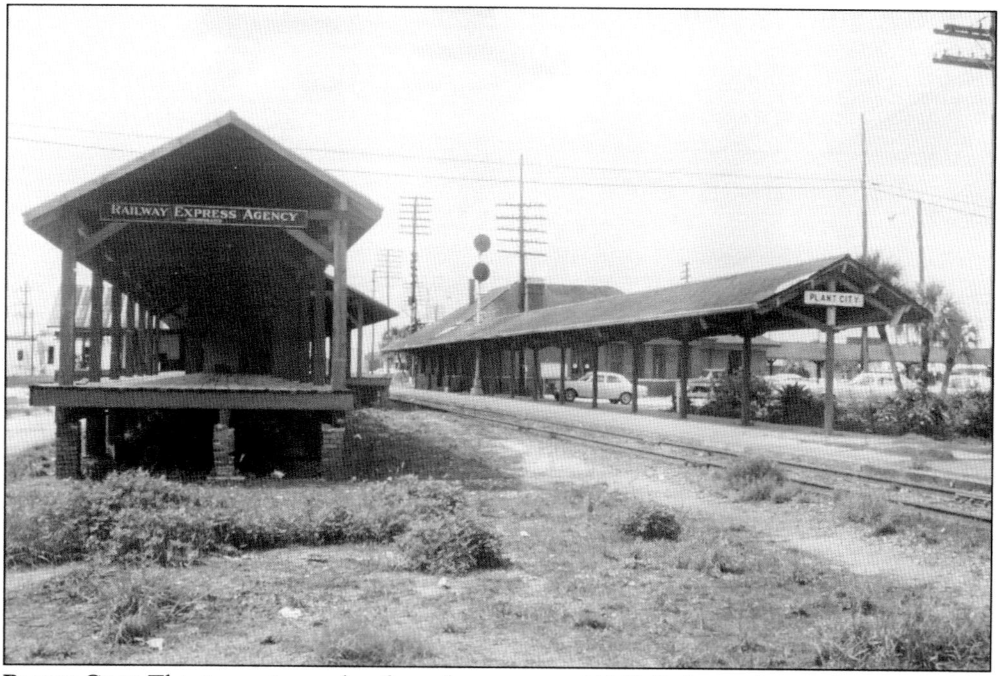

PLANT CITY. This image is another from the summer of 1968. It shows the northern end of the Plant City passenger platform and the Railway Express Agency loading dock on the opposite side of the former Seaboard tracks, which run north-south. (Courtesy of R. Randolph Stevens.)

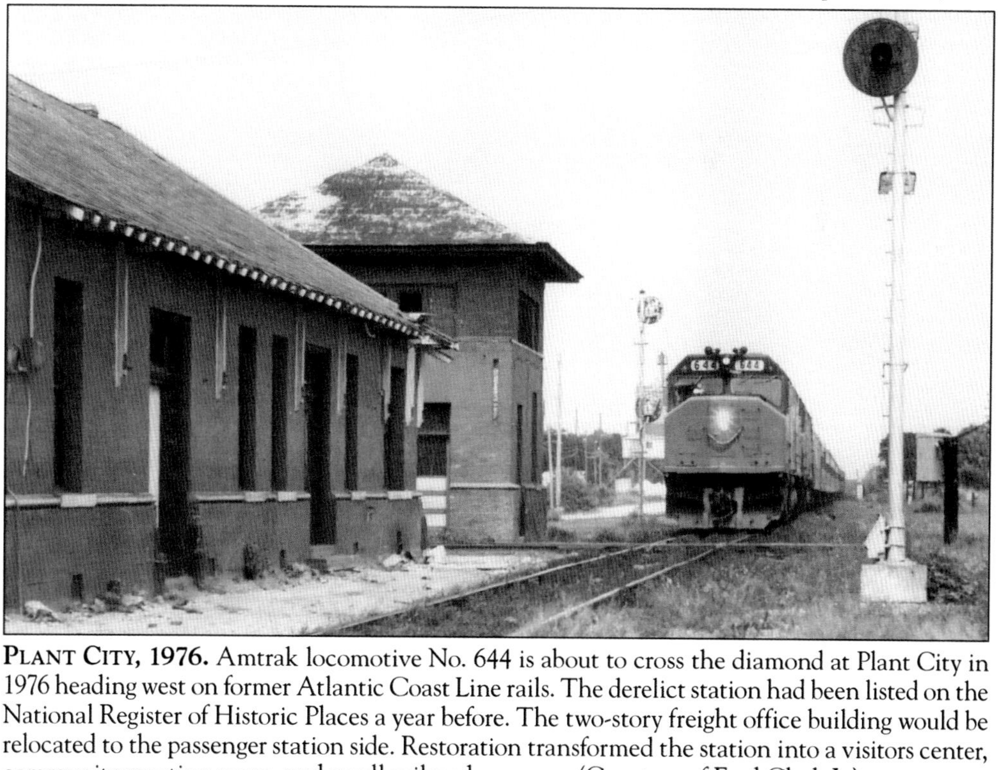

PLANT CITY, 1976. Amtrak locomotive No. 644 is about to cross the diamond at Plant City in 1976 heading west on former Atlantic Coast Line rails. The derelict station had been listed on the National Register of Historic Places a year before. The two-story freight office building would be relocated to the passenger station side. Restoration transformed the station into a visitors center, community meeting room, and small railroad museum. (Courtesy of Fred Clark Jr.)

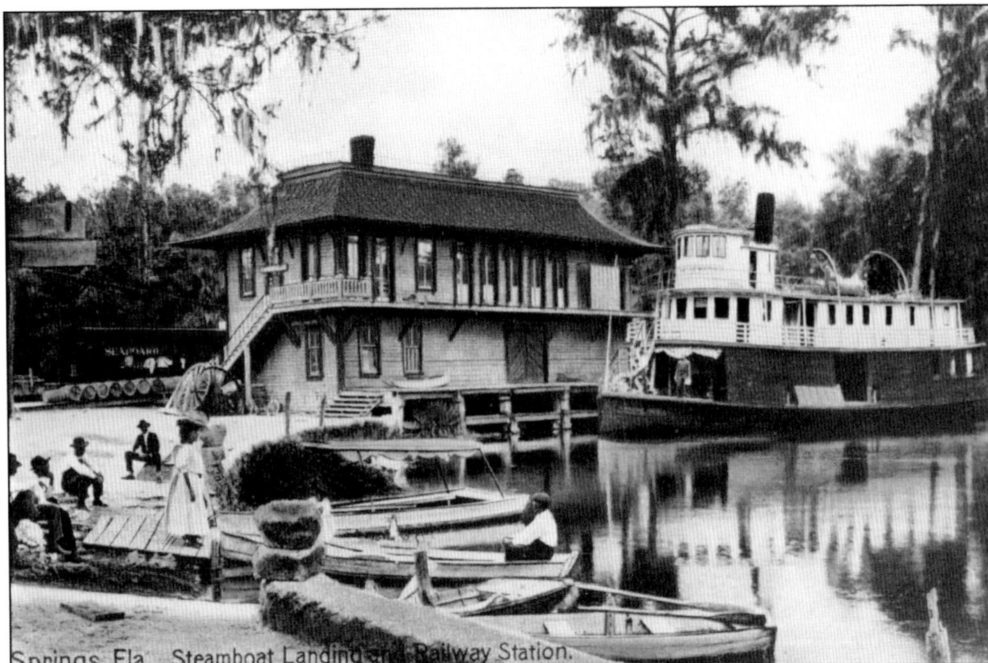

Silver Springs. Railroads and steamboats shared facilities in some Florida locations early in the railroad era. Therefore, these facilities would qualify as Union Stations. Most of these would be gone by the start of the 1920s. Silver Springs was one such location. Seaboard served the railway station along with steamers like the *William Howard*. Seaboard would cancel service to Silver Springs in 1915. This scene is about 1905. (Courtesy of Florida State Archives.)

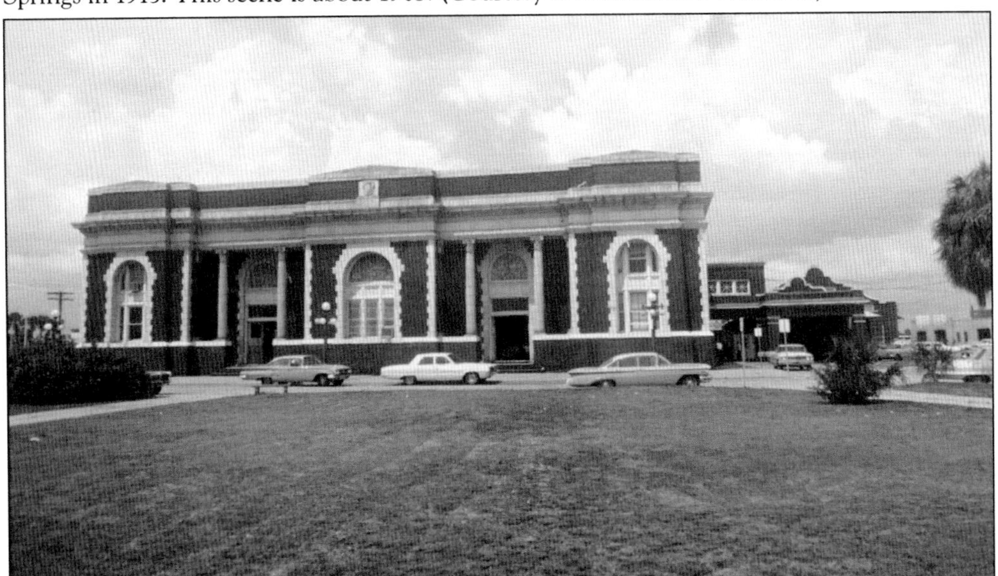

Tampa. Atlantic Coast Line, Seaboard Air Line, and Tampa Northern Railroads agreed to provide $250,000 to build Union Station for Tampa. The building opened in 1912. Its deteriorated condition would force Amtrak to close it in 1984. It reopened in 1998 after an extensive renovation, but in 2008, Amtrak trains only stop here twice per day. Forty years ago, it was the subject of this picture, taken on a summer day. (Courtesy of R. Randolph Stevens.)

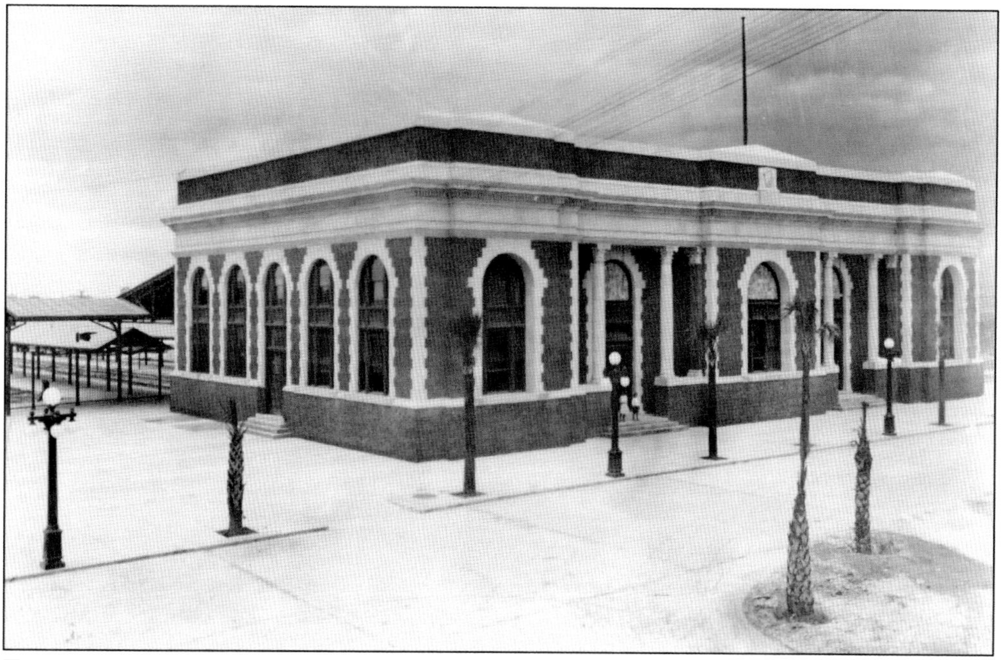

TAMPA UNION STATION, 1912. Tampa's Union Station was designed in the Italian Renaissance style with Corinthian columns. Tampa's Burgert Brothers Studio was present on opening day, May 15, 1912, to capture the facility on film (above). Burgert Brothers would visit Union Station many times over the years. Another visit on August 16, 1957, produced the scene below of the station lunchroom entrance located by the track platforms. Tampa Union Station is thoroughly covered in Arcadia Publishing's *Tampa Union Station* by Jackson McQuigg (published in 1998). (Both courtesy of Tampa-Hillsborough Public Library.)

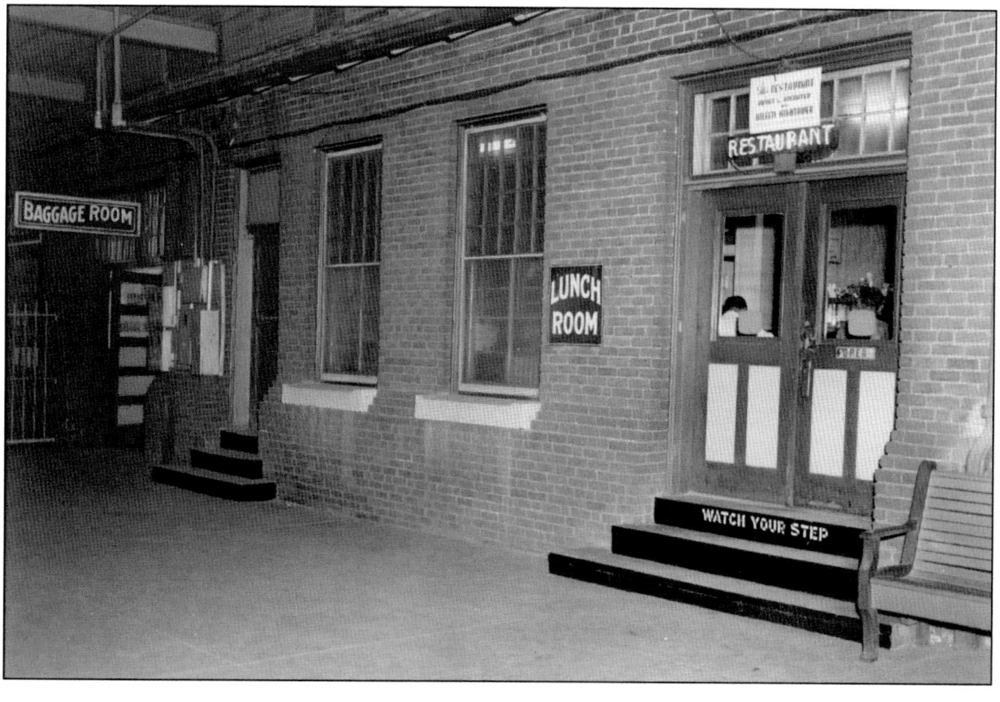

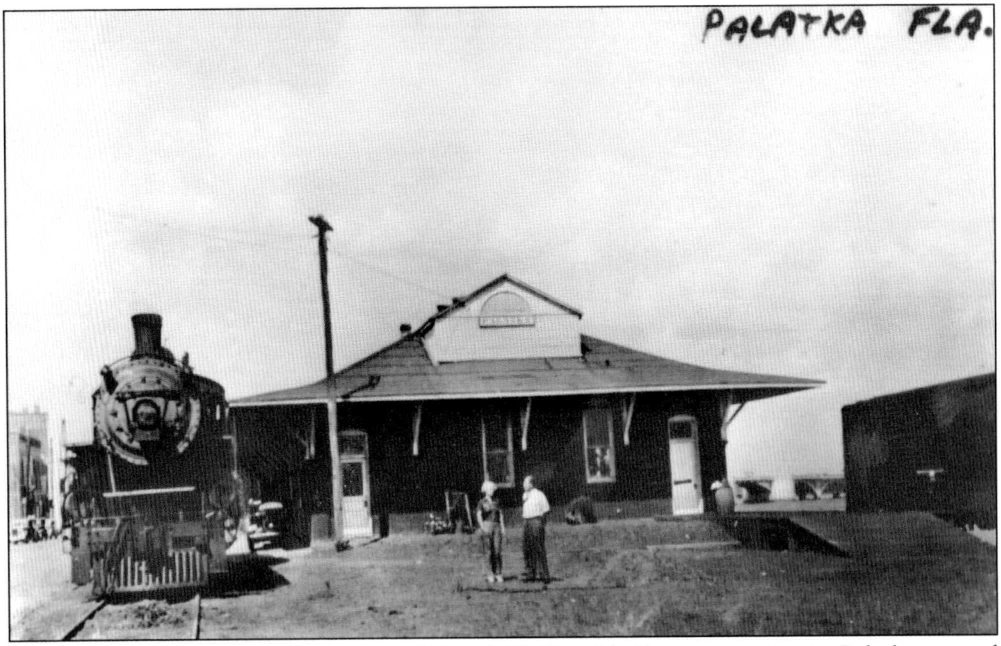

PALATKA, 1940. Georgia Southern and Florida Railroad built a new station in Palatka around 1905. Sometime around 1912, Ocklawaha Valley Railroad, originally the Ocala Northern, used the station over the next decade or so. Locomotive No. 8253, a 4-6-0 type, sits alongside the depot in this scene from 1940. At that time, the station was served by a mixed train daily except Sunday, originating from Valdosta, Georgia, a distance of 133 miles. (Courtesy of Florida State Archives.)

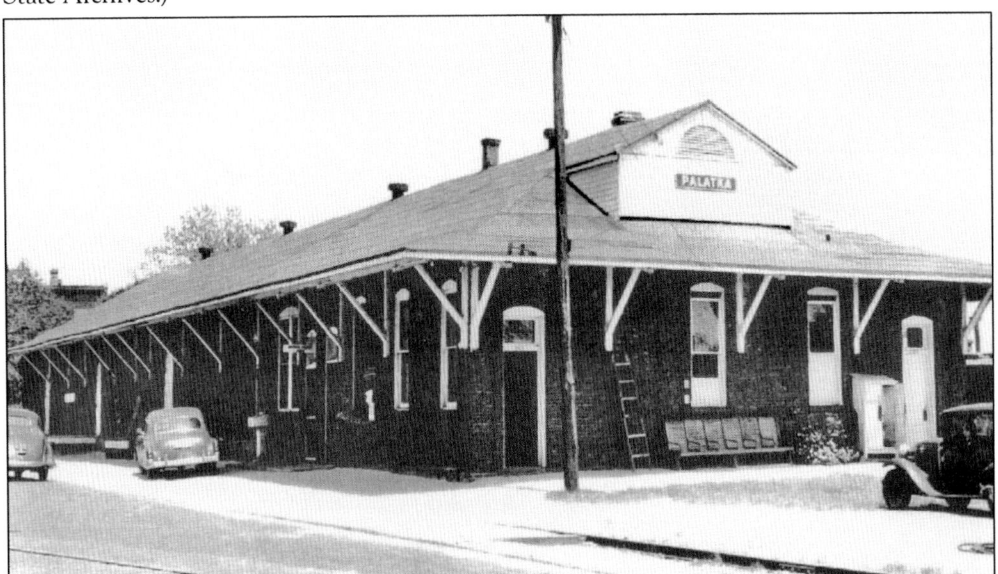

PALATKA, 1950. Georgia Southern and Florida would continue operating mixed trains to Palatka into the late 1950s. This photograph shows the waiting room end of the station around 1950. The "white" room is on the left and "colored" on the right. An exact year of the building's demolition is unknown, but it is believed to be in the early 1970s. A city park now occupies the location. (Courtesy of Putnam County Library System.)

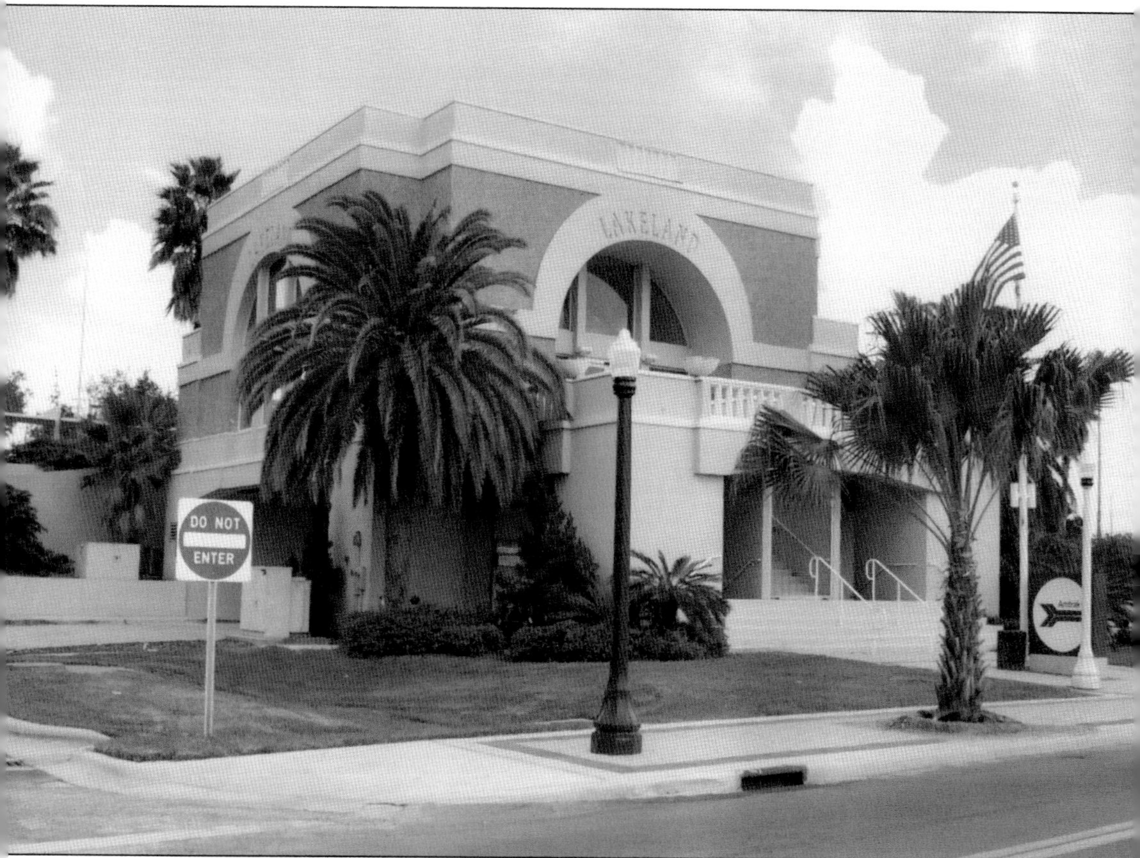

LAKELAND AMTRAK, 1998. Lakeland's "new" Amtrak station provides a glimmer of hope that passenger rail service has a future in Florida and the nation. This station boarded almost 21,000 ticketed passengers in 2007. Opened in 1998, the building is architecturally impressive by the building standards of today. Perhaps travel by train will grow and became a significant part of our transportation options. Our state and nation will need alternatives as we move into the future. (Courtesy of Mike Mulligan.)

Consistent with our mission to preserve history on a local level, this book was printed in South Carolina on American-made paper and manufactured entirely in the United States. Products carrying the accredited Forest Stewardship Council (FSC) label are printed on 100 percent FSC-certified paper.

MADE IN THE USA